"Carrie Booth Walling has written... trains about human rights in a college or a community, providing just the right mix of history and theory with stories of emblematic activists and their struggles. An amazing toolkit for advocacy at the end helps the reader put it all into action."

Kathryn Sikkink, *Harvard University*

"What does it really mean to make human rights change? Everyone demands it; so few do it well. As Carrie Walling's unique book teaches through gripping real-life stories, the necessary skills in messaging, organization, and advocacy can be taught. Additionally, human rights work also requires insight, commitment, ingenuity, sweat, and optimistic persistence. And most importantly, the book illustrates the necessity of believing in a better world, a world for which one is willing to fight and die."

Harold Hongju Koh, *former Assistant Secretary for Democracy, Human Rights, and Labor, US Department of State*

"*Human Rights and Justice for All* takes on the complex topic of universal human rights and explains what these rights are, and how they are protected (or not) in the world today. By sharing the stories of advocates around the world, author Carrie Walling emphasizes the human part of human rights, in addition to the historical and legal aspects. This is an indispensable text for students and lifelong learners seeking to understand how to utilize the human rights framework to ensure respect for the rights and dignity of all people."

Jill Savitt, *National Center for Civil and Human Rights*

"Carrie Walling's book is a must-read for anyone looking to make sense of human rights and justice on the local, national, and international level. This is an accessible and comprehensive introduction to rights that concern us all and provides an unmissable resource for students, teachers, and practitioners alike. The book explores a wide array of different human rights issues and highlights areas in which they have come under threat. This contested nature of human rights is brought to life through numerous case studies from across the world which provide grounds for hope and optimism that ordinary individuals can (and do) make a difference to protect and promote justice and rights. This book is also a call to action by providing a human rights advocacy toolkit that will inspire readers to become human rights defenders themselves and transform their ideas into action. Carrie Walling shows that human rights matter and that we all can make a real difference."

Andrea Birdsall, *University of Edinburgh*

HUMAN RIGHTS AND JUSTICE FOR ALL

Human rights is an empowering framework for understanding and addressing justice issues at local, domestic, and international levels. This book combines US-based case studies with examples from other regions of the world to explore important human rights themes – the equality, universality, and interdependence of human rights, the idea of international crimes, strategies of human rights change, and justice and reconciliation in the aftermath of human rights violations. From Flint and Minneapolis to Xinjiang and Mt. Sinjar, this book challenges a wide variety of readers – students, professors, activists, human rights professionals, and concerned citizens – to consider how human rights apply to their own lives and equip them to be changemakers in their own communities.

Carrie Booth Walling is Professor of Political Science and Faculty Director of the Gerald R. Ford Institute for Leadership in Public Policy and Service at Albion College. Her research interests are in human rights, international politics, transitional justice, and the United Nations. Walling is a Security Fellow with the Truman National Security Project and teaches for the Inside-Out Prison Exchange Program which brings incarcerated and non-incarcerated people together to study justice behind prison walls.

INTERNATIONAL STUDIES INTENSIVES
Series Editors: Shareen Hertel and Michael J. Butler

Series Description

International Studies Intensives (ISI) is a book series that springs from the desire to keep students engaged in the world around them. ISI books are meant to offer an intensive introduction to subjects often left out of the curriculum. Our authors are from a range of disciplines and employ many different methodological approaches to teaching about international issues. Yet each and every ISI book packs a wealth of information into a small space, and does so in ways that students find compelling and instructors find useful. ISI books are relatively short, visually attractive, and affordably priced. Examination/inspection copies for course adoption may be requested from the Webpage of any book in the series. Book proposals for the series should be directed to the co-editors: shareen.hertel@uconn.edu and mbutler@clarku.edu.

Recent Books in the Series:

U.S. Foreign Policy and the Politics of Apology
Loramy Gerstbauer

American Exceptionalism Reconsidered
U.S. Foreign Policy, Human Rights, and World Order
David P. Forsythe and Patrice C. McMahon

All the World's a Stage
The Theater of Political Simulations
Hemda Ben-Yehuda

Human Rights and Justice for All
Demanding Dignity in the United States and Around the World
Carrie Booth Walling

HUMAN RIGHTS AND JUSTICE FOR ALL

Demanding Dignity in the United States and Around the World

Carrie Booth Walling

Routledge
Taylor & Francis Group

NEW YORK AND LONDON

Cover image: "We the People Must Come Together," was created by Kelly Simpson Hagen, www.kellysartfromthesoul.com.

First published 2022
by Routledge
605 Third Avenue, New York, NY 10158

and by Routledge
2 Park Square, Milton Park, Abingdon, Oxon OX14 4RN

Routledge is an imprint of the Taylor & Francis Group, an informa business

© 2022 Taylor & Francis

Library of Congress Cataloging-in-Publication Data
Names: Walling, Carrie Booth, author.
Title: Human rights and justice for all : demanding dignity in the United States and around the world / Carrie Booth Walling.
Description: New York, NY : Routledge, 2021. |
Series: International studies intensives | Includes bibliographical references and index. |
Identifiers: LCCN 2021040712 (print) | LCCN 2021040713 (ebook) |
ISBN 9780367902124 (paperback) | ISBN 9781032189093 (hardback) |
ISBN 9781003256939 (ebook)
Subjects: LCSH: Human rights--United States. | Justice, Administration of--United States. | Human rights--Case studies. | Justice, Administration of--Case studies. | Social justice--Case studies.
Classification: LCC KF4749 .W357 2021 (print) | LCC KF4749 (ebook) |
DDC 341.4/8--dc23/eng/20211004
LC record available at https://lccn.loc.gov/2021040712
LC ebook record available at https://lccn.loc.gov/2021040713

ISBN: 978-1-032-18909-3 (hbk)
ISBN: 978-0-367-90212-4 (pbk)
ISBN: 978-1-003-25693-9 (ebk)

DOI: 10.4324/9781003256939

Typeset in Bembo
by Taylor & Francis Books

Access the Support Material:
www.routledge.com/9780367902124 and www.albion.edu/human-rights

Dedicated to my students who have also been my teachers. Incarcerated and free, both have demonstrated the power that comes from breaking free from the prisons of our minds and the opening of our hearts.

CONTENTS

ILLUSTRATIONS

Figures

Tables

Boxes

ACKNOWLEDGMENTS

The seeds for this book were planted more than two decades ago and nurtured by years of personal and professional experience with human rights as a student, advocate, citizen, teacher, and scholar. But the idea to write this book emerged from a late-night conversation about the state of human rights with my mentor and friend, Shareen Hertel, in an overcrowded lobby of a conference hotel in Toronto. Without Shareen's vision and encouragement, this book might still be living inside me waiting to be written.

This book was written and shaped in the context of two pandemics that have urgently revealed the vast inequities and injustices in our world, and the importance of human rights, however imperfect, as a tool for addressing them. The COVID-19 pandemic and the pandemic of racism directed at people of African descent in the United States and around the world have highlighted the contingency of human rights. They also reveal how human rights violations compound – violations of one human right can trigger the violations of other human rights. We live in a time characterized by democratic backslide, human rights reversals, unraveling multilateralism, and significant fear of others. Human rights are under threat; so is democracy and the rule of law that allow human rights to flourish. Yet, it is also a moment characterized by significant human rights advances secured through global solidarity movements and local organizing. Each semester I witness students organize our campus community against threats to justice and rights, applying human rights concepts learned in the classroom to real world challenges that threaten their values. The contemporary struggle to determine whether human rights will expand or contract reminds me that human rights do not progress in a linear fashion. The story of human rights is one of advances and reversals accompanied by fissures, cracks, and contestation. It is likely that human rights will never be fully realized. But it is also true that human rights empower people to demand dignity, pursue equality, and struggle for justice. And sometimes they win. This book is my personal response to the assault on human rights in the United States and abroad. It is my effort to join the fight on behalf of human rights and to push for more wins.

There are many people that have shaped my relationship with human rights who deserve recognition. My undergraduate academic advisor at James Madison College (Michigan State University), Michael Schechter, encouraged my interest in human rights, introduced me to new authors and ideas, and planted the idea of graduate school. Ken Booth at the University of Wales Aberystwyth taught me to put people and their emancipation at the center of my thinking about international politics. At Women for Women International, Zainab Salbi taught me how passion could be mobilized into action and that individuals working collectively with a common purpose can change their communities and their own lives. Ibadete Bytiqi showed me what it looks like to live human rights and to experience human wrongs. I learned from her that struggle for recognition, dignity, and rights is always local. Kenneth Waltzer taught me to be ethically responsible with the difficult and intimate knowledge that comes from human testimony. Kathryn Sikkink taught me more about living a human rights consistent life than can be recounted here. Through years of mentorship, she has shown me that it is possible to produce scholarship that pushes the boundaries of human rights and at the same time be an inspiring teacher and encouraging mentor dedicated to developing human rights teacher-scholars. Barbara Frey got me excited about advocacy and along with Shareen Hertel helped me see the links between the local and the global. Maryam Zarneger-Deloffre has been a steadfast colleague and friend – someone who will edit the ugliest of drafts with encouragement and who can finish my sentences. Helen Kinsella helped me find and gain confidence in my voice.

I am thankful to the Michigan Society of Fellows and the Gerald R. Ford School of Public Policy at the University of Michigan for providing a nurturing environment from which to launch an academic career. I am especially thankful to Susan Waltz who has helped me dream bigger through collaboration. It's a privilege to have colleagues that encourage you to spread your wings, celebrate your successes, and give you more credit than you often deserve – thank you Andrew Grossman and Bill Rose who have mentored me at Albion College. A special thank you to my incarcerated (and now formerly incarcerated) students who renewed my love of teaching. Behind the walls of the G. Robert Cotton Correctional Facility, you showed me the transformative power of human rights education, how to build community across difference, and the importance of empathy in the pursuit of justice. My human rights students at Albion College have taught me the importance of seeing human rights close to home, the value of applying the human rights framework to the US context, and how human rights education empowers advocacy. It has been a great joy to collaborate with Morgan Armstrong, Marco Colmenares Jr., and Caitlin Cummings to create the human rights toolkit found at the end of this book. They have been my teachers as much as I have been theirs. I am also thankful to Caitlin for additional editorial assistance on the text. Student participation in the project was funded by Albion College through a Foundation for Undergraduate Research, Scholarship, and Creative Activity (FURSCA) Academic Year Grant, the Associate Professor Summer Fellowship, and Faculty Development research grant.

I regularly teach my students that scholarship is a collaborative exercise. We are all teachers and learners. Thank you to the many individuals who read drafts of chapters and offered suggestions on how to strengthen them: Andrea Birdsall, Alison Brysk, Shareen Hertel, Courtney Hillebrecht, Helen Kinsella, Joel Pruce, Dominick Quinney, Dayne Walling, Susan Waltz, and Maryam Zarneger-Deloffre. Dayne Walling read and commented on the entire draft and was a sounding board for ideas throughout the entire creation process. I owe a debt of gratitude to several anonymous reviewers who offered helpful constructive feedback, the members of the editorial team Jennifer Knerr, Shareen Hertel, and Michael J. Butler for their guidance and support, and the entire team of people at Routledge, Taylor & Francis Group that touched this project and helped bring it to fruition, including Jacqueline Dorsey, Emily Boyd, and Francesca Tohill. The book is better for all their interventions though I must claim any remaining errors as my own.

The cover art for this book, "We the People, Must Come Together," was created by Kelly Simpson Hagen, www.kellysartfromthesoul.com. Hagen describes her painting as "about the need for us to start coming together again and stop the hateful words toward people we don't agree with. We are all unique and we each have a story to tell. We need to come together and fight for a better world." This painting and the sentiment that inspired its creation align with the central message of this book – all people are equally deserving of dignity, rights, and justice. Thank you to Kelly and *Kelly's Art from the Soul* for generously allowing me to use her beautiful artwork to represent the book.

I am especially grateful for my family who offered unending patience and support (and quiet spots for writing) through a long and often challenging writing process. Bennett and Emery Walling and their generation represent our greatest hope in securing a world of more dignity, justice, and human rights.

INTRODUCTION

Beliefs and ideas shape our world. They structure our expectations and give birth to our practices. This book is about the powerful idea of human rights and the belief that all people are equally deserving of dignity and rights. It is an idea that resonates with people from all cultures, religions, nationalities, gender identities, sexualities, races, ethnicities, abilities, and economic backgrounds, in all regions of the world. Human rights issues are all around us. If we look closely, we can find them in our neighborhoods, on our college campuses, and even in our own closets. We can advance human rights by placing the well-being and dignity of other human beings at the center of the decisions we make personally and as a community. By understanding human rights, we can help make their enjoyment a reality. And that is the purpose of this book: to offer tools and strategies for fighting discrimination, expanding inclusion, and increasing access to rights and justice.

The meaning and content of human rights are described in the Universal Declaration of Human Rights, which in turn has prompted the creation of more than 70 human rights treaties that codify these norms into law. Yet human rights are contested, frequently violated by powerful actors, and insufficiently protected by states and the institutions designed to help fulfill them. The story of human rights, then, is a story about political struggles to define the practices of people, institutions, and states. Human rights is greater than an academic concept; it is fundamental to our lived experiences and can empower (and sometimes disappoint) us in quests for justice.

This book explores the claims to human rights that people make; the ways that governments (democratic and non-democratic alike) violate human rights; and the processes, strategies, and institutions that foster human rights change. The text explores important human rights themes using case examples drawn from every

DOI: 10.4324/9781003256939-1

region of the world – equality and non-discrimination, interdependence, the idea of international crimes, strategies of human rights change, and justice and reconciliation in the aftermath of human rights violations. Cases invite us to study the struggle over human rights up close and in context, allowing us to develop a deeper understanding and to draw stronger conclusions about their meaning. Frequently, people conceive of human rights as belonging to other people in other places without considering how they relate to their own lives and experiences. For this reason, this book includes cases drawn from the developed as well as the developing world, from democracies as well as autocracies, and with the United States as a rights violator and not simply a rights proponent. From Flint and Minneapolis to Xinjiang and Mt. Sinjar, this book challenges readers to consider how human rights apply to their own lives and equips them to be changemakers in their own communities.

Each chapter features human rights defenders – people working individually or collectively to advance human rights in their own communities with extraordinary achievement. In practice, human rights are used by defenders in three different ways. First, human rights are a *framework of analysis* for making sense of injustice. When we analyze problems from a human rights perspective, we center the lived experience of human beings and how they experience the law and other social, political, and economic practices. We also can identify who wields power and who feels its effects. Second, human rights is a *language of dispossession* that is used to make rights and justice claims. Although human rights belong to all people by right of birth, they are unequally respected, protected, and fulfilled. The language of human rights allows us to claim the violation of rights as an injustice – a theft of an entitlement we were given ownership to at birth. Third, human rights laws and norms are *tools* that are used to promote social, economic, political, and legal change. They are used to promote a human rights culture, convince others that we are deserving of our rights, and hold states and institutions accountable to their human rights responsibilities. As an illustration, Cédric Herrou is a human rights defender who uses human rights as a framework of analysis to understand the global refugee and migration crisis. He uses the language of human rights to object to the unjust treatment of migrants by the French government and to demand that displaced people be afforded the human rights they deserve. Herrou uses human rights standards as a tool to pressure France to protect the rights of non-citizens.

Cédric Herrou, Citizen Activism, and the Global Refugee and Migration Crisis

At the end of 2019, there were more than 79.5 million forcibly displaced people in the world. This amounts to one in every 97 people in the world fleeing persecution, conflict, violence, and human rights violations. This is more than at any other time since the end of World War II and the highest number ever recorded

FIGURE 0.1 Cédric Herrou
Source: Vianney Le Caer/Invision/AP.

since the United Nations High Commissioner for Refugees (UNHCR) began collecting statistics on human displacement.[1] As the number of asylum seekers, refugees, internally displaced, and stateless people increase, their access to basic necessities has decreased.[2] Countries are accepting only a limited number of displaced persons for resettlement and closing their borders. Few of the displaced can return home because the conditions that forced them to flee persist. The global refugee and migrant crisis is a widespread, growing, long-term, persistent problem. The human rights implications are catastrophic.

Human rights violations are a major cause of the movement of people from their countries of origin and the persistence of those human rights violations is a barrier to their return. Yet refugees, displaced, and stateless persons also are disproportionately vulnerable to human rights violations from their displaced status. These include the inability to access their rights to water, food, sanitation, and healthcare as well as the direct violation of their rights by states through forcible deportation to places where their human rights or freedom is endangered, or by non-state actors who target them for physical violence, forced labor, and sexual exploitation.

Since 2015, European governments and European Union (EU) institutions have bolstered efforts to keep migrants from accessing Europe by intercepting them at sea, detaining them in overcrowded facilities, tightening asylum rules, and suspending its system of open borders, earning the region the nickname "fortress Europe." Informal grassroots networks of solidarity have emerged in which ordinary people offer humanitarian assistance to asylum seekers and migrants where European governments have not. One such place is along the rugged, snow-capped alpine border between Italy and France. In the Roya valley, villagers troubled by the growing sight of young African migrants lost along French roadsides suffering from hypothermia and hunger have risked arrest to respond to their suffering.[3] One of the most principled and vocal among them, Cédric Herrou, a French olive farmer, has openly defied national laws prohibiting citizens from aiding migrants entering the country illegally.

Cédric Herrou has been arrested and harassed by government authorities for aiding the illegal entry of African migrants into France and running a makeshift refugee camp.[4] His defense is that as a farmer it is his job to feed hungry people, not to determine who is legal or illegal. He argues that his humanitarian actions actually defend French values of liberty, equality, and fraternity while the government's behavior betrays them.[5] He used the media attention surrounding his prosecution to denounce the French state for violating asylee rights and illegally deporting unaccompanied minors.[6] Herrou says he must protect his fellow human beings because his government does not. In 2018, the *Cour de Cassation* – France's court of final appeals – ruled in favor of Mr. Herrou, overturning a previous conviction, arguing that in aiding migrants Herrou acted within his rights. The court ruled, "the principle of fraternity confers the freedom to help others for humanitarian purposes, regardless of the legality of their presence on national territory."[7] Cédric Herrou, a farmer and human rights defender, is an advocate for the rights of all people. He has provided life-saving assistance to more than 200 migrants, inspired an informal network of collective resistance to government injustice, and set a new precedent in French law to include a humanitarian exemption from prosecution for "crimes of solidarity."

Wai Wai Nu's Fight for Gender Equality and the Recognition of Identity

Wai Wai Nu is another example of a human rights defender. She shows it is possible to be a victim of human rights violations and still be a defender of human rights. Like Herrou, Nu uses human rights to frame the injustices experienced by Rohingya women, as a language for claiming their equal rights, and as a tool of gender equality. Nu is the Founder and Executive Director of the Women's Peace Network and Founder of the Yangon Youth Leadership Center. She is an advocate for gender equality, peace building, and youth empowerment. Nu became a human rights defender out of necessity rather than desire. Her personal experience with the injustice of religious, ethnic, and gender discrimination motivates her to stand up for her community when she would rather live a normal personal and professional life.[8] Nu was imprisoned with her family at the age of 18. Her only "crime" was that she was the daughter of a political activist who opposed the ruling government of Myanmar (formerly known as Burma)[9]

FIGURE 0.2 Wai Wai Nu.
Source: Oslo Freedom Forum via Wikimedia Commons.

and was a member of a persecuted indigenous group – the Rohingya. Greatly influenced by the human rights violations she witnessed during her seven years as a political prisoner, Nu has dedicated her post-imprisonment life to empowering women and youth from marginalized communities.

Discrimination against women is deeply ingrained in all aspects of society in Myanmar – education, healthcare, the economy, personal life, government policy, and access to decision-making. It is even more difficult for Rohingya women and girls, who face added ethnic and religious discrimination including the risk of sexual violence from security forces, deprivation of nationality, and discriminatory birth control policies, including restrictions on the ability to marry and the number of children that Rohingya women are permitted to birth.[10] After earning her law degree, Nu co-founded Justice For Women in Yangon, a network of women lawyers providing legal and educational assistance to victims of gender-based violence. The Women's Peace Network, which Nu also founded, seeks to build peace and understanding between different ethnic communities in Myanmar, aiming to reduce discrimination and hatred between Buddhist and Muslim women. The organization empowers and advocates for the rights of all marginalized women throughout Myanmar in addition to advocating for the human rights of the Rohingya people.[11]

Nu is also focused on empowering the next generation of leaders. She founded the Yangon Youth Leadership Center as a space where youth from diverse backgrounds can build trusting relationships, gain civic and leadership skills, and participate in peace-building efforts. She has been recognized as a "Champion of Prevention" by the United Nation's Office on the Prevention of Genocide and Responsibility to Protect and has received numerous prestigious awards and distinctions for her human rights, peace building, and gender equality work.[12]

Nu has said, "I believe in the universality of human rights and I want to promote the advancement of human rights around the world. However, I work for my own community, the Rohingya community, as well."[13] The Rohingya have been persecuted for decades by Myanmar's government due to their identity. In 2017 that persecution turned genocidal. In 2017 the Myanmar Army, Air Force, Police Force, and armed civilians carried out widespread and systematic attacks against Rohingya civilians in Rakhine state. The mass atrocities included killing, gang rape, arbitrary arrest, and forced expulsion/ethnic cleansing.[14] In January 2020 the International Court of Justice ordered Myanmar's authorities to protect Rohingya Muslims from genocide after the Gambian government brought a charge of genocide against Myanmar to the high court.[15] This is just a first step toward justice. Justice for the Rohingya also means "being able to return to their places of origin, being recognized as a group native to Burma, and having their full citizenship and other equal rights restored" according to Nu.[16] Wai Wai Nu says that she will not be free until her community and country are free. She will continue her defender work until all the women of Rakhine are respected, safe and secure, and have equal rights and freedom.[17]

Organization of the Book

Cases like the refugee and migration crisis in Europe and rights defenders like Cédric Herrou and Wai Wai Nu animate this book, highlighting the contested political terrain of human rights. The following chapters are designed to help make sense of rights and justice concerns at local, national, and international levels, and illustrate how ordinary people make human rights claims to challenge the practices of powerful states and other institutions. The cases, drawn from all regions and from countries at all levels of economic development, demonstrate how rights and justice issues are cultural and geographic variations of common political, social, and economic problems. Each chapter begins by introducing a theme central to understanding human rights and then provides a set of conceptually connected, but geographically and culturally distinct, empirical case studies. Each chapter also includes bibliographic profiles of human rights defenders, working individually and collectively, to promote human rights change.

Chapter 1 introduces the concept of human rights and how it is put into practice domestically and internationally. It provides an overview of the international human rights framework, including its defining attributes, its historical and political origins, key elements of international human rights law, why human rights violations happen, and how the content and meaning of human rights evolve over time. Chapter 1 introduces the framework necessary to explore the subsequent chapters on major themes with examples.

Equality and non-discrimination are at the heart of the human rights project, and inequality and discrimination are at the root of most human rights violations. Each core human rights treaty contains a provision guaranteeing the rights it protects to apply to all human beings equally without distinction of any kind. Chapter 2 examines the equality and non-discrimination requirement of human rights. Yet, an investigation of policing and incarceration practices in the United States reveals a high level of racial discrimination, violating multiple international human rights standards and especially the Convention on the Elimination of All Forms of Racial Discrimination. Protests following the murder of a Black American, George Floyd, by police officers in Minneapolis, Minnesota in May 2020 went global, prompting criticism of American racism (and human rights hypocrisy) but also initiating a global conversation about systemic discrimination against people of African descent worldwide. China's repression of Uyghur Muslims in government-run concentration camps is also the subject of Chapter 2. China has enacted a series of repressive measures against the entire Uyghur community based on their ethnicity and religion. Rather than countering terrorism as the government claims, the goal is to eliminate the distinctive Uyghur identity. States frequently invoke threats to national security to disingenuously justify repressive practices that violate human rights. These two cases illustrate how government policy has had discriminatory and unequal effects on members of their population and how advocates use human rights laws and norms to fight identity-based persecution including racial and religious discrimination.

Chapter 3 focuses on the interdependent and interconnected character of human rights. Political and civil rights are necessary for identifying and fulfilling economic, social, and cultural needs. Similarly, violations of socio-economic rights limit our ability to exercise our political and civil rights. Chapter 3 explores two cases that illustrate how the violation of any rights diminish the ability to exercise the others. The Flint Water Crisis (US) demonstrates how the violation of political rights in the city led to the violation of the right to water, threatening the rights to health and life. The fight for clean water in Flint, Michigan is directly related to the struggle for democratic governance. The second case – ISIS and sexual violence against Yazidi women in northern Iraq – shows that violations of women's political, economic, and social rights are interconnected and that gender discrimination in peace translates into gender-based atrocities during war. Sexual violence perpetrated against Yazidi women by ISIS was at once a genocidal act intended to destroy the Yazidi people and their culture, and an assertion of patriarchal power over women's bodies. Both cases challenge the idea that one set of human rights is more important than another.

Despite cultural variation in the interpretation of human rights, there are some human rights violations that are universally recognized as criminal and a grave matter of international concern. They are classified as "international crimes" and generate a collective responsibility to respond to their breach. Chapter 4 considers the crimes of genocide, crimes against humanity, and war crimes within the context of Rwanda and Syria. Despite promises of "Never Again," genocide and mass atrocity crimes remain a persistent practice in international politics. Yet, strengthened human rights norms have generated new forms of response and an increased expectation of an international responsibility to protect populations.

Chapter 5 tackles the question of how people can learn to live together and trust their governments in the aftermath of widespread human rights violations. It opens with an overview of the global transitional justice framework – the set of judicial and non-judicial measures used by societies to redress the legacies of human rights abuse. Focusing on human rights trials and truth commissions, the cases upend conventional wisdom by illustrating how new human rights ideas and practices flow from the global south to the global north and not simply the reverse. Human rights trials in Argentina and the experiences and practices of Argentinian advocates (especially women), human rights lawyers, government officials, and domestic courts have shaped the global justice and accountability norms now championed by the United Nations and replicated by other states. The South African Truth and Reconciliation Commission (SATRC) is a global model for truth-telling bodies, highlighting the importance of documenting the truth for both restorative and retributive forms of justice. Examining the legacy of the SATRC shows the importance of addressing economic inequities alongside political ones for achieving justice and reconciliation. Finally, the chapter concludes with an example of a local, non-governmental truth process. The Greensboro Truth and Reconciliation Commission – the first truth commission in the United States – illustrates that transitional justice is an effective means for strengthening human rights practices even in absence of government support and when faced with official opposition.

Human rights belong to all people, but they are not equally respected, protected, or fulfilled in different communities and countries. Achieving a world in which all humans are equal in dignity and rights requires challenging the people and power structures that perpetuate oppression, inequality, discrimination, and injustice. Chapter 6 explores the people, processes, and places of human rights change. It identifies the best practices of human rights advocacy and investigates the strengths and weaknesses of existing mechanisms of human rights monitoring and enforcement using real world illustrations.

The book closes with a human rights advocacy toolkit of practical ideas for building more inclusive communities, preventing bias, challenging hate, and increasing access to rights and justice. Here readers learn how to become human rights defenders in their own communities. Inspired by contemporary campus activism in the United States and people in communities large and small who have taken to the streets to demand recognition of their human rights, the toolkit provides a framework for advocates-in-the-making. The toolkit includes fact-sheets and sample activities, designed, in part, by citizen activists who are working to: end discrimination; broaden LGBTQIA, racial, and religious inclusion; and increase access to justice on their own college campuses and in their home communities. The toolkit is designed for use in contexts where the rights to protest and freedom of assembly, opinion, and information are legally protected. Advocates must assess the context and their positionality within that context for safety. You must protect your own safety if you want to protect the safety of others. Readers can also access additional support material including human rights resources online (see www.routledge.com/9780367902124 and www.albion.edu/human-rights. Human rights are only respected, protected, and fulfilled to the extent that people, individually and collectively, demand that they are. We all have responsibilities for human rights. It's time to get started.

Notes

1 United Nations High Commissioner for Refugees (UNHCR), "Figures at a Glance," www.unhcr.org/en-us/figures-at-a-glance.html, accessed 6/18/2020.
2 An asylum seeker is a person seeking international protection. Internally displaced people seek safety in other parts of their own country. Refugees are persons fleeing persecution or conflict, and stateless people have been denied their right to nationality. UNHCR, "Who We Help," www.unhcr.org/en-us/who-we-help.html, accessed 11/18/2020.
3 Adam Nossiter, "Farmer on Trial Defends Smuggling Migrants: 'I Am a Frenchman'," *The New York Times*, January 5, 2017, https://nyti.ms/2j8RigR, accessed 11/18/2020.
4 International Federation for Human Rights, "France: The Harassment of Cédric Herrou, Defender of Migrants' Rights Must End," April 9, 2017, www.fidh.org/en/issues/human-rights-defenders/france-the-harassment-of-cedric-herrou-defender-of-migrants-rights, accessed 11/18/2020.
5 Nossiter, "Farmer on Trial."; Adam Nossiter, "When Journalism Meets Civil Disobedience," *The New York Times*, January 19, 2017, https://nyti.ms/2jDKWJZ, accessed 11/18/2020.
6 International Service for Human Rights, "Human Rights Defender's Profile: Cédric Herrou from France," March 22, 2019, www.youtube.com/watch?v=04V-Bo-JQLA, accessed 11/18/2020.
7 Elian Peltier and Richard Pérez-Peña, "Fraternité Brings Immunity for Migrant Advocate in France," *The New York Times*, July 6, 2018, https://nyti.ms/2Nxd26a, accessed 11/18/2020.
8 Equal Rights Trust, "Layers of Marginalisation: Life for Rohingya Women: Testimony from Myanmar," *The Equal Rights Review*, 16 (2016), 223–227; Feliz Solomon, "The Activist Bridging a Democratic Divide," *Time*, March 2, 2017, https://time.com/collection-post/4684884/wai-wai-nu-next-generation-leaders/, accessed 12/5/2020.
9 The military junta officially changed the country's name to Myanmar which has been formally recognized by the United Nations. Some countries, including the US and UK, continue to refer to the country as Burma as a matter of official policy which they justify on the basis that the government changed the name without reference to the will of its people.
10 Equal Rights Trust 2016, p. 225.

11 Women's Peace Network, www.womenspeacenetwork.org, accessed 7/2/2021.
12 US Holocaust Memorial Museum, "Wai Wai Nu: Genocide Prevention Fellow," Simon-Skjodt Center, www.ushmm.org/genocide-prevention/simon-skjodt-center/fellows/wai-wai-nu, accessed 12/4/2020.
13 Equal Rights Review 2016, p. 224.
14 Fortify Rights and Simon-Skjodt Center for the Prevention of Genocide, United States Holocaust Memorial Museum, *They Tried to Kill Us All: Atrocity Crimes against Rohingya Muslins in Rakhine State, Myanmar*, November 2017, p. 1.
15 Human Rights Watch, "International Court of Justice Orders Burmese Authorities to Protect Rohingya Muslims from Genocide," interview of Reed Brody with Democracy Now! January 24, 2020, www.hrw.org/news/2020/01/27/international-court-justice-orders-burmese-authorities-protect-rohingya-muslims, accessed 12/6/2020.
16 Wai Wai Nu and Naomi Kikoler, "Anniversary of Genocidal Attacks on Rohingya Reminds Us They are Still at Risk," *Just Security*, August 28, 2020, www.justsecurity.org/72194/anniversary-of-genocidal-attacks-on-rohingya-reminds-us-they-are-still-at-risk/, accessed 12/5/2020.
17 Office of the High Commissioner for Human Rights, "Wai Wai Nu, Rohingya Activist: 'I Am Not Free. My Community Is Not Free. My Country Is Not Free'," www.ohchr.org/EN/NewsEvents/Pages/WaiWaiNu.aspx, accessed 12/6/2020.

1

dignity – state of respect

UNDERSTANDING HUMAN RIGHTS AS LIVED EXPERIENCE

argument

We experience human rights or their violation in deeply personal ways. We advance human rights or we fuel human wrongs through our choices, actions, and inactions. This book is about the fight for human rights – the contestation over their meaning, the politics of their recognition, the struggle by people for their realization, and the tools and tactics that support political change. For while we each have a claim to our human rights, too often they remain unfulfilled or are actively challenged by the decisions of political leaders and the practices of powerful institutions. When human rights are denied, they must be demanded and fought for. When they are achieved, they must be regularly exercised and actively protected. The claim to rights, and the responsibilities for them, belong to people in all regions of the world, all forms of government, and countries at all stages of economic development. Whether respect for human rights grows or their disregard widens depends on our embrace of equality or discrimination, pursuit of inclusion or exclusion, and support for justice or impunity. We learn more about human rights and human wrongs by examining them in the contexts in which they occur. The case studies in this text and the stories of the people who have struggled within them invite us to link ideas with practices and to consider how we can build a more equal, just, and rights-filled world. They invite us to imagine how we might "live human rights" at home and abroad.

Human rights are the rights every human being is born with. Human rights are about more than survival; they include those things that are essential to a life of dignity. These rights never go away even if those in power do not recognize them – they are inalienable. Human rights are universal. They are different than the rights granted by governments to their citizens. All human beings are born with human rights, do nothing to earn them, and their rights travel with them wherever they reside and no matter what border they cross. All human beings are equal in dignity and rights. Equality means that they apply to all persons regardless

DOI: 10.4324/9781003256939-2

universal

of gender, sex, race, religion, nationality, economic status, ability, sexual orientation, ethnicity, political belief, age, or any distinction of any kind. Importantly, all human rights are interdependent and interrelated. This means that human beings must have access to all their rights to achieve dignity. The violation of any single right limits the enjoyment of other rights. Human rights are an entitlement. They are not simply good or desirable. They are not a gift. People suffer harm when they are deprived of the human rights to which they are entitled. Although human rights are seldom fully realized, and often violated, that does not mean they do not exist. Rather, it is the deprivation of our human rights that mobilizes political action to claim them. In sum, human rights are the rights that every human is entitled to and are necessary for a life of dignity. Human rights are inalienable, equal, and interdependent.

The content of our human rights are described in the Universal Declaration of Human Rights (UDHR) which passed without dissent in 1948 by the United Nations (UN) General Assembly, is legally codified in multiple international treaties, and was reaffirmed by UN members from all regions of the world through regional treaties and at the World Conference of Human Rights in 1993 and again in the UN 75 Declaration of 2020.[1] Available in more than 500 languages and dialects, the UDHR is the most widely translated document in the world. The UDHR is composed of 30 articles which promote a shared vision of basic human rights and dignities that apply to all people in all nations (see Box 1.1). The preamble identifies respect for these human rights as, "the foundation of freedom, justice and peace in the world," and disregard for human rights as barriers to their achievement. The 30 articles entail a variety of civil, political, economic, social, and cultural rights. These include the right to life (Article 3), peaceful assembly (Article 20), religion (Article 18), free and fair trial processes and humane treatment (Articles 5, 8–10), as well as reasonable work conditions, fair pay (Article 23), access to education (Article 26), and participation in cultural life and scientific advances (Article 27). By presenting these rights in a single document, the drafters signaled that these basic rights were interrelated and mutually reinforcing. For example, Article 6 says that everyone has the right to recognition as a person before the law – the right to a legal identity. The right to a legal identity is connected to every other human right in the UDHR and all the rights examined in this book. A legal identity is needed to access healthcare, education, to vote, to cross an international border, to open a bank account which is necessary for employment in the formal job sector, and to own property. Without access to a legal identity, people are uncounted and unprotected. Children without a legal identity are vulnerable to labor exploitation, human trafficking and enslavement, forced marriage, involuntary military service, and with no legal record of their existence there may be no record that they are missing. The World Bank estimates that more than 1 billion people worldwide lack a legal identity.[2] The loss of this single right makes it more likely their other human rights also will be violated.

BOX 1.1 THE 30 ARTICLES OF THE UNIVERSAL DECLARATION OF HUMAN RIGHTS

Article 1: Right to Equality

Article 2: Freedom from Discrimination

Article 3: Right to Life, Liberty and Personal Security

Article 4: Freedom from Slavery

Article 5: Freedom from Torture and Degrading Treatment

Article 6: Right to Recognition as a Person before the Law

Article 7: Right to Equality before the Law

Article 8: Right to Remedy by Competent Tribunal

Article 9: Freedom from Arbitrary Arrest and Exile

Article 10: Right to a Fair Public Hearing

Article 11: Right to be Considered Innocent until Proven Guilty

Article 12: Prohibition on Interference with Privacy, Family, Home and Correspondence

Article 13: Right to Free Movement in and out of the Country

Article 14: Right to Seek Asylum in other Countries from Persecution

Article 15: Right to a Nationality and Freedom to Change Nationality

Article 16: Right to Marriage and Family (and equal rights within it)

Article 17: Right to Own Property

Article 18: Freedom of Belief and Religion

Article 19: Freedom of Opinion and Information

Article 20: Right of Peaceful Assembly and Association

Article 21: Right to Participate in Government and in Free Elections

Article 22: Right to Social Security

Article 23: Right to Desirable Work and to Join Trade Unions

Article 24: Right to Rest and Leisure

Article 25: Right to Adequate Standard of Living

Article 26: Right to Education

Article 27: Right to Participate in Cultural Life of Community and Share in Scientific Advances

Article 28: Entitlement to a Social and International Order Protective of Human Rights

Article 29: Everyone has Duties to Community and to Allow the Exercise of Rights of Others

Article 30: Freedom from State of Personal Interference in the Realization of these Rights

The UDHR provides a guiding framework but putting human rights into practice involves struggle over their meaning and how they should be applied in specific contexts. In practice, even interdependent rights can come into conflict.

My claim to a right might conflict with the fulfillment of yours, or an individual rights claim might conflict with the rights claim of a group. For any of us to enjoy human rights, others must be allowed to exercise their rights as well.[3] How to do so justly and in an equitable manner is a source of contestation. Yet everyone has the responsibility to respect human rights (Article 29) and to create a world in which they can be realized (Article 28). Furthermore, governments have a special three-fold responsibility to uphold human rights. Governments have an obligation to respect human rights and not violate rights themselves. Governments have a second obligation to protect human rights, meaning that governments must protect individuals and groups from having their rights violated or abused by others. Governments also have an obligation to fulfill human rights. They must take positive action to facilitate the enjoyment of basic rights by their people. This tripartite understanding of duty-bearer responsibilities is commonly referred to as a "human rights-based approach (HRBA)."[4] When governments fail to offer these protections, they are guilty of human rights violations.

The Universal Declaration of Human Rights (UDHR)

The Universal Declaration of Human Rights is a politically negotiated text that reflects the shared values of its drafters, who were drawn from all regions of the world. A global consensus in support of human rights emerged at the end of World War II but the groundwork for the Universal Declaration was laid in earlier decades by non-state actors, lawyers, and diplomats.[5] The horrors of the Holocaust and the devastating effect of the war mobilized support for an internationally recognized set of human rights and made its adoption politically possible.[6] The diverse origins of the UDHR are often overlooked. It is a common critique to suggest that human rights are not truly universal but rather reflect the values of western industrialized states.[7] This claim overlooks the vital contribution that small states and states from the global south made to the inclusion of human rights in the Charter of the United Nations (UN) and the substantive content of human rights in the UDHR. It also underestimates great power ambivalence toward human rights at the time of their adoption.[8] In fact, both the US and the UK faced significant domestic opposition to the UDHR from constituencies afraid its adoption would force a reckoning on racial segregation and colonialism, respectively.[9]

While human rights are mentioned seven times in the UN Charter, their inclusion was the result of extensive lobbying by the Non-Governmental Organization (NGO) community, small states (especially from Latin America), and states representing the global south. It was not driven by the great powers; some of whom were deeply ambivalent about the project.[10] Later, the Universal Declaration was created to clarify and develop a common understanding of human rights, which were adopted as a core purpose of the UN alongside the maintenance of peace and security and economic development. The drafting commission included individuals of varying religious, cultural, and political backgrounds. Most prominent among them were the representatives of France, China, Lebanon, the United States, and Canada. Latin American states were particularly influential having drafted the first intergovernmental declaration of rights – the American Declaration on the Rights and Duties of Man.[11] Delegates from small and developing states worked to remove gender bias from the final text of the UDHR. The representatives from India and the Dominican Republic fought for inclusive language so that women's rights would not be overlooked.[12] The Latin American delegates of Chile, Panama, and Uruguay, accompanied by Syria, Saudi Arabia, the Philippines, China, and Pakistan, were champions of social and economic rights.[13] Article 2, which prohibits discrimination on the basis of identity and personal attributes, had wide support among most delegates and the language extending equal human rights to colonized peoples, crafted by the Egyptian delegate, was included in the final version despite opposition from colonial powers.[14] Each of these examples challenge the idea that human rights reflect the principles of a single set of political, geographic, or cultural interests and problematize the idea that they were crafted by the most powerful states for imposition on the powerless. The UDHR was negotiated and shaped by a diversity of contributors. In the words of human rights scholar-practitioner Susan Waltz, the UDHR can be "claimed as heritage for all."[15]

To give the Universal Declaration the binding force of international law, the newly established UN Commission on Human Rights was tasked with formalizing the content of the UDHR by codifying it in a legally binding international treaty. These efforts were disrupted by the political divisions that emerged between the United States and the Soviet Union during the Cold War (see Chapter 3). For political expediency, the indivisible rights of the UDHR were separated into two different treaties – one codifying political and civil rights and the other codifying economic, social, and cultural rights. Combined, these three documents make up what is known as "the International Bill of Human Rights."[16] They form the foundation of international human rights law and are viewed as the authoritative source on the meaning of human rights. Today there are nine core human rights treaties (also called instruments) that further elaborate the human rights of specific populations and prohibit additional government violations:

- International Convention on the Elimination of All Forms of Racial Discrimination (ICERD)
- International Covenant on Economic, Social and Cultural Rights (ICESCR)
- International Covenant on Civil and Political Rights (ICCPR)
- Convention on the Elimination of Discrimination against Women (CEDAW)
- Convention against Torture and Other Cruel, Inhuman or Degrading Treatment (CAT)

- Convention on the Rights of the Child (CRC)
- International Convention on the Protection of the Rights or All Migrant Workers and Members of their Families (ICRMW)
- International Convention on the Rights of Persons with Disabilities (ICRPD)
- International Convention for the Protection of All Persons from Enforced Disappearance (ICED)

Dozens of other international and regional human rights treaties also exist.

BOX 1.2 DEFENDING HUMAN RIGHTS: BEATRICE MTETWA AND THE RULE OF LAW

Beatrice Mtetwa is among the most widely respected human rights lawyers internationally and in her country of Zimbabwe. She is known for speaking

FIGURE 1.1 Beatrice Mtetwa
Source: AP Photo/Stuart Ramson

out against unjust governmental action including government violation of constitutional and human rights. For more than 30 years, Mtetwa has defended journalists, members of the political opposition, peace activists, and human rights practitioners who have been harassed, arrested, and abused by the Zimbabwean government. She defends freedom of peaceful assembly, association and speech, freedom of the press, the empowerment of women, and respect for rule of law. Mtetwa's success in high profile human rights cases has made her a target of physical abuse and judicial harassment by government authorities.[19]

Beatrice Mtetwa has received numerous recognitions and awards for her unwavering commitment to human rights, her struggle to protect the rule of law, and her efforts to prevent the Zimbabwean government from using the law as a weapon against its people. According to Mtetwa, "I am not an activist because there is glory or cash to it and not because I'm trying to antagonize the government...I'm doing it because it is a job that's got to be done."[20] Beatrice Mtetwa is a member of the Zimbabwean Lawyers for Human Rights. She is a recipient of the US State Department's International Women of Courage Award, the American Bar Association's International Human Rights Award, and the Burton Benjamin Award for lifetime achievement by the Committee to Protect Journalists. She has also received the prestigious Ludovic-Trarieux International Human Rights Prize – the oldest and most prestigious award given to a lawyer by fellow lawyers for defense of human rights. In her acceptance speech, Beatrice Mtetwe argued her receipt of the award illustrated the universality of human rights.

> My nomination for this award demonstrates that the defence of human rights knows no culture, language barriers, continental locations or other differences. My nomination therefore serves to confirm the universality of human rights and those who argue, particularly in Africa, that Human Rights are a Eurocentric concept do so from a perspective where they want Africans to enjoy a lesser standard of human rights than their counterparts elsewhere.[21]

Beatrice Mtetwa is a human rights defender who believes that all people are equally deserving of dignity and rights and must be able to live in a society governed by the rule of law. Though her body has been bruised, her spirit remains strong as she fights for human rights for all.

The law can be a powerful tool in defense of human rights, but the law can also be abused by governments and used to subvert rights rather than protect them. To safeguard against such abuse, the United Nations promotes the *rule of law* – a principle of governance in which all people and institutions (including government officials and the state itself) are accountable to laws that are publicly declared, equally enforced, independently judged, and consistent with human rights norms.[17] Rule of law is the mechanism that translates human rights standards into lived practice. There can be no meaningful rule of law in societies that systematically violate human rights, and human rights cannot be protected in societies without a strong rule of law.

The World Justice Project identifies four principles that constitute a working definition of the rule of law. The first is accountability. This means everyone is equally accountable under the law, including government officials and private actors. The second principle is that laws must be just. They must be clear, publicized, stable, applied consistently, and protect human rights. The third principle is about transparency and openness. The law must be enacted, administered, and enforced fairly without corruption. Finally, the justice system must be administered by competent, ethical, and independent tribunals adequately resourced and representative of the communities they serve.[18] Human rights practitioners like Beatrice Mtetwa (see Box 1.2) champion the rule of law both for its inherent value and because it is necessary for safeguarding all other human rights.

Human Rights as a 20th and 21st Century Political Project

This book examines human rights as a 20th and 21st century political project rather than simply a legal or philosophical one. A political approach focuses attention on contestation and the human struggle at the center of human rights. Human rights norms have emerged, gained legitimacy, and become formalized through a process characterized by activism, intentional labor, and resistance. People make claims to rights. They can be supported by movements, organizations, lawyers, and diplomats. These rights are frequently contested by governments and other powerful actors. Recognition of rights claims is either achieved through political struggle grounded in human rights advocacy or successfully resisted by powerful opposing forces who benefit from the status quo. Throughout, the advancement or failure of human rights change is further mediated by political contingencies beyond the control of any single actor.

Focusing on the politics of human rights means being agent-centered, listening to the voices, experiences, and actions of victims, survivors, and defenders. It draws attention to how people working individually and collectively through organizations, networks, movements, and occasionally governments make human rights change happen. While international human rights law is a powerful tool for advancing human rights, the international human rights movement is not limited by the law. Instead, it advances new norms and develops new standards that may eventually be incorporated into the law but that are won first in the realm of politics.

Finally, approaching human rights as a political project reduces the need to forge agreement on the theoretical and philosophical origins of human rights.

Instead, the legitimacy of the human rights project can be derived from the overlapping consensus that produced the UDHR itself – the creation and adoption of universal standards by peoples and governments from every region of the world as represented in the International Bill of Human Rights and the core human rights treaties.[22] These standards also have been by supported through the adoption of additional regional and international declarations and treaties. Examples include the American Declaration of the Rights and Duties of Man adopted prior to the UDHR in 1948, the American Convention on Human Rights (1969), the European Convention on Human Rights (1950), the African Charter on Human and Peoples' Rights (1981), and the Cairo Declaration on Human Rights in Islam (1990). Each regional conference reaffirmed the UDHR preceding the World Conference on Human Rights in 1993 which produced the Vienna Declaration and Programme of Action – a direct rebuke to rights-challenging narratives of cultural relativism and Asian values.[23] Human rights have been validated multiple times since then and most recently were endorsed by the world's governments and peoples in the UN 75 Declaration and the UN75 People's Declaration respectively. Peoples' charters have also emerged from Asia including the Asian Human Rights Charter (1998) and the Charter 08 manifesto published by Chinese intellectuals and human rights activists (2008).

This book promotes an empowerment model of human rights. Despite wide acceptance of human rights, human rights practitioners should respect diversity, variations in interpretation, and elevate the interests, needs, and voices of those making human rights claims. Human rights practitioners risk falling prey to ethnocentrism and betraying a core principle of human rights – honoring human dignity – if they adopt the role of savior seeking to rescue victims.[24] Human rights must be claimed by those that seek them and supported by other defenders in their struggle to achieve them. They cannot be imposed by others.

Causes of Human Rights Violations

Understanding human rights as a political project also helps us understand the underlying causes of human rights violations. We know that war, authoritarianism, and exclusionary ideologies and dehumanizing language are key triggers for human rights violations and mass atrocity crimes.[25] We also know that large-scale instability, past armed conflict, and a societal history of discrimination and unpunished violence also are associated with human rights violations and mass atrocity crimes.[26] But not all cultures characterized by racial, religious, or cultural difference violate human rights; and not all strong authoritarian states or weak and unstable ones assail people and groups they see as threats. Further, democratic states also violate the rights of their citizens and may support or turn a blind eye to human rights violations in other states when they perceive it to be in their interest to do so. While it is true that certain conditions like war, authoritarianism, economic displacement, or societal disorder create opportunities for and increase the likelihood of human rights violations, it takes deliberate choices by leaders to put systemic human rights violations into motion. The willingness of ordinary people to participate in human rights violations and the tolerance or readiness of bystanders to look the other way also are necessary for them to succeed.

The motives behind these choices vary among decision-makers, the ordinary people who implement rights-violating policies, and the bystanders who choose inaction in the face of injustice. Leaders often make conscious decisions to violate human rights when they perceive it to be to their benefit – as a way to impose stability, secure their hold on political power, or because it gives them an advantage, either economically or socially. Leaders also may be motivated by a commitment to an exclusionist ideology – a system of belief that justifies violence or discrimination to advance a vision of a "better society," often freed of those who oppose that vision.[27] Sometimes the two work in tandem. A context of war, domestic insecurity, or severe economic displacement can increase fear and uncertainty, increasing the appeal of exclusionary ideologies that assign blame to "outsiders," or "enemy others." Exclusionist ideologies associated with human rights violations can include racism and other discriminatory ideologies, anticommunism, neoliberal economic orthodox, or the adoption of a national security or antiterrorism doctrine (see Chapter 2).[28] In social environments characterized by these exclusionary ideologies, the idea of repression is seen as an appropriate response to the circumstances. By labeling categories of people as "outsiders" or "others," promoters of these ideologies dehumanize their targets making it easier for ordinary people to participate in or accept human rights violations.

An unsettling finding of social scientific research is that under the right social conditions, ordinary people can become perpetrators of human rights violations. Indeed, most rights-violators are not uniquely evil or violent individuals. Instead, most perpetrators are ordinary people.[29] A series of well-known social psychology experiments known as the Milgram experiments and the Stanford Prison Project showed that ordinary people will harm others under orders or when the social context incentivizes them to do so. While people with a predisposition of obedience to authority may be more susceptible to harming others when ordered to do so, people also can be trained to torment others through processes of indoctrination, peer pressure, coercion, fear, greed, and opportunity.[30] Based on their research of how Greek military police were trained as torturers by that country's former military regime, Janice Gibson and Mika Haritos-Fatouros created a simple model to explain the training techniques designed to instill unquestioning obedience to commit torture.[31] Essentially, the sense of bondedness people feel when they join others in obeying authority must be greater than the strain they experience when they obey an order to physically harm another person (especially if they were previously taught it was morally wrong). When feelings of camaraderie and belonging are more powerful than the strain of cooperating with an order to harm others, people will do what they are told. Conversely, when strain is greater, they are more likely to disobey.[32] Leaders, organizations, and movements use a variety of techniques to decrease the strain of obeying orders to commit human rights violations including scapegoating and dehumanizing victims, physically and psychologically intimidating perpetrators-in-the making, rewarding those who comply with orders and punishing those that do not, and socializing group members through incremental steps like watching others be rewarded for violent acts until they have been desensitized enough for them to appear routine.[33] Initiation processes like these that introduce people into a new social order with new rules and norms are not uncommon, even on a college campus. Such processes may be used to train people toward empathy and inclusion or toward hostility and exclusion.

Social science research also shows that a small number of perpetrators can succeed if the majority of people in society – those that are neither perpetrators or victims of human rights violations – stay silent.[34] Being a bystander normalizes human rights violations and makes resistance to them more difficult. Holocaust survivor Elie Wiesel argued that the indifference of bystanders benefits the perpetrators and magnifies the pain of their victim.[35] Silence in the face of injustice is often interpreted by both perpetrators and victims of human rights violations as approval of them. Disrupting human rights violations, then, requires addressing the choices that political leaders, perpetrators, and bystanders make. At the political level, Kathryn Sikkink proposes six policy tools that help diminish human rights violations: 1) decreasing war and seeking nonviolent solutions to conflict; 2) promoting democracy and strengthening existing ones; 3) guarding against dehumanizing and exclusionary ideologies about race, religion, gender, or any other status; 4) encouraging states to ratify human rights treaties and to enforce human rights laws and norms nonviolently; 5) ending impunity for human rights violations by supporting domestic and international accountability to deter future violations; and 6) supporting domestic and transnational human rights advocacy.[36] Ordinary people also can be trained to identify injustice and courageously resist it, rather than perpetrate it. The authors of *Courageous Resistance: The Power of Ordinary People*, propose several actions that make people more likely to defend human rights: 1) cultivating bonds with others; 2) practicing empathy by actively imagining the experiences and perspectives of other people; 3) consistently performing care-giving work; 4) diversifying relationships by deliberately connecting with people from different groups to deepen mutual respect and understanding; 5) developing networks and connections with like-minded people who support justice and share human rights values; and 6) imagining a better world is possible.[37] Resisting injustice and defending human rights requires gaining and exercising the skills that foster them.

The Emergence of New Human Rights

International human rights have evolved and expanded over time, but that process has not been linear, progressive, or uncontested. Rather, debates about their content, force, and legitimacy have accompanied the development of human rights. Taking a long view, it is possible to see periods of both progress and regression. A broad-based coalition of domestic and international actors uses the power of the human rights idea, the tool of human rights law, and credible evidence of rights violations to promote human rights change. These human rights practitioners rarely started out with the intention of building normative standards and legal instruments but often found it necessary to fulfill their mandates.[38] For example, Amnesty International was founded to defend the rights of prisoners of conscience – someone who has not used or advocated violence but who is imprisoned because of who they are or what they believe.[39] As Amnesty International began working to protect and free prisoners of conscience they discovered other related rights violations that demanded their attention – like torture and other forms of ill-treatment – which prompted them to collaborate in international efforts to draft, get states to adopt into law, and then enforce the Convention against Torture and Other Cruel, Inhuman or Degrading Treatment or Punishment.[40]

Rights-violating governments also learn to innovate and adapt, attempting to circumvent the legal prohibitions imposed by human rights standards. When political opinion in 1970s Chile and Argentina would not support open violation of citizens' human rights by their military governments, those governments created new practices to avoid detection of their crimes. Human rights organizations and lawyers began noticing that many of their clients had "disappeared." To avoid public scrutiny of their human rights violations – arbitrary detention, torture, unlawful killing – governments kidnapped their political opponents and detained them in irregular facilities beyond the reach of the regular judicial system.[41] Sometimes people reappeared and revealed what had happened to them; often they were killed. Many remain missing. Advocates had to create new human rights standards to adjust to these new human rights violations. Today the International Convention for the Protection of All Persons from Enforced Disappearances prohibits,

> the arrest, detention, abduction or any other form of deprivation of liberty by agents of the State or by persons or groups of persons acting with the authorization, support or acquiescence of the State, followed by a refusal to acknowledge the deprivation of liberty or by concealment of the fate or the whereabouts of the disappeared person, which places such a person outside the protection of the law.[42]

Countries as diverse as Argentina, Guatemala, the Philippines, Sri Lanka, and Syria have engaged in the practice of enforced disappearance. Implementation of the 2010 treaty is monitored by the Committee on Enforced Disappearance – a United Nations treaty body (see Chapter 6).

BOX 1.3 DEFENDING HUMAN RIGHTS: XIYE BASTIDA

Climate change poses a clear and fundamental threat to the enjoyment of basic human rights. The work for climate justice is being led by youth climate activists who adopt an intersectional approach and focus their intervention on collective decision-making rather than individual behavior. The world's youth are tired of waiting on decision-makers who continue to fail to act. "If you adults won't save the world, we will," says Xiye Bastida, a youth climate activist and member of the indigenous Mexican Otomi-Toltec nation.[46] An outspoken critic of environmental exploitation and injustice, Bastida fights for equity and inclusion within the climate movement. That involves highlighting the link between climate justice and indigenous rights and fighting to ensure that "a rainbow of diverse voices," including indigenous voices, are included in decision-making.[47] Motivated by the belief that people should "leave everything better than you found it," Bastida is a lead organizer with Fridays for Future (a global school strike movement for climate), a coordinator of the Re-Earth Initiative, and sits on the administrative committee for the People's Climate movement – intersectional organizations that promote equity and inclusion in climate advocacy. Bastida writes, "Being an activist means lending

FIGURE 1.2 Xiye Bastida (left) with fellow climate change activists, Alexandria Villasenor and Greta Thunberg, at an August 2019 meeting with the UN General Assembly prior to the United Nations Climate Action Summit on September 23
Source: AP Photo/Mary Altaffer

your skills toward a cause that furthers justice. And all these voices must be uplifted equitably."[48] Xiye Bastida received "The Spirit of the United Nations" award in 2018 when she was only 16 years old. In September 2019 she organized 300,000 people to strike for climate in New York and participated in the United Nations Climate Summit.

BOX 1.4 DEFENDING HUMAN RIGHTS: VANESSA NAKATE

FIGURE 1.3 Vanesa Nakate speaks via video call at the Desmond Tutu International Peace Lecture in October 2020

Source: AP Photo/Ronald Zak, File

Vanessa Nakate is a Ugandan climate justice advocate and founder of the Youth for Future Africa and the Rising Up Movement. A vocal advocate for diversity in environmental activism, Nakate argues that the world must listen to voices from the global south.[49] She criticizes the culture that silences marginalized communities disproportionately affected by the climate crisis. Nakate, who has experienced this marginalization firsthand, argues that if we don't tell the stories of those affected most by the climate crisis, the solutions to it and environmental justice will remain out of reach.[50] According to Nakate, who led a strike outside the Ugandan Parliament, the global south may not be on the front page of the media coverage but it is on the frontline of the climate crisis.[51]

BOX 1.5 DEFENDING HUMAN RIGHTS: JAMIE MARGOLIN

FIGURE 1.4 Jamie Margolin
Source: AP Photo/Ted S. Warren

Jamie Margolin is a Colombian American student, climate activist, and author of *Youth to Power: Your Voice and How to Use it.* Margolin argues that the fights for social justice and environmental justice are inseparable. She calls for the climate justice movement to build meaningful coalitions with people on the frontlines of the climate crisis. This means supporting the #Black-LivesMatter movement and making room for people of color, people in the global south, indigenous peoples, poor people, people with disabilities, women, youth, queer and trans people, and people of marginalized faiths.[52] She is a co-founder of the youth climate organization Zero Hour which fights for all individuals in all communities to have access to clean air, water, and public land, and strives to hold adults and elected officials accountable on climate.[53]

Which human rights ideas gain traction and develop into norms hinges on many factors, including political events and international advocacy efforts. The idea that there is a human right to a healthy climate has gained significant international traction in large part due to the advocacy work of the world's youth. The human rights dimensions of the climate crisis are many and varied. A clean and healthy environment is necessary for the enjoyment of human rights, and climate change poses a direct threat to a full range of fundamental human rights including the right to life, health, food, water and sanitation, a healthy environment, an adequate standard of living, housing, property, self-determination, development and culture.[43] The negative effects of climate change disproportionately affect people living in poverty, those whose contributions to the problem are minimal, and those with limited access to the resources necessary to protect themselves or to adapt. This violates other core human rights standards like the right to equality and non-discrimination. Human rights defenders working on environmental issues are particularly vulnerable to having their rights violated or abused by state and non-state actors like multinational corporations (MNCs) or rebel groups that seek to silence them. Indeed, a ground-breaking regional agreement for the Americas – the Escazú Agreement – provides special protection for human rights defenders working on environmental issues. The Escazú Agreement also guarantees the right to environmental information, public participation in environmental decision-making, and access to justice in environmental matters.[44]

A forward-looking rights-based approach to climate change focuses on the human rights of all people as well as the human rights of future generations. It prioritizes justice and equity within and between nations, as well as across generations. The responsibility for protecting and implementing these human rights is collective, requiring the participation of state and non-state actors, including individuals.[45] Global youth are at the forefront of the worldwide climate justice movement that is challenging and changing global norms.

Like many rights defenders, Xiye Bastida, Vanessa Nakate, and Jamie Margolin urge us to focus on their movement rather than individual activists, but their voices remind us of the dangers of homogenization. They illustrate the collective power that comes from demanding all people and voices be included within rights and justice movements. Climate is an intersectional issue. Climate change, racial injustice, and income inequality are linked. And sustainable solutions must address the inequalities being exposed by climate change and protect the equal enjoyment of human rights.

Conclusion

Human rights are both simple and challenging. They belong equally to everyone, including those who violate the human rights of others. But human rights are not equally recognized in practice.

It may seem unfair for victims to struggle for their human rights to be protected, but when not freely given, human rights must be claimed and fought for. And even those who have achieved rights must regularly exercise and monitor them to ensure their enforcement. This makes human rights intensely political – not in the sense of partisanship but because they uncover and reveal systems of power. The story of human rights is a story about people exercising their agency in pursuit of dignity, equality, and justice. This book broadens understanding of essential rights using case studies to illustrate what human rights mean in practice, how human rights are violated, and the means and venues that support human rights change. The toolkit that follows the text offers strategies, tactics, and tools for working individually and collectively to advance equality, promote justice, and secure human rights.

Notes

1 You can read the entire Universal Declaration of Human Rights at www.un.org/en/universal-declaration-human-rights/, accessed 12/9/2020.
2 The World Bank, Identification for Development (ID4D) global dataset, https://id4d.worldbank.org/global-dataset, accessed 3/11/2021; Vyjayanti T. Desai, Anna Diofasi, and Jung Lu, "The Global Identification Challenge: Who Are the 1 Billion People Without Proof of Identity?" April 25, 2018.
3 Eric D. Weitz, *A World Divided: The Global Struggle for Human Rights in the Age of Nation-States* (Princeton University Press, 2019), p. 9.
4 OHCHR, "International Human Rights Law," www.ohchr.org/en/professionalinterest/pages/internationallaw.aspx#:~:text=By%20becoming%20parties%20to%20international,and%20to%20fulfil%20human%20rights.&text=The%20obligation%20to%20fulfil%20means,enjoyment%20of%20basic%20human%20rights, accessed 12/11/2020.
5 Kathryn Sikkink, *Evidence for Hope: Making Human Rights Work in the 21st Century* (Princeton University Press, 2019), p. 62.
6 These states included several Latin American states and notably Panama and Chile as well as New Zealand, Australia, Philippines, Lebanon, and France. Susan Waltz, "Reclaiming and Rebuilding the History of the Universal Declaration of Human Rights," *Third World Quarterly*, 23:3 (2002), pp. 438, 444; Sikkink, *Evidence for Hope*, pp. 65–68.
7 For an overview of the cultural relativism and Asian values debates see Amartya Sen, "Human Rights and Asian Values," *The New Republic*, 1997; Thomas M. Franck, "Are Human Rights Universal?" *Foreign Affairs*, 80:1 (2001).
8 Waltz, "Reclaiming and Rebuilding"; Sikkink, *Evidence for Hope*.
9 For a detailed account of US ambivalence toward human rights including domestic political opposition see Christopher N. Roberts, *The Contentious History of the International Bill of Human Rights* (Cambridge University Press, 2014). To learn more about US opposition to human rights due to racial segregation and its history of slavery see Carol Anderson, *Eyes off the Prize: The United Nations and the African American Struggle for Human Rights, 1944–45* (Cambridge University Press, 2003).
10 Only China was deeply committed to the inclusion of the idea of human rights.
11 Kathryn Sikkink, "Latin American Countries as Norm Protagonists of the Idea of International Human Rights," *Global Governance*, 20 (2014), pp. 391, 397.
12 Waltz, "Reclaiming and Rebuilding," p. 444.
13 Waltz, "Reclaiming and Rebuilding," p. 444.
14 Waltz, "Reclaiming and Rebuilding," p. 445.
15 Waltz, "Reclaiming and Rebuilding," p. 447.
16 The International Covenant on Civil and Political Rights also has two optional protocols. The first allows the Human Rights Committee to receive complaints from individuals and the second abolishes the death penalty. An optional protocol may provide procedures related to a treaty or address in more detail a substantive area related to a treaty. Optional protocols are independent treaties in their own right and are open to ratification (but ratification is not required) by members of the original treaty that they are related to.
17 United Nations, "What is the Rule of Law?" www.un.org/ruleoflaw/what-is-the-rule-of-law/, accessed 12/12/2020.

18 World Justice Project, "What is Rule of Law?" https://worldjusticeproject.org/a bout-us/overview/what-rule-law, accessed 12/12/2020.

19 International Federation of Human Rights, "Zimbabwe: Judicial Harassment of Mr. Hopewell Chin'ono's lawyer Ms. Beatrice Mtetwa," August 20, 2020, www.fidh.org/ en/issues/human-rights-defenders/zimbabwe-judicial-harassment-of-mr-hopewell-chi n-ono-s-lawyer-ms, accessed 12/20/2020; International Bar Association, "Comment On the Call for the Prosecution and Disqualification of Beatrice Mtetwa in Zim-babwe," September 3, 2020, www.ibanet.org/Article/NewDetail.aspx?ArticleUid= 341f01c7-30b5-41c1-8a34-d22f89441922, accessed 12/20/2020.

20 Frontline Defenders, "Beatrice Mtetwa," www.frontlinedefenders.org/en/case/ca se-history-beatrice-mtetwa, accessed 12/10/2020.

21 Ludovic Trarieux Prize 2009, Beatrice Mtetwa acceptance speech, www.ludovictra rieux.org/uk-page3.remplt2009.htm, accessed 12/20/2020.

22 See Jack Donnelly, "The Relative Universality of Human Rights," *Human Rights Quarterly*, 29:2 (May 2007), 281–306 and Jack Donnelly and Daniel J. Whelan, *International Human Rights: Dilemmas in World Politics*, Fifth edition (Westview Press, 2017) for detailed treatment of the overlapping political consensus on human rights. See also the response by Michael Goodhart, "Neither Relative nor Universal: A Response to Donnelly," *Human Rights Quarterly*, 30:1 (February 2008), 183–193.

23 Cultural relativism questions the universality and cultural neutrality of human rights. Cultural relativists argue that a person's, society's, or government's practices should be evaluated based on their own cultural values and norms and not be judged against universal human rights standards. Cultural relativists argue that human rights are not universal but reflect western cultural values. The Asian values critique of human rights claims that Asian values are less supportive of freedom and more concerned with order and discipline than western values, making political and civil rights less appropriate in Asia than in the west and that Asian values prioritize community and economic and social rights.

24 See the critique made by Makua Mutua, "Savages, Victims, and Saviors: The Metaphor of Human Rights," *Harvard International Law Journal*, 42:1 (2001), 201–245.

25 Sikkink, *Evidence for Hope*; Scott Straus, *Fundamentals of Genocide and Mass Atrocity Prevention* (United States Holocaust Memorial Museum, 2016).

26 Straus, *Fundamentals of Genocide*, pp. 56–60.

27 Sonia Cardenas, *Human Rights in Latin America: A Politics of Terror and Hope* (University of Pennsylvania Press, 2009); Straus, *Fundamentals of Genocide*.

28 Cardenas, *Human Rights in Latin America*.

29 Janice T. Gibson and Mika Haritos-Fatouros, "The Education of a Torturer," *Psychology Today* (November 1986); Philip Zimbardo, "When Good People Do Evil," *Yale Alumni Magazine* (January/February 2007); Ervin Staub, *The Roots of Evil* (Cambridge University Press, 1989); Kristina E. Thalhammer, Paula O'Loughlin, Myron Peretz Glazer, and Nathan Stoltzfus, *Courageous Resistance: The Power of Ordinary People* (Palgrave Macmillan, 2007); Daniel Goldhagen, *Worse Than War: Genocide, Eliminationism and the Ongoing Assault on Humanity* (PublicAffairs, 2009); Straus, *Fundamentals of Genocide*; Christopher Browning, *Ordinary Men: Reserve Battalion 101 and the Final Solution in Poland* (Harper Perennial, 1992).

30 Straus, *Fundamentals of Genocide*, pp. 99–104.

31 Gibson and Haritos-Fatouros, "The Education of a Torturer."

32 Gibson and Haritos-Fatouros, "The Education of a Torturer," p. 57.

33 Gibson and Haritos-Fatouros, "The Education of a Torturer," p. 57.

34 Staub, *The Roots of Evil*; Thalhammer, et al., *Courageous Resistance*.

35 Elie Wiesel, "The Perils of Indifference: Lessons Learned from a Violent Century," *Seventh White House Millennium Evening*, April 12, 1999, www.pbs.org/eliewiesel/ resources/millennium.html, accessed 9/23/2021.

36 Sikkink, *Evidence for Hope*, pp. 183–184.

37 Thalhammer, et al., *Courageous Resistance*, pp. 165–181.

38 See the *Human Rights Advocacy and the History of International Human Rights Standards* website, www.humanrightshistory.umich.edu, accessed 9/23/2021.

39 To learn more about Amnesty International and its influence in the human rights movement, see Ann Marie Clark, *Diplomacy of Conscience: Amnesty International and Changing Human Rights Norms* (Princeton University Press, 2001).

40 Nigel Rodley, "Torture," in Carrie Booth Walling and Susan Waltz, *Human Rights: From Practice to Policy* (University of Michigan, 2011); also available at: http://huma nrightshistory.umich.edu/files/2012/08/Rodley.pdf, accessed 3/11/2021.

41 José Zalaquett, "The Emergence of 'Disappearances' as a Normative Issue," in Carrie Booth Walling and Susan Waltz, *Human Rights: From Practice to Policy* (University of Michigan, 2011), pp 14–18; also available at: http://humanrightshistory.umich.edu/files/2012/07/Zalquette.pdf, accessed 3/11/2021.

42 OHCHR, "International Convention for the Protection of All Persons from Enforced Disappearance," www.ohchr.org/en/hrbodies/ced/pages/conventioncoed.aspx, accessed 12/12/20.

43 United Nations Human Rights Special Procedures, *Safe Climate: A Report of the Special Rapporteur on Human Rights and the Environment*, A/74/161, July 15, 2019, p. 18.

44 Regional Agreement on Access to Information, Public Participation and Justice in Environmental Matters in Latin America and the Carribbean, adopted at Escazu, Costa Rica on March 4, 2018, https://repositorio.cepal.org/bitstream/handle/11362/43583/1/S1800428_en.pdf, accessed 6/8/2021.

45 Kathryn Sikkink, *The Hidden Face of Rights: Toward a Politics of Responsibilities* (Yale University Press, 2020), pp. 54–58.

46 Xiye Bastide, "If You Adults Won't Save the World, We Will," TED2020, September 21, 2020, www.ted.com/talks/xiye_bastida_if_you_adults_won_t_save_the_world_we_will?language=en#:~:text=Xiye%20Bastida%3A%20If%20you%20adults,world%2C%20we%20will%20%7C%20TED%20Talk, accessed 6/8/2021.

47 Xiye Bastide, "My Name is Not Greta Thunberg: Why Diverse Voices Matter in the Climate Movement," The Elders intergenerational blog, June 19, 2020, www.theeld ers.org/news/my-name-not-greta-thunberg-why-diverse-voices-matter-climate-m ovement, accessed 11/20/2020; Olivia Riggio, "Xiye Bastida: Making Room for Climate Activists of All Backgrounds," KCET, September 12, 2020, www.kcet.org/shows/tending-nature/xiye-bastida-making-room-for-climate-activists-of-all-ba ckgrounds, accessed 6/27/2021; Anna Lucente Sterling, "This Teen Climate Activist if Fighting to Ensure Indigenous and Marginalized Voices are Being Heard," *HuffPost*, September 25, 2019, www.huffpost.com/entry/xiye-bastida-climate-activism_n_5d8a 7ec9e4b0c6d0cef3023e, accessed 6/27/2021.

48 Bastide, "My Name is Not Greta Thunberg."

49 Vanessa Nakate, "The Climate Crisis is Already Here: Why we Must Listen to the Voices of the Global South," The Elders, intergenerational blog, May 1, 2020, www.theelders.org/news/climate-crisis-already-here-why-we-must-listen-voices-global-south, accessed 11/20/2020

50 Nakate, "The Climate Crisis is Already Here."

51 Nakate, "The Climate Crisis is Already Here."

52 Jamie Margolin, "Why the Climate Movement Must United Behind the Black Lives Matters Movement," The Elders intergenerational blog, June 8, 2020, www.theelders.org/news/why-climate-movement-must-unite-behind-black-lives-matter-movement, accessed 11/19/2020.

53 Zero Hour, "Who We Are," http://thisiszerohour.org/who-we-are/, accessed 11/20/2020.

2

EQUALITY AND NON-DISCRIMINATION

Equality and non-discrimination are at the heart of the human rights project and foundational to international human rights law. The two concepts are inextricably linked for the effective protection of human rights. Equality can only be achieved through a prohibition of discrimination.[1] Every core human rights treaty contains a provision guaranteeing that the rights it protects apply to all human beings equally without distinction of any kind and several human rights treaties were specifically drafted to elaborate the human rights of groups of people who are particularly vulnerable to discrimination. This chapter explores the equality and non-discrimination requirement of human rights, how it is violated by democratic and authoritarian states alike, and how targeted populations and their allies use the equality and non-discrimination articles of human rights instruments to fight for recognition and realization of their rights. Two case studies elaborate these dynamics: systemic racism in law enforcement in the United States; and the religious persecution of Uyghur Muslims in Xinjiang, China.

Article 1 of the Universal Declaration of Human Rights (UDHR) proclaims that "all people are born free and equal in dignity and rights." The language of dignity indicates that all human beings have intrinsic worth and the language of rights underscores that human rights are an entitlement for all people, in all places, always – not a reward for good behavior or preferred identity. Equality is enshrined in human rights law as a universal goal and provides a legal foundation for those struggling to have their equality recognized.[2] That human rights belong to everyone is further elaborated in Article 2 which proclaims, "Everyone is entitled to all the rights and freedoms set forth in this Declaration, without distinction of any kind, such as race, colour, sex, language, religion, political or other opinion, national or social origin, property, birth or other status." The language "other status" indicates that the types of discrimination prohibited in Article 2 are illustrative rather than exhaustive. The inclusion of the phrase "other status" has frequently been used to expand the list of

DOI: 10.4324/9781003256939-3

people protected by human rights law (e.g. indigenous, children, refugee, and people with disabilities) and the types of discrimination that is prohibited (e.g. sexual orientation, gender identity, and economic class).

Equality and non-discrimination are a cross-cutting concern of various human rights instruments. These principles are enshrined in both the International Covenant on Civil and Political Rights (Articles 2, 3, 4, and 26) and the International Covenant on Economic, Social and Cultural Rights (Article 2). Regional human rights instruments also recognize the universality of rights, prohibit discrimination, and promote equal treatment including the American Convention on Human Rights, the African Charter on Human and Peoples Rights, and the European Convention on Human Rights. Indeed, the Inter-American Court of Human Rights in a 2003 advisory opinion ruled that the principles of equality before the law, equal protection before the law, and non-discrimination have achieved the status of *jus cogens* – a peremptory norm that is accepted by the international community of states as a norm that must always be followed. This means they are fundamental, overriding principles of international law upon which the entire legal structure of national and international public order rests.[3] The right to non-discrimination is called a non-derogable right.

Simply including the right to equality and non-discrimination in the International Bill of Human Rights, however, does not protect all populations. In reality, many governments respect, protect, and fulfill human rights for a portion of their population while failing to do the same for others. Groups particularly vulnerable to discrimination because of their identity or belief often require specific protection and further elaboration of their rights. Therefore, several human rights instruments have been created to specifically address the human rights of groups, including women, indigenous peoples, migrants, people with disabilities, minorities, children, and racial and religious groups. Each prioritizes equality and non-discrimination. Efforts are underway to specify that discrimination due to sexual orientation and gender identity is also prohibited by international human rights law (see Box 2.1).

BOX 2.1 DEFENDING HUMAN RIGHTS: THE UNITED NATIONS' FREE & EQUAL CAMPAIGN FOR LGBTI RIGHTS[4]

That all human beings are born free and equal in dignity and rights is the foundation of international human rights law and every United Nations human rights instrument. According to the United Nations (UN) Human Rights Council's ground-breaking report, *Free and Equal*, "human rights are for everyone, without exception: lesbian, gay, bisexual, trans, and intersex (LGBTI) people are just as entitled to protection, respect, and fulfilment of their human rights as everyone else, including protection from discrimination, violence and torture."[5]

These protections include rights to life; security of person and privacy; the right to be free from torture, arbitrary arrest, and detention; freedom from discrimination; equality before the law; and the right to freedom of expression,

FIGURE 2.1 Free & Equal Campaign
Source: Screenshot via UN Human Rights channel on YouTube (www.youtube.com/watch?v=KgFlf_jQZhc&list=PLYUVFvBU-lofhW23ryCB1S1Gkvp_l6gyE&index=2)

association, and peaceful assembly.[6] Yet more than a third of the world's countries criminalize consensual same-sex relationships in violation of basic rights and even more have laws that discriminate on the bases of sexual orientation, gender identity, and sex characteristics.[7] The UN Free & Equal campaign is a global public information campaign aimed at promoting equal rights and fair treatment of LGBTI people.[8] The idea is that protection of LGBTI people does not require the passage of new laws. Rather, it requires the recognition and enforcement of their existing rights, including their right to non-discrimination which is contained in every human rights treaty. In addition to the campaign, the UN Human Rights Council has passed two resolutions condemning violence and discrimination and appointed an Independent Expert on Sexual Orientation and Gender Identity whose purpose it is to investigate, monitor, advise, and publicly report on matters related to human rights violations against LGBTI people. According to the UN, the core legal obligations of all states include:

1. protecting people from homophobic and transphobic violence;
2. preventing the torture and ill treatment of LGBTI persons;
3. repealing laws that criminalize homosexuality and transgender people;
4. prohibiting and addressing discrimination based on sexual orientation, gender identity, and sex characteristics; and
5. safeguarding freedom of expression, and peaceful assembly and association for all LGBTI people.[9]

Human rights must be demanded, claimed, and fought for and when achieved they must be regularly exercised, monitored, and enforced. Human rights demand equality of rights and equality of dignity. Complete respect for human rights means respecting the right to be different – and not to be discriminated against because of those differences.[10] Importantly, these instruments do not mandate uniformity because equality does not mean sameness. The equality and non-discrimination articles contained in the core human rights treaties are valuable tools for protecting the human rights of people who are frequently discriminated against. Two treaties – the Convention on the Elimination of All Forms of Discrimination against Women (CEDAW) and the International Convention on the Elimination of All Forms of Racial Discrimination (ICERD) – are entirely dedicated to the fight against discrimination. Despite formal equality in human rights law, gender inequality and gender subordination remain serious barriers to women's equal enjoyment of human rights. CEDAW was created to elevate women's human rights globally and address the main barriers to their realization.[11] Women's rights are human rights and human rights are women's rights.[12]

The International Convention on the Elimination of All Forms of Racial Discrimination

Racial and ethnic discrimination denies people the human rights they are entitled to and fuels hatreds that can destroy lives and communities. History is filled with wars and conflicts over racial animosities. The fight against racial and ethnic superiority is a priority for the United Nations' global membership and the principle of equality between and within states is enshrined in the UN Charter and the Universal Declaration of Human Rights. The International Convention on the Elimination of All Forms of Racial Discrimination (ICERD) is devoted in its entirety to promoting racial equality and prohibiting racial discrimination. It was unanimously adopted by the UN General Assembly in 1965. It has been ratified by 182 countries (94% of UN member states) and requires governments and other actors to not only respect the equal rights of all people but to adopt measures to eradicate the conditions that create and perpetuate racial discrimination and its unequal effects. Only 15 states, including Malaysia, Myanmar, and North Korea, have not ratified ICERD.[13]

The Convention defines racial discrimination as:

> any distinction, exclusion, restriction or preference based on race, colour, descent, or national or ethnic origin which has the purpose or effect of nullifying or impairing the recognition, enjoyment or exercise, on an equal footing, of human rights and fundamental freedoms in the political, economic, social, cultural or any other field of public life.[14]

This means governments are responsible not just for their deliberate actions but also the differential effects of their laws and actions on racial groups.[15] Importantly, ICERD equally protects the rights of citizens and non-citizens. It specifically condemns racial segregation, apartheid, and all institutions based on theories of superiority of one race, ethnicity, or color over others. The Convention forcefully condemns doctrines of racial differentiation and superiority as "scientifically false, morally condemnable, socially unjust and dangerous" and without justification.[16] ICERD guarantees the right to equal treatment before the law and in the administration of justice. It requires the protection of all racial groups by the state from bodily harm whether inflicted by government officials or any other group or institution. The Convention elaborates that all individuals and groups have equal political, civil, economic, social, and cultural rights and that governments have an equal responsibility to protect them. The United States ratified the ICERD in 1994.

Systemic Racism in Law Enforcement in the United States of America

"I can't breathe." On May 25, 2020, George Floyd, a Black American, uttered this phrase more than a dozen times as he struggled against the weight of a white Minneapolis, Minnesota police officer's knee pressed against his neck. Officer Derek Chauvin killed Floyd in public view on a busy city street. Chauvin held Floyd down while three other officers assisted or prevented bystanders from

FIGURE 2.2 Marchers at a justice rally for George Floyd
Source: Fiora Watts / Shutterstock.com

interfering. A 17-year-old high school student, Darnella Frazier, documented the police killing on her cellphone and published it on Facebook because "the world needed to see what I was seeing" and know the truth of what really happened to George Floyd.[17] In the weeks following his murder, up to 26 million Americans took to the streets to participate in demonstrations protesting police violence and racial discrimination organized by Black Lives Matter.[18] Global demonstrations in solidarity with American racial protests occurred throughout the world in what was described by a United Nations human rights expert as, "the largest transnational mobilization against systemic racism in law enforcement."[19] The police killing of George Floyd and the global outrage that followed shone a light on the persistence of systemic racism in law enforcement in the United States and other racially inspired human rights violations against people of African descent in the United States and around the world. Systemic racism refers to legal rules, policies, practices, and predominant cultural attitudes in either the public or private sector that create relative disadvantages for some racial groups, and privileges for other racial groups. The UN prohibits systemic discrimination and requires governments to eliminate it and offer a remedy to the victims of its harms.[20]

The United States imprisons more people – in absolute numbers and per capita – than any other country and has an incarceration rate five to ten times higher than other western democracies.[21] With 5% of the world's population, the United States' prison population represents 25% of the world's incarcerated.[22] In 2018, the prison and jail population was 2.1 million people with another 6.4 million individuals under some form of correctional control – about one in 40 adult US residents.[23] The rise in the US prison population has far outpaced US population and crime rates. Since 1970, the US prison population increased 700% even as crime rates were in decline.[24] While these numbers alone are disturbing, the racial disparity that pervades the US criminal justice system demonstrates an alarming pattern of racial discrimination. According to The Sentencing Project, "African Americans are more likely than white Americans to be arrested; once arrested, they are more likely to be convicted; and once convicted, they are more likely to experience lengthy prison sentences."[25] In the United States, people of color make up 27% of the US population, but make up 67% of the incarcerated population.[26] The US Bureau of Justice's own statistics show that in 2019 the imprisonment rate of Black males was 5.7 times the imprisonment rate of white males and Black males aged 18 and 19 were 12 times as likely to be imprisoned as white males of the same age group. Hispanic males were 2.5 times as likely to be incarcerated than whites.[27] Importantly, these incarceration rates do not reflect higher involvement in criminal activity by racial groups. Rather, they illustrate the prevalence of racial disparity and bias within the US criminal justice system where racial profiling is prevalent, communities of color are overpoliced, and white defendants are undercharged.[28] The comparatively and historically excessive use of incarceration and correctional control in the United States, which is characterized by the imprisonment of overwhelmingly poor and disproportionately Black and brown Americans, is referred to as mass incarceration.[29]

Racial discrimination in the US criminal justice system manifests in multiple forms and at multiple stages of law enforcement – policing, trial rights, incarceration, sentencing, conditions of detention, and the administration of the death penalty, among others. Black Americans are 3.7 times more likely to be arrested than white Americans for marijuana possession despite a comparable rate of marijuana use.[30] Black and Hispanic drivers are more likely to be stopped by police than whites, more likely to be stopped for discretionary reasons than actual traffic violations, and are three times more likely to be searched and twice as likely to be arrested than whites.[31] Racial disparity is also pervasive within the US juvenile justice system.[32] Black youth are frequently treated more harshly than whites and low-income youth accused of crimes are denied basic rights.[33] Rather than reflecting individual prejudice or personal-level bias, these racial disparities are the result of systemic discrimination deeply embedded in the structures of the US criminal justice system.

White supremacy is an enduring legacy of American race-based slavery. Enslaved black people in the US were denied their basic human rights and the narrative of white superiority and Black inferiority used to justify slavery created a racial hierarchy that has been sustained by America's most powerful political and legal institutions.[34] After emancipation, "slavery evolved but did not end," according to Bryan Stevenson.[35] A racial caste system of Jim Crow laws[36] enforced segregation and racial supremacy formally, while racial terror lynching and other forms of brutal violence did so informally. Stevenson and other justice advocates identify the death penalty and mass incarceration as contemporary manifestations of these earlier practices and reflective of the persistence of racial inequality.[37] The United Nations Human Rights Council agrees. In a 2016 fact-finding report, independent human rights experts argued that "a systemic ideology of racism ensuring the domination of one group over another continues to impact negatively on the civil, political, economic, social and cultural rights of African Americans."[38] Their investigation identified pervasive racial bias in the US criminal justice system. They warned of "alarming levels of police brutality and excessive use of lethal force by law enforcement officials, committed with impunity against people of African descent in the United States," and criticized the low rate of accountability for police crimes.[39]

Increased contact between police and people of African descent in the US also increases the risk that Black Americans like George Floyd, Tamir Rice, and Breonna Taylor will have a violent encounter with a police officer. Data from multiple independent databases that track fatal shootings by on-duty police officers in the United States reveals that the number of fatal shootings by police nationwide remains relatively constant at approximately 1,000 people annually between 2015 and 2020.[40] Of these, Black Americans are killed at more than twice the rate of white Americans and were slightly more likely to be unarmed and less likely to be threatening someone when they were killed.[41] In 2020, most police killings (approximately 58%) "began with police responding to suspected non-violent offenses or cases where no crime was reported."[42] Indeed, levels of police violence are not related to levels of violent crime. Instead, contemporary data suggests that there is "strong and statistically reliable evidence of anti-Black racial disparities in the killing of unarmed Americans by police."[43]

Racially discriminatory policing practices, including the excessive use of force, police killings, and the disproportionate incarceration of people of color, directly violate the human rights treaties to which the US is legally bound. The United States ratified ICERD in 1994 and is legally obligated to condemn racial discrimination, eradicate practices of racial discrimination, ensure its domestic law and practices conform to the treaty, and eliminate racial discrimination at the national, state, and local level. Specifically, the US is bound by Article 5 "to guarantee the right of everyone, without distinction as to race, colour, or national or ethnic origin, to equality before the law." This includes "the right to equal treatment before tribunals and all other organs administering justice," and "the right to security of person and protection by the State against violence or bodily harm, whether inflicted by government officials or by any individual group or institution."[44] Racially discriminatory law enforcement practices violate these provisions whether those practices are the result of official government policy (acts of commission) or a consequence of unintentional action (acts of omission). ICERD requires the United States to eliminate both.[45] The US has consistently violated these legal obligations.

United States policing and criminal justice practices also violate the equality and non-discrimination clause (Article 2) of the International Covenant on Civil and Political Rights (ICCPR), which the US ratified in 1992. US failure to protect the human rights of a portion of its population based on racial identity means that the US is violating other human rights protected by the ICCPR, including the right to life and human dignity, equality before the law, freedom from torture and ill-treatment, freedom from arbitrary arrest and detention, and the right to a fair trial. Unlawful police killings specifically violate Article 6 "no one shall be arbitrarily deprived of his life," Article 10 "All persons deprived of their liberty shall be treated with humanity and with respect for the inherent dignity of the human person," and Article 14 "Everyone charged with a criminal offense shall have the right to be presumed innocent until proven guilty."[46] The United States violates human rights when its policies, actions, and laws are contrary to its international human rights commitments, when they have differential effects on racial groups, and when the government fails to sincerely investigate and punish violations.

The unlawful killing of George Floyd tapped into a long history of police killings of Black people with impunity in the United States, sparking what may be the largest protest movement in US history. Between May 26 and June 28, 2020 more than 4,700 Black Lives Matter demonstrations condemning police brutality (an average of 140 a day) were held in approximately 2,500 small towns and large cities representing more than 40% of counties in the United States.[47] Many of these peaceful demonstrations were dispersed with excessive police force. In one particularly brutal illustration, police and security forces wearing riot gear and gas masks used chemical irritants, projectiles, explosive devices, and batons to forcibly disperse peaceful demonstrators who had been protesting police brutality outside the White House.[48] UN human rights experts condemned the killing of Floyd as a "modern-day racial terror lynching" and warned that given "impunity for racial violence of this nature in the United States, Black people have good reason to fear for their lives."[49] In a subsequent official statement, UN human rights experts called the disproportionate and excessive use of force against peaceful demonstrators "inexcusable," and "especially distressing" because the demonstrators were calling for accountability on police brutality and systemic racism in policing. At the same time, they credited the "innovation" of US civil society for "putting forward ideas to recreate public security grounded in human rights."[50]

Targeted populations and their allies have used the equality and non-discrimination articles of human rights instruments like the ICERD to fight for recognition and realization of their rights. Domestic justice advocates in the US have taken to the courts and the streets demanding recognition of their equality and human dignity. And the widespread racial protests in the US in the summer of 2020 inspired similar protests abroad calling for the dismantling of systems of racism and oppression worldwide.[51] Human rights practitioners based in the United States and elsewhere also appealed to the UN for help protecting the rights of Black Americans. Less than two weeks after George Floyd's murder, family members of several victims of police violence joined over 600 rights groups from more than 60 countries to demand the UN Human Rights Council launch an independent inquiry into US violations of international human rights law in the context of policing, protests, and assemblies.[52] They warned of an "unfolding grave human rights crisis" in the United States and called on the UN to hold the US accountable for its racist policing, repression of nationwide protests, and violence against journalists covering them – all human rights violations.[53] Members of the African Group – the largest United Nations regional group – responded to the appeal by calling for an urgent meeting of the Human Rights Council on human rights violations against people of African descent.

The Human Rights Council held an urgent debate on "current racially inspired human rights violations, systemic racism, police brutality against people of African descent and violence against peaceful protests" on June 17, 2020 in Geneva. Opening the proceedings, Michelle Bachelet, the UN High Commissioner for Human Rights, called the killing of George Floyd an "act of gratuitous brutality" and said that it was the result of "the systemic racism that harms millions of people of African descent."[54] She argued that failures to address the legacies of colonialism and the transatlantic slave trade manifest today in racial violence, systemic racism, and discriminatory policing. She demanded swift and decisive reform by states nationally and internationally.[55] Professor E. Tendayi Achiume, the Special Rapporteur on contemporary forms of racism, racial discrimination, xenophobia, and related intolerance, concurred. Referring to a joint statement issued by 47 UN human rights experts, Achiume reminded the US it must take steps in law, policy, and practice to ensure equal rights. She explained that it was the job of the UN human rights system to "sound the alarm" when grave human rights violations occur and to ensure that people subjected to human rights violations have recourse for protection when their national authorities are unable or unwilling to protect their human rights.[56] Citing the systemic nature of racial injustice in law enforcement, the experts urged the Human Rights Council (HRC) to create a thematic commission of inquiry to investigate systemic racism in law enforcement globally and especially in countries that participated in colonialism and the transatlantic trade and enslavement of people. "What is at stake here," Professor Achiume concluded, "is the lives and lived experiences of human beings who deserve fundamental human rights protections, and who should not be denied these rights on the basis of the color of their skin."[57]

In a rare break from procedure, the brother of George Floyd, Philonese Floyd, was invited to address the HRC. He said the murder of his brother is representative of how Black people are treated in the American justice system. In an emotional appeal, he asked the UN to help American families touched by police violence get justice.[58] Thirty member countries, 59 observer states, four international organizations, and 26 civil society organizations participated in the debate that followed.[59] All denounced the scourge of racism and persistent human rights violations directed at people of African descent, yet they disagreed whether the UN should address it as a common global problem or single out specific UN members for particularly egregious conduct. Racist violence directed at people of African descent spans history and transcends borders.[60] And yet, many member countries specifically demanded the US resolve the structural inequality that had sparked the events leading to the emergency meeting. The HRC unanimously adopted a resolution condemning racially discriminatory and violent practices and human rights violations perpetrated by law enforcement agencies against Africans and people of African descent. The resolution specifically condemned the death of George Floyd.[61] While the UN initially declined an international investigation, it committed the Office of the High Commissioner for Human Rights (OHCHR) to reporting on systemic racism and rights-violating police practices (including the incident leading to George Floyd's death), examining government responses to anti-racism protests, and regularly updating the HRC on police brutality against Africans and people of African descent worldwide. In June 2021, Bachelet called on UN members to stop denying and start dismantling racism. In

July, the HRC established a panel of experts to investigate systemic racism in policing around the world but the resolution establishing the panel specifically references the murder of George Floyd, ensuring that the United States will be investigated alongside other states.[62]

The Right to Freedom of Religion or Belief

The right to freedom of religion or belief is protected in multiple human rights instruments and features prominently in both the Universal Declaration of Human Rights (Article 18) and the International Covenant on Civil and Political Rights (Article 2, 5, 18, 26, and 27). Article 27 of the ICCPR declares,

> In those states in which ethnic, religious or linguistic minorities exist, persons belonging to such minorities shall not be denied the right, in community with other members of their group, to enjoy their own culture, to profess and practice their own religion, or to use their own language.

Elements of this right are connected to provisions in the International Covenant on Economic, Social and Cultural Rights, the convention prohibiting racial discrimination (ICERD), the women's convention (CEDAW), the children's convention (CRC), the torture convention (CAT), the migrant workers convention, the genocide convention and convention relating to the status of refugees.[63] Discrimination based on religion or belief is defined in the 1981 Declaration on the Elimination of All Forms of Intolerance and Discrimination Based on Religion or Belief as:

> any distinction, exclusion, restriction or preference based on religion or belief and having as its purpose or as its effect the nullification or impairment of the recognition, enjoyment or exercise of human rights and fundamental freedoms on an equal basis.

The Declaration describes religious discrimination as "an affront to human dignity and a disavowal of the principles of the Charter of the United Nations." It condemns religious discrimination as a violation of human rights and as an obstacle to peace.[64]

Human rights standards on the right to freedom of religion and belief protect: 1) the freedom to adopt, change, or renounce a religion or belief; 2) freedom from coercion due to that religion or belief; 3) the right to exercise one's religion or belief; and 4) the prohibition of discrimination due to religion or belief. Religious hatred, incitement to discrimination, and deprivation of life and freedom are also prohibited. The equality and non-discrimination principles ensure these rights for all people including children, women, and men, and ethnic, religious, and linguistic minorities. Freedom of religion or belief is a fundamental right. It cannot be suspended even in time of emergency or because of national security concerns. The OHCHR warns states to avoid equating certain religions with terrorism because it may breach the right to freedom of religion or belief of all members of the concerned religious communities or communities of belief.[65]

China's Repression of Uyghurs Under the Guise of Counterterrorism

The Uyghur community is a Turkic Muslim ethnic group of more than 11 million people who mostly live in the northwest region of China in the province of Xinjiang also known as the Uyghur region or Uyghur homeland. The indigenous Uyghur people possess a shared culture expressed through their distinct language, traditions, and largely the same religion of Islam. China formally recognizes the Uyghurs as an "ethnic minority" and has sought to forcibly assimilate them into the majority Han culture by suppressing their identity for decades. In the late 2010s, these efforts expanded and evolved into a campaign to destroy the Uyghur people through the eradication of their identity, language, culture, and religion. Under the guise of eliminating terrorism and violent extremism, China's government has enacted a series of repressive measures against the entire Uyghur community based on their ethnicity and religion. These include the enactment of discriminatory laws, mass social and technological surveillance, arbitrary and extra-judicial detention, family separation, forced labor, and processes of indoctrination. The goal is to eliminate the distinctive Uyghur identity and fully integrate and assimilate the Uyghur people and territory into modern China.[66] These practices are grave violations of human rights, violating key provisions of multiple core human rights treaties and violating the equality and non-discrimination provisions of them all. Indeed, there is reasonable evidence that China's practices in Xinjiang qualify as crimes against humanity and possibly genocide against the Uyghurs (see Table 2.1).[67]

TABLE 2.1 Defining Crimes Against Humanity and Genocide

Crimes Against Humanity	Genocide
Large-scale and systematic violence directed against a civilian population.	Deliberate, organized, large-scale violence directed at a specific national, ethnical, racial or religious group. People are targeted because they are members of the targeted group. The goal is to destroy the group.
Types of violence may include: murder; extermination; enslavement; imprisonment; torture; persecution; apartheid; sexual violence; and inhumane acts intended to cause physical or mental suffering.	Types of violence may include: killing; causing serious bodily or mental harm; imposing conditions intended to cause physical destruction; prevention of births; and removal of children.

Identity-based persecution of Uyghurs in Xinjiang is multi-faceted, systematic, and pervasive. Uyghurs are barred from openly practicing their religion, speaking their language, or expressing their cultural and religious identity through food or dress.[68] Government authorities have eliminated Uyghur language education; targeted religious and cultural leaders for prolonged detention and death; restricted freedom of movement; and have destroyed mosques, sacred cultural sites, and Uyghur architecture.[69] Defiance of these policies, open expression of religious devotion and Islamic tradition, or evidence of non-assimilationist tendencies can result in arrest or detention for the offender and often their family members. To neutralize resistance, the Chinese government has enacted a vast system of mass internment, arbitrary imprisonment, and constant surveillance of the population.

It is estimated that up to 3 million Uyghurs have been detained in mass internment camps since 2016.[70] Researchers have verified the existence of over 380 new or expanded detention centers across the Uyghur region since 2017, bringing the total number of these facilities to above 1,000. Most of these new facilities are highly fortified with barbed wire-fencing, perimeter walls and watchtowers, and the capacity to hold tens of thousands of internees outside the traditional criminal justice system.[71] The International Consortium of Investigative Journalists (ICIJ) calls it "the biggest interment of an ethnic-religious minority since World War II."[72] Former inmates report torture, forced labor, and indoctrination inside the camps. Detainees are constantly surveilled, prohibited from speaking their language, forced to denounce their religion, and must attend "re-education classes" where they learn Mandarin, participate in regular "repentance and confession," sing songs, and make statements swearing allegiance to the Communist Party. Hundreds of these detention facilities have on-site factories where detainees are reportedly forced to work.[73] Detainees are forcibly separated from their families and prevented from communicating with them. Frequently, they are held incommunicado without charge or trial for periods of months and years. In cases where both parents are detained, children are sent to government-run boarding schools where they are trained in Mandarin and Han culture. Former female detainees report forced sterilization, having intrauterine contraceptive devices (IUDs) forcibly implanted, and non-consensual abortions inside the camps. These practices have been corroborated by independent doctors and the government's own data, as well as shocking drops in the Uyghur birthrate.[74]

The Chinese government maintains control over the Uyghur people outside the camp system through mass surveillance, social monitoring and control, and fear. Security officials have implemented what they describe as a proactive approach to combating the "three evil forces" of terrorism, separatism, and extremism. The policy involves thousands of "convenience police stations" in towns and cities, security checkpoints, cameras with facial recognition technology, surveilling mobile and online communications, confiscating passports and travel documents of all Uyghurs, and installing GPS tracking devices on all vehicles.[75] Under the "Strike Hard Campaign," regional authorities have gathered biometric data, including DNA samples, fingerprints, iris eye scans, blood, and voice samples of all residents between the ages of 12 and 65.[76] The surveillance continues within the walls of Uyghur homes through the "Unite as One Family" program, which places Han Chinese citizens in Uyghur households to conduct in-person monitoring. Reports by monitors that Uyghur families are engaging in Uyghur cultural practices or the refusal by Uyghur families to permit homestays can result in arrest or detention.[77] Even Uyghurs living abroad are surveilled and threatened to prevent them from protesting Chinese policies in the Uyghur region. Retaliation against Uyghur rights activists includes punishing family members within China by denying them jobs and education or imprisoning them.[78]

China is obligated to respect, protect, and fulfill the human rights guaranteed by the treaties it has ratified including the Universal Declaration of Human Rights; the International Covenant on Economic, Social and Cultural Rights; the International Convention on the Elimination of All Forms of Racial Discrimination; and the Convention against Torture. Identity-based repression of the Uyghurs violates the right to be free from discrimination; the right to freedom of thought, conscience, and religion; the freedom of opinion and expression; and the right to education. Its detention and surveillance practices violate the right to a fair trial, freedom of movement, the right to not be deprived arbitrarily of liberty, the prohibition on torture and cruel and degrading treatment, and the right to privacy. Because these practices are specifically targeted at Uyghurs, they directly violate ICERD and the non-discrimination requirement of all the human rights treaties China is legally obligated to respect. Human rights experts also have concluded the widespread and systematic practices of enslavement, imprisonment, torture, enforced sterilization, enforced disappearance, and persecution amount to crimes against humanity. They also meet key elements of the genocide convention: causing serious bodily and mental harm to members of an ethnical group; deliberately inflicting conditions intended to bring about the physical destruction of the group (in whole or in part); imposing measures intended to prevent births within the group; and forcibly transferring children from the group to another.[79]

China denies that its practices violate human rights. Authorities claim internment camps are vocational training centers designed to help Uyghurs better integrate into Chinese society and the economy. It justifies its system of detention and surveillance as a legitimate and effective response to an existential national security threat – Uyghur Islamic terrorism. By labeling Uyghurs terrorists and invoking the language of national security threat, the Chinese government argues that the suspension of human rights is justified. This repeats an argument commonly made in the context of the Global War on Terror – that human rights can be suspended when a nation is under threat and that terrorists are not deserving of rights.[80] There are three major problems with China's argument. First, claims of widespread Uyghur terrorism prior to the implementation of China's security measures are not credible.[81] Second, it violates human rights to classify an entire people as terrorists due to their ethnicity or religion. Third, many of China's policies against the Uyghurs violate what are known as "non-derogable" rights – human rights that can never be suspended even in times of public emergency that threaten the life of the nation. These non-derogable rights include: the freedom of thought, conscience, and religion; prohibition of torture and cruel or unusual punishment; prohibition of enslavement; prohibition of medical experimentation without consent; prohibition of collective punishment; prohibition of arbitrary deprivation of liberty; and the right of those deprived of their liberty to be treated with humanity.[82] In short, national security is not a permissible grounds for restricting religion or belief, opinion or conscience. In the very narrow circumstances when permitted, the suspension of any other human rights for national security purposes may not be done in a discriminatory manner, according to human rights law. The right to equality and non-discrimination itself is non-derogable. Crimes against humanity and genocide are prohibited international crimes (see Chapter 4) and grounds for criminal prosecution.

Fear of being swept up into China's vast internment system and the threat of retaliation against family have prevented many Uyghurs inside and outside of China from directly challenging Chinese authorities with their rights claims. Yet individual activists, human rights NGOs, international lawyers, UN experts, and other governments are using the human rights framework to challenge China's repressive policies. Individual activists and former detainees are sharing their experiences with the media and elected officials despite great personal risk. NGOs like Human Rights Watch, the Uyghur Human Rights Project, the Global Center for Responsibility to Protect, International Crisis Group, and the Asia Pacific Partnership for Atrocity Prevention are corroborating that testimony with their independent research. The Worker Rights Consortium and the Coalition to End Forced Labor in the Uyghur Region, a broad network of human rights, labor rights, and Uyghur rights organizations, are asking apparel brands and retailers to stop outsourcing products from the Uyghur region and to cut ties with companies implicated in Uyghur forced labor.[83] Independent experts, international lawyers, and regional specialists are using their expertise to interpret that evidence while UN agencies including UN Human Rights and peer governments are demanding China comply with international human rights standards.

Conclusion

Equality and non-discrimination are a fundamental requirement of human rights. The case studies in this chapter have illustrated how the prohibition on discrimination is intimately connected to the protection of all other human rights. Yet in practice, democratic and authoritarian governments alike may honor their obligations to respect, protect, and fulfill human rights for some parts of their population while denying those same rights to others. When governments fail to fulfill their human rights obligations, they are guilty of human rights violations.

The human rights-based approach requires governments to avoid violating human rights, to equally protect its people from the human rights violations of others, and to take proactive measures to create the conditions necessary for the fulfillment of human rights for all people under their jurisdiction. Governments are responsible for eradicating systemic and institutionalized forms of discrimination. The desire for law and order, claims of necessity for national security purposes, and counterterrorism efforts cannot be used to justify suspending fundamental human rights, including the right to equality and non-discrimination.

Notes

1 Rhona K.M. Smith, *Textbook on International Human Rights*, Fifth edition (Oxford University Press, 2012), p. 196.
2 OHCHR, "Universal Declaration of Human Rights at 70: 30 Articles on 30 Articles – Article 1," www.ohchr.org/EN/NewsEvents/Pages/DisplayNews.aspx?NewsID= 23857&LangID=E, accessed 12/22/2020.
3 Inter-American Court of Human Rights, Advisory Opinion OC-18/03 of September 17, 2003, Juridical Condition and Rights of Undocumented Migrants, para. 101 in International Commission of Jurists, "Universality, Equality and Non-Discrimination," www.icj.org/sogi-casebook-introduction/chapter-two-universality-equality-and-non-discrimination/, accessed 12/22/2020.
4 The United Nations uses LGBTI to refer to lesbian, gay, bisexual, transgender, and intersex persons. The acronym LGBTQI is the more common usage in North American and European contexts and includes the letter "Q" to refer to individuals who identify as queer or are questioning their sexual or gender identity. Sometimes the letter "A" is also included to refer to individuals who identify as asexual and the sign "+" can be included to encompass spectrums of sexuality and gender.
5 OHCHR, *Born Free and Equal: Sexual Orientation, Gender Identity and Sex Characteristics in International Human Rights Law*, Second edition (United Nations, 2019) HR/PUB/ 12/06/Rev1.
6 OHCHR, *Born Free and Equal*, p. 2.
7 OHCHR, "The United Nations Global Campaign Against Homophobia and Transphobia," www.unfe.org/about-2/, accessed 2/20/2021.
8 OHCHR, "The United Nations Global Campaign."
9 OHCHR, "The United Nations Global Campaign"; OHCHR, *Born Free and Equal*, p. 7.
10 See United Nations Study on the Current Dimension of the Problems of Intolerance and of Discrimination Groups of Religion or Belief, UN Doc E/CN.4/Sub.2/1987/ 27, para. 17 cited in Smith, *Textbook on International Human Rights*, pp. 214–215.
11 OHCHR, "Convention on the Elimination of All Forms of Discrimination Against Women, New York, 18 December 1979," www.ohchr.org/en/professionalinterest/pa ges/cedaw.aspx, accessed 12/29/2020.
12 Hillary Clinton, then first lady of the United States, popularized this phrase used by gender advocates in a 1995 speech. Hillary Clinton, "Remarks for the United Nations Fourth World Conference on Women," September 5, 1995, www.un.org/esa/gop her-data/conf/fwcw/conf/gov/950905175653.txt, accessed 12/29/2020.
13 OHCHR, "Committee on the Elimination of Racial Discrimination," www.ohchr. org/en/hrbodies/cerd/pages/cerdindex.aspx, accessed 6/26/2021.
14 OHCHR, "International Convention on the Elimination of All Forms of Racial Discrimination (ICERD)," December 21, 1965, www.ohchr.org/en/professionalinterest/pa ges/cerd.aspx, accessed 12/30/2020.

15 Bandana Purkayastha, Aheli Purkayastha, and Chandra Waring, "From International Platforms to Local Yards: Standing Up for the Elimination of Racial Discrimination in the United States," in William T. Armaline, Davita Silfen Glasberg, and Bandana Purkayastha (eds.), *Human Rights in Our Own Backyard: Injustice and Resistance in the United States* (University of Pennsylvania Press, 2011), pp. 181 and 187.

16 OHCHR, "ICERD."

17 Paul Walsh, "Teen Who Recorded George Floyd Video Wasn't Looking to be a Hero, Her Lawyer Says," *Star Tribune*, June 11, 2020, www.startribune.com/teen-who-shot-video-of-george-floyd-wasn-t-looking-to-be-a-hero-her-lawyer-says/571192352/, accessed 1/16/2020.

18 Larry Buchanan, Quoctrung Bui, and Jugal K. Patel, "Black Lives Matter May Be the Largest Movement in U.S. History," *The New York Times*, July 3, 2020, https://nyti.ms/2ZqRyOU, accessed 1/16/2020.

19 OHCHR, *Statement from the UN Special Rapporteur on Contemporary Forms of Racism, Racial Discrimination, Xenophobia and Related Intolerance and The Working Group of Experts on People of African Descent. Joined by the Special Rapporteur on the Rights of Freedom of Assembly and Association, and the Coordination Committee of the UN Human Rights Special Procedures*, Urgent Debate of the Human Rights Council on "the current racially inspired human rights violations, systemic racism, police brutality and the violence against peaceful protest," Human Rights Council, June 17, 2020, www.ohchr.org/EN/NewsEvents/Pages/DisplayNews.aspx?NewsID=25969&LangID=E, accessed 10/06/2021.

20 United Nations Committee on Economic, Social and Cultural Rights, *General Comment No. 20* (E/C.12/GC/20), July 2, 2009, https://docstore.ohchr.org/SelfServices/FilesHandler.ashx?enc=4slQ6QSmlBEDzFEovLCuW1a0Szab0oXTdImnsJZZVQdqeXgncKnylFC%2blzJjLZGhsosnD23NsgR1Q1NNNgs2QltnHpLzG%2fBmxPjJUVNxAedgozixcbEW9WMvnSFEiU%2fV, accessed 6/28/2021.

21 American Civil Liberties Union (ACLU), *Overcrowding and Overuse of Imprisonment in the United States: American Civil Liberties Union Submission to the Office of the High Commissioner for Human Rights*, May 2015, p. 1.

22 ACLU, "Mass Incarceration," www.aclu.org/issues/smart-justice/mass-incarceration, accessed 6/26/2021.

23 Laura M. Maruschak and Todd D. Minton, "Correctional Populations in the United States, 2017–2018," *Bureau of Justice Statistics*, August 2020, www.bjs.gov/content/pub/pdf/cpus1718.pdf, accessed 1/24/2021.

24 ACLU, *Overcrowding and Overuse of Imprisonment*, p. 1.

25 The Sentencing Project, "Report of The Sentencing Project to the United Nations Special Rapporteur on Contemporary Forms of Racism, Racial Discrimination, Xenophobia, and Related Intolerance: Regarding Racial Disparities in the United States Criminal Justice System," March 2018, www.sentencingproject.org/wp-content/uploads/2018/04/UN-Report-on-Racial-Disparities.pdf, accessed 9/23/2021.

26 Rafael Khachaturian, "How the Criminal Justice System Preys on the Poor," *Dissent Magazine*, April 6, 2020.

27 E. Ann Carson, US Bureau of Justice Statistics, *Prisoners in 2019*, October 2020, p. 16.

28 The Sentencing Project, "Report," pp. 2–3. N. Ghandnoosh, *Race and Punishment: Racial Perceptions of Crime and Support for Punitive Policies* (The Sentencing Project, 2014), www.sentencingproject.org/wp-content/uploads/2015/11/Race-and-Punishment.pdf, accessed 9/23/2021.

29 See ACLU, *Overcrowding and Overuse of Imprisonment*, p. 1.

30 E. Edwards, W. Bunting, and L. Garcia, *The War on Marijuana in Black and White* (American Civil Liberties Union, 2013); The Sentencing Project, "Report," p. 4.

31 The Sentencing Project, "Report," p. 5, citing US Bureau of Justice Statistics, *Police Behavior during Traffic and Street Stops, 2011* (September 2013); and the Stanford Open Policing Project, available at: https://openpolicing.stanford.edu/findings/.

32 William T. Armaline, "Caging Kids of Color," in William T. Armaline, Davita Silfen Glasberg, and Bandana Purkayastha (eds.), *Human Rights in Our Own Backyard: Injustice and Resistance in the United States* (University of Pennsylvania Press, 2011), pp. 189–198; National Council on Crime and Delinquency, *And Justice for Some: Differential Treatment of Youth of Color in the Justice System* (Oakland, California, 2007).

33 Richard Pérez-Peña, "St. Louis County Biased Against Black Juveniles, Justice Department Finds," *The New York Times*, July 31, 2015, www.nytimes.com/2015/08/01/us/st-louis-county-biased-against-black-juveniles-justice-department-finds.html?mwrsm=Email, accessed 2/6/2021; United States Department of Justice Civil Rights Division, *Investigation of the S. Louis County Family Court St. Louis, MO*, July 15, 2020, https://njdc.info/wp-content/uploads/2015/07/St.-Louis-County-Family-Court-Findings-Report-7.31.15.pdf, accessed 2/6/2021.

34 Equal Justice Initiative (EJI), *The Legacy Museum: From Enslavement to Mass Incarceration* (Equal Justice Initiative, 2018).

35 Bryan Stevenson, *Just Mercy: A Story of Justice and Redemption* (Spiegel & Grau, 2014); EJI, "The Legacy Museum."

36 The name Jim Crow refers to a Black minstrel show character that demeaned African Americans. Jim Crow laws were the variety of state and local statutes that legalized racial segregation.

37 Stevenson, *Just Mercy*; Michelle Alexander, *The New Jim Crow: Mass Incarceration in an Age of Colorblindness* (The New Press, 2012).

38 Human Rights Council, *Report of the Working Group of Experts on People of African Descent on its mission to the United States of America*, A/HRC/33/61/Add.2, August 18, 2016, p. 4.

39 Human Rights Council, *Report*, p. 7.

40 "Police Shootings Database 2015–2021," *The Washington Post*, www.washingtonpost.com/graphics/investigations/police-shootings-database/, accessed 9/23/2021; Mapping Police Violence, https://mappingpoliceviolence.org/, accessed 9/23/2021.

41 "Police Shootings Database 2015–2021"; and Mapping Police Violence, *2020 Violence Report*, https://policeviolencereport.org//, accessed 9/23/2021. The *Washington Post* database provides data on individuals fatally shot by on-duty police officers. It relies primarily on news accounts, social media postings, and police reports. The project began after an investigation into the police shooting of Michael Brown (an unarmed Black man killed by police in Ferguson, Missouri) revealed that the FBI consistently undercounts fatal police shootings because many police departments fail to report police killings to the FBI. *Mapping Police Violence* is a research collaborative that collects data on police killings in the United States to quantify the impact of police violence on communities. The data is collected from media reports, obituaries, public records, police reports, criminal records databases, and other databases including Fatal-Encounters.org, the US Police Shooting Database, and KilledbyPolice.net. The *Mapping Police Violence* database includes data on all police killings whatever the means of death (shooting, taser, chokehold) committed by on-duty and off-duty police officers.

42 Mapping Police Violence, *2020 Violence Report*.

43 Mapping Police Violence, *2020 Violence Report*; Cody Ross, Bruce Winterhalder, and Richard McElreath, "Racial Disparities in Police Use of Deadly Force Against Unarmed Individuals Persist After Appropriately Benchmarking Shooting Data on Violent Crime Rates," *Social Psychological and Personality Science*, 12:3 (June 18, 2020), https://doi.org/10.1177/1948550620916071.

44 OHCHR, "ICERD."

45 Purkayastha, Purkayastha, and Waring, "From International Platforms to Local Yards," in Armaline, Glasberg, and Purkayastha (eds.), *Human Rights in Our Own Backyard* (2011), pp. 181 and 187.

46 OHCHR, "International Covenant on Civil and Political Rights (ICCPR)," December 16, 1966, www.ohchr.org/EN/ProfessionalInterest/Pages/CCPR.aspx, accessed 1/30/2021.

47 Buchanan, Bui, and Patel, "Black Lives Matter May Be the Largest Movement in U.S. History," *The New York Times*.

48 Katie Rogers, "Protesters Dispersed with Tear Gas So Trump Could Pose at Church," *The New York Times*, June 1, 2020.

49 OHCHR, "UN Experts Condemn Modern-Day Racial Terror Lynchings in the US and Call for Systemic Reform and Justice," June 5, 2020, www.ohchr.org/EN/NewsEvents/Pages/DisplayNews.aspx?NewsID=25933, accessed 9/23/2021.

50 OHCHR, "United States: UN Experts Condemn Crackdown on Peaceful Protests and Highlight Calls to Overhaul Policing," June 10, 2020, www.ohchr.org/EN/NewsEvents/Pages/DisplayNews.aspx?NewsID=25948&LangID=E, accessed 1/9/2021.

51 Borzou Daragahi, "Why the George Floyd Protests Went Global," *New Atlanticist*, June 10, 2020; Mary Dudziak, "George Floyd Moves the World: The Legacy of Racial Protest in America and the Imperative to Reform," *Foreign Affairs*, June 11, 2020.

52 American Civil Liberties Union (ACLU), Coalition Letter – Request for U.N. Independent Inquiry into Escalating Situation of Police Violence and Repression of Protests in the United States, "Re: Request for the Convening of a Special Session on the Escalating Situation of Police Violence and Repression of Protests in the United States," June 8, 2020, www.aclu.org/letter/coalition-letter-request-un-independent-inquiry-escalating-situation-police-violence-and?redirect=letter/coalition-letter-request-un-investigation-escalating-situation-police-violence-and-repression, accessed 9/23/2021.

53 American Civil Liberties Union (ACLU), "Families, Rights Groups Demand UN Investigate US Brutality, Protest Suppression," June 8, 2020, www.aclu.org/press-releases/families-rights-groups-demand-un-investigate-us-police-brutality-protest-suppression?utm_source=PassBlue+List&utm_campaign=f2879db445-PB_RSS_Fordham-Jun2020&utm_medium=email&utm_term=0_4795f55662-f2879db445-55011693, accessed 9/23/2021.

54 OHCHR, Statement by Michelle Bachelet, 43rd Session of the Human Rights Council Urgent Debate on current racially inspired human rights violations, systemic racism, police brutality against people of African descent and violence against peaceful protests, June 17, 2020.

55 OHCHR, Statement by Michelle Bachelet.

56 OCHRH, Statement from the UN Special Rapporteur on Contemporary Forms of Racism, Racial Discrimination, Xenophobia and Related Intolerance and the Working Group of Experts on People of African Descent joined by The Special Rapporteur on the Rights of Freedom of Assembly and Association, and the Coordination Committee of the UN Human Rights Procedures, June 17, 2020.

57 OHCHR, Statement from the UN Special Rapporteur.

58 Universal Rights Group, "Report of the Council's Urgent Debate on Currently Racially Inspired Human Rights Violations, Systemic Racism, Police Brutality against People of African Descent and Violence against Peaceful Protesters During HRC43," June 19, 2020, www.universal-rights.org/blog/report-of-the-councils-urgent-debate-on-current-racially-inspired-human-rights-violations/, accessed 2/12/2021.

59 Universal Rights Group, "Report of the Council's Urgent Debate."

60 Statement by Deputy Secretary-General of the United Nations, Amina Mohammed, Universal Rights Group, 2020.

61 United Nations Human Rights Council, Resolution 43/1 (A/HRC/RES/43/1), June 19, 2020.

62 Nick Cummings-Bruce, "U.N. to Form Panel to Investigate Systemic Racism in Policing," *The New York Times*, July 13, 2021, www.nytimes.com/2021/07/13/world/united-nations-panel-human-rights-council-racism.html, accessed 7/23/2021.

63 OHCHR, *Rapporteur's Digest on Freedom of Religion or Belief*, excerpts of the Reports from 1986 to 2011 by the Special Rapporteur on Freedom of Religion or Belief Arranged by Topics of the Framework for Communications, p. 4. See also ICESCR (Articles 2 and 13), ICERD (Article 5), CRC (Articles 14 and 30), CEDAW (Article 2), CAT, ICMW (Article 12), PPCG and CSR (Articles 4 and 33).

64 Declaration on the Elimination of All Forms of Intolerance and of Discrimination Based on Religion or Belief, 25 November 1981 (General Assembly resolution 36/55), www.ohchr.org/EN/ProfessionalInterest/Pages/ReligionOrBelief.aspx, accessed 12/31/2020.

65 OHCHR, *Rapporteur's Digest*, p. 98 citing E/CN.4/2005/61, paras 59–60.

66 Sean R. Roberts, *The War on the Uyghurs: China's Internal Campaign against a Muslim Minority* (Princeton University Press, 2020).

67 Dozens of governments, human rights NGOs, and mass atrocity prevention organizations have called these practices crimes against humanity while dozens of other independent experts on human rights, war crimes, and international law (and some governments) label them genocide. See United States Holocaust Memorial Museum (USHMM), Simon-Skjodt Center for the Prevention of Genocide, "The Uyghurs in China"; the Asia Pacific Partnership for Atrocity Prevention (APPAP), Members Statement on the Uighurs, February 19, 2021, https://appap.group.uq.edu.au/files/1670/APPAP%20statement%20-%20China%20February%202021_FINAL.pdf, accessed 6/26/2021; Newlines Institute for Strategy and Policy, *The Uyghur Genocide: An Examination of China's Breaches of the 1948 Genocide Convention*, March 2021; Roberts, *The War on the Uyghurs*.

68 USHMM Simon-Skjodt Center for the Prevention of Genocide, "The Uyghurs in China."

69 Newlines Institute for Strategy and Policy, *The Uyghur Genocide: An Examination of China's Breaches of the 1948 Genocide Convention*, March 2021, p. 4; OHCHR, "Convention on the Prevention and Punishment of the Crime of Genocide," December 9, 1948, www.ohchr.org/EN/ProfessionalInterest/Pages/CrimeOfGenocide.aspx, accessed 10/6/2021; ICC, "Rome Statute of the International Criminal Court," 2011, www.icc-cpi.int/resource-library/documents/rs-eng.pdf, accessed 10/6/2021.

70 USHMM Simon-Skjodt Center for the Prevention of Genocide, "The Uyghurs in China."

71 Newlines, *The Uyghur Genocide*, p. 23; Global Centre for the Responsibility to Protect, "Populations at Risk: China," January 15, 2021, www.globalr2p.org/countries/china/, accessed 3/1/21.

72 Hannah Knowles, Kim Bellware, and Lateshia Beachum, "Secret Documents Detail Inner Workings of China's Mass Detention Camps for Minorities," *The Washington Post*, November 24, 2019.

73 Global Centre for the Responsibility to Protect, "Populations at Risk: China"; Newlines, *The Uyghur Genocide*.

74 The region is responsible for 80% of new IUD placements in China and the Uyghur birthrate dropped about 33% between 2017 and 2018 alone. For detailed data on the prevention of births in the Uyghur community backed by Chinese government statistics see Newlines, *The Uyghur Genocide*, pp. 30–33. See also, Ben Westcott and Rebecca Wright, "First Independent Report into Xinjiang Genocide Allegations Claims Evidence of Bejing's 'Intent to Destroy' Uyghur People," CNN, March 9, 2021.

75 Newlines, *The Uyghur Genocide*; Global Centre for the Responsibility to Protect, "Populations at Risk: China"; ICERD, Committee on the Elimination of Racial Discrimination, "Concluding Observations on the Combined Fourteenth to Seventeenth Periodic Reports of China," September 19, 2018 (CERD/C/CHN/CO/14–17), p. 7.

76 Human Rights Watch, *China's Algorithms of Repression: Reverse Engineering a Xinjiang Police Mass Surveillance App*, May 1, 2019.

77 USHMM Simon-Skjodt Center for the Prevention of Genocide, "The Uyghurs in China."

78 Nury Turkel, "China's Repression and Internment of Uyghurs: US Policy Responses," written testimony, House Committee on Foreign Affairs Subcommittee on Asia and the Pacific, September 26, 2018.

79 Rome Statute of the ICC; Genocide Convention; Newlines Institute; Alison Macdonald QC, Jackie McArthur, Naomi Hart, and Lorraine Aboagye, *International Criminal Responsibility for Crimes against Humanity and Genocide Against the Uyghur Population in the Xinjiang Uyghur Autonomous Region*, January 26, 2021.

80 Roberts, *The War on the Uyghurs*.

81 Roberts, *The War on the Uyghurs*.

82 OHCHR, "Core Human Rights in Two Covenants," September 2013, https://nhri. ohchr.org/EN/IHRS/TreatyBodies/Page%20Documents/Core%20Human% 20Rights.pdf, accessed 3/13/21.

83 Worker Rights Consortium, "Ending Uyghur Forced Labor," www.workersrights. org/our-work/forced-labor/, accessed 7/29/2021; and End Uyghur Forced Labor, "The Coalition to End Forced Labor in the Uyghur Region," https://enduy ghurforcedlabour.org/, accessed 7/29/2021.

3

THE INTERDEPENDENCE OF HUMAN RIGHTS

Political and civil rights are deeply intertwined with economic, social, and cultural (ESC) rights. Consider two examples. The Flint Water Crisis (US) demonstrates how the violation of political rights in Flint, Michigan led to the violation of the right to water which threatened the rights to life and health. These rights violations were compounded by preexisting racial, economic, and environmental disparities – violations of the right to non-discrimination. The fight for clean water in Flint, then, is directly related to the struggle for democratic governance, fundamental equality, and justice. In northern Iraq, ISIS's use of sexual violence against Yazidi women also demonstrates the interdependence of human rights. Violations of women's political and ESC rights are interconnected; and in wartime, gender discrimination translates into gender-based atrocities. Both examples illustrate the interdependence of human rights.

Human rights are equal, interdependent, and require universal protection. To say that human rights are interdependent is to say that the enjoyment of any single right or group of rights requires the enjoyment of other rights.[1] This means that political and civil rights are necessary for formulating and fulfilling ESC needs.[2] Similarly, violations of socio-economic rights limit our ability to exercise our political and civil rights. In short, human beings must possess the entire spectrum of human rights to lead a life of dignity. Governments cannot simply pick and choose which human rights to respect, protect, and fulfill. They are required to protect them all; although in practice, many governments privilege some rights over others.

The interdependence of human rights is not just a conceptual argument about the equal value of all rights. And it is not just a principled commitment to common aspirations for a dignified life. Human rights are interdependent in practice. It is difficult to participate fully in the governance of your country (a

DOI: 10.4324/9781003256939-4

political right) if you do not have access to education (a social right), lack the means to meet basic food and health needs (economic rights), lack freedom of the press or are denied freedom of expression (civil rights). While the basic idea is that true achievement of human rights requires recognition of all of them, the relationship between specific rights vary. Sometimes one human right will protect against the violation of a related right. The right to freedom of movement also protects the right to freedom of assembly.[3] One human right might justify the need for another human right – fulfillment of the right to life requires the right to an adequate standard of living and the right to water. Other rights are mutually reinforcing like the freedom of association and the right to form a trade union.[4] Effective fulfillment of free and fair trial rights and access to courts can provide a remedy when other human rights are violated. The right to vote can pressure government leaders to protect other human rights and can hold them accountable for human rights violations. One set of rights can be used to identify, exercise, and protect other rights.[5]

 The cases in this chapter are examples of what Michael Goodhart calls "negative interdependence" – the idea that the insecurity of some rights make other rights insecure.[6] Human rights violations are frequently "intersectional" meaning that multiple forms of discrimination are often at work simultaneously.[7] This chapter explores how political and civil rights are intricately connected to ESC rights; how the violation of some rights can initiate a "chain reaction" triggering the violation of other rights; and how the effective fulfilment of human rights requires the enjoyment of all categories of rights without privileging one set of rights above the others.

The United Nations (UN) asserted the interdependent character of human rights from the earliest negotiations on the Universal Declaration of Human Rights (UDHR). The principle of interdependence continues to shape the approach of UN human rights bodies today. Yet the passage of the UDHR was followed by the drafting of two separate human rights covenants in 1966 rather than a single treaty – the International Covenant on Civil and Political Rights (ICCPR) and the International Covenant on Economic, Social, and Cultural Rights (ICESCR). This implied that there was a notable distinction between them. Some self-interested governments instrumentalized the separation of human rights for their own political purposes, in some cases defending a hierarchy of rights, and in others claiming that some human rights are aspirational rather than necessary.[8] Yet the separation of human rights into two covenants is best explained by the character of international politics rather than the character of these rights.

The UN Commission on Human Rights was tasked with elaborating the meaning of these rights and setting the standards of appropriate state conduct in legally binding treaties. The drafters disagreed whether all human rights could be implemented the same way – many governments argued it was more challenging to translate state duties and obligations of human economic and social practice

Justiciability

into rights.[9] These governments claimed that political and civil rights were justiciable but ESC rights were not. Justiciability refers to the ability for a court to exercise its legal authority. The drafters ultimately decided it was functionally difficult to combine different types of government obligations into a single human rights instrument.[10] This distinction is reflected in the different language found in the two covenants. The ICCPR uses the language of immediate obligation to uphold rights (e.g. undertakes to respect and ensure) while the ICESCR uses the language of progressive realization of rights (e.g. undertakes to take steps).[11]

challenge

Second, the United States and other western countries demanded the separation of the covenants because they considered the idea of justiciable economic and social rights "unpalatable and politically untenable."[12] Separation suited American political interests during the Cold War by allowing the US to exert leadership on civil and political rights as a way to undermine the Soviets and to simultaneously lessen the saliency of ESC rights which the USSR privileged and the US rejected.[13] Finally, human rights were codified into two distinct covenants for pragmatic reasons. Simply put, the negotiation process was taking too long. States reached agreement on political and civil rights long before they did on ESC rights. To pass, any treaty would need majority support from UN members, and some states, including the US, would not ratify a human rights treaty that included economic rights. The concern was that further delay could doom the entire standard-setting project. Separation was considered a pragmatic political concession. If support for a single treaty could not be reached, the option of two treaties would mean that most states would ratify at least one, making both more likely to pass.[14] The separation of human rights into two covenants does not mean the human rights norms contained within them are separable.[15] Yet, the decision to draft two covenants limits the enjoyment of human rights for people living within countries that have ratified one but not both treaties.

The Flint Water Crisis

①water → health issue → high rates of infertility & miscarriage

At first glance, the Flint Water Crisis seems to be all about the water. In 2014, after the City of Flint changed its municipal water source as a cost-saving measure, residents started to complain about the color, taste, and smell of the water. They also reported mysterious rashes and illnesses. By October 2015, a local pediatrician made the awful discovery that tens of thousands of Flint's children had been exposed to dangerously high levels of lead through the drinking water, threatening their health, growth, and neurological development. Later, the water would be identified as the likely source of a Legionella outbreak that killed at least a dozen residents and associated with higher rates of infertility and miscarriage in pregnancies.[16] But the water crisis wasn't just about poisoned water and its devastating impact on Flint's population. It was about how the people of Flint came to be harmed by their water in the first place. They were poisoned

cause

through governmental decision – by policy.[17] And that policy was made by a series of unelected emergency financial managers appointed by the State of Michigan in contravention of the democratic political rights of Flint citizens.

In November 2011, on election day, Governor Rick Snyder declared a financial emergency in Flint. A month later, he appointed the first of four emergency managers to run Flint's municipal affairs, vacating the effect of local elections. Under Michigan's emergency manager law, emergency managers (EMs) have the authority to suspend, even dissolve, the power of local elected officials and legislate in their place.[18] The move eliminated the traditional checks and balances that come with democratic governance. Charged with cutting expenditures to address fiscal distress and insulated from public accountability for their actions, Flint's EMs made a series of decisions that privileged state interest and financial status above citizen safety and public health. One of those decisions was to cut costs by relying on the Flint River as the primary source for drinking water despite opposition from the local community, their elected representatives, and municipal officials who were ill prepared and lacked the scientific expertise to safely treat the water. The EMs were solely accountable to the Governor that appointed them rather than the people impacted by their decisions. They, along with other state and municipal authorities, ignored citizen complaints about water quality, dismissed and discredited evidence that water treatment had been mismanaged, and in some cases, conspired to conceal evidence that prolonged harm to public health.[19] These actions added insult to injury and both extended and deepened the harm caused by the water crisis. The social, health, and economic impacts are difficult to calculate – lost lives, damaged health, increased medical costs, a destroyed water infrastructure, plunging housing values, soaring unemployment rates, lost business development, and irreversible harm to children. The loss of democratic accountability in Flint stripped its people of self-governance and encouraged EMs to recklessly endanger their safety and their rights.[20]

cause

What happened in Flint was not only an injustice – it was a violation of fundamental human rights by decision-makers with political power. Article 21 of the Universal Declaration of Human Rights (UDHR) guarantees all people the right to participate in political governance either directly or through freely chosen representatives. It also declares that everyone has the right of equal access to public services and that the will of the people shall be the basis of political authority expressed through free and fair elections. When Governor Snyder appointed an emergency manager to Flint, he overturned a democratic election, denying Flint citizens their right to choose their political representatives and removing the political authority of duly elected local officials.

The political participation rights found in Article 21 of the UDHR are also guaranteed by Article 25 of the International Covenant on Civil and Political Rights (ICCPR) which the United States ratified in 1992. Article 25 also enables popular influence in public debate and dialogue. This means that citizens have the right to engage in the decision-making processes that affect them.[21] Yet Flint's

Article 21 & 25 — violated

EMs denied citizens the right to participate in decision-making, consistently ignored popular opinion, and refused to offer opportunities for meaningful debate and dialogue on policy and its impacts. According to Article 25 these rights must be applied equally without distinction of any kind. And while Article 25 does not require a specific electoral system, it is based on the principle of one person, one vote and requires that the vote of one elector be equal to the vote of another elector.[22] Governor Snyder applied the EM law as a fiscal correction tool in some of Michigan's distressed communities but not dozens of others. Those where emergency management was applied – Flint, Benton Harbor, Pontiac, Detroit, and Ecorse – were disproportionately comprised of Black and other minority communities.[23] At one point about half of Michigan's African American population lived under the rule of an EM.[24] In comparison, only 2% of the white population did.[25] One vote in Flint or Detroit was hardly equal with a vote in majority white surrounding communities where elections were not disregarded and democratically elected authority was not suspended. In Flint, each element of Article 21 in the UDHR and Article 25 of the ICCPR was violated.

The Flint Water Crisis is an example of negative interdependence – the insecurity of political rights made ESC rights insecure. The right to water is derived from two articles of the International Covenant on Economic, Social, and Cultural Rights (ICESCR): the right to an adequate standard of living (Article 11) and the right to health (Article 12).[26] The right to water is also indispensable to the right to life (Article 6 of the ICCPR) and a "prerequisite for the realization of other human rights."[27] The UN Committee on Economic, Social and Cultural Rights (CESCR) has identified five normative criteria that specify the content of this right. Water must be available (sufficient), quality (safe), acceptable, accessible, and affordable for personal and domestic use.[28] These criteria were reaffirmed in UN General Assembly Resolution 64/292 on "the human right to water and sanitation" in 2010. The UN defines availability to mean sufficient and continual access to water for drinking, personal sanitation, washing of clothes, food preparation, personal and household hygiene. Quality means that water must be safe to drink; be an acceptable color, odor, and taste; and be free from threats to human health.[29] Water must be physically and safely accessible within a reasonable distance to one's home. It must be affordable (meaning that the cost does not encroach on the fulfillment of other human rights) and be provided in a culturally acceptable manner.[30] Everyone is entitled to water adequate for human dignity, life, and health.

Governments have an obligation to respect, protect, and fulfill human rights (see Chapter 1), including the right to water. Governments must not pollute or contaminate the water supply or interfere (directly or indirectly) with the enjoyment of the right to water. Governments must prevent others from interfering with the right to water. And governments must adopt appropriate legal, administrative, budgetary, scientific, and other measures necessary to ensure people can realize their right to water. In Flint, the federal, state, and local government failed in all three obligations. Due to government action and inaction (altering the water source, failing to properly treat the water, and disregarding evidence of contamination), the availability, quality, accessibility, and affordability requirements of the right to water were violated with devastating results. Contaminated water threatened the health and life of Flint's more than 100,000 residents and thousands of Flint kids were exposed to lead poisoning with lifelong consequences. Water accessibility decreased because residents could not safely use tap water at home, school, or work. Water became increasingly unaffordable. Flint's disproportionately poor population was required to pay disproportionately high rates for unusable water, and were forced to rely on bottled water and water filters to remove contaminants from unsafe municipal water. As a result, the availability of safe water was insufficient to meet the personal and household needs of Flint families. Human rights violations in Flint were the result of government decision-making. Government failure to fulfill its representative function was connected to its failure to serve its protective function.[31]

One of the notable characteristics of the Flint Water Crisis was citizen activism. It was the collective action of ordinary residents – primarily women and mothers – that built a justice movement, attracted national media attention, put government officials at the state and federal level on the defensive, and eventually restored their own rights. From the very beginning, Flint's citizen water movement argued that the denial of democracy was the cause and reason for the severity of the water crisis.[32] Justice was rooted in the restoration of democracy, realization of the right to water, and reparations for harm done, including replacement of local water infrastructure, individual compensation, and community revitalization.[33]

With the traditional routes of constituent lobbying closed off to them by the replacement of elected officials with appointed emergency managers, Flint activists vocally protested the condition of the water in the streets, on the lawn of City Hall, the steps of the State Capitol, and at every available public information session. When their voices and experiences were ignored, they became citizen scientists working with independent researchers, scientists, and national environmental activists to gather data and create the evidence base to support their claims of water contamination.[34] They coordinated with nonprofit organizations, local churches, and rallied national celebrities to help mitigate the impacts of the crisis through bottled water donations, water filter drives, and financial donations to help residents fill the gaps left by the State of Michigan's and the Federal Government's lackluster response to the crisis. Finally, they went to the courts, the halls of the US Congress, and the United Nations to demand the restoration of their human rights. The world was listening. In 2016, the UN Special Rapporteurs on extreme poverty and safe drinking water described lack of regular access to safe drinking water in Flint as a potential violation of human rights. They suggested that if Flint's population had been well-off or overwhelmingly white, government officials would not have acted with such callous disregard for their health and safety.[35] In 2019, the UN Human Rights Council demanded that the US government remedy the water crisis in Flint and ensure that all citizens have access to safe and clean water as part of its periodic review of the US human rights record.[36]

In Flint, the violation of political participation rights caused the violation of the right to water which in turn threatened the right to life, health, and an adequate standard of living. Emergency managers appointed by the State of Michigan were responsible for the decision to change the source of the drinking water. They and other government officials shared responsibility for the mismanagement and contamination of the water, the devastating health effects on the population, and destruction of water infrastructure citywide. If the political rights of Flint's people had been protected, the water source never would have been changed over citizen objection, would have been treated properly, and citizen safety would have been prioritized above monetary savings.[37] No emergency manager, no water crisis. It is also likely that without citizen activism, there would not have been a remedy. The Flint water movement revealed the extent of the water crisis, compelled the State of Michigan to allow the city of Flint to reconnect to a safe water source, and pressured the State of Michigan and federal government into providing emergency relief. The people of Flint were responsible for realizing their own human rights. At the time of this writing, citywide lead levels are within the range that the US government deems safe and nearly 10,000 lead lines have been replaced by court order.[38] A multi-million-dollar class action legal settlement has been reached and an additional civil and criminal litigation remains pending. Yet for many Flint families, like families in other American communities without reliable access to safe drinking water like Detroit and Pittsburgh, lack of faith in government and lack of trust in the safety of the water remains.[39] In fact, the US government does not formally recognize the right to water and has not ratified the International Covenant on Economic, Social, and Cultural Rights (ICESCR).

BOX 3.1 DEFENDING HUMAN RIGHTS: FAITH SPOTTED EAGLE AND THE YANKTON SIOUX NATION FIGHT THE DAKOTA ACCESS PIPELINE

Faith Spotted Eagle is a member of the Yankton Sioux Nation, a tribal elder, water protector, and human rights activist. A leader of the Keystone XL Pipeline and Dakota Access Pipeline (DAPL) protests, Spotted Eagle has dedicated her life to safeguarding the rights of indigenous people, their lands, water, and culture. The DAPL runs just north of the Standing Rock Sioux Tribe Reservation on land that was inhabited by indigenous ancestors for generations. Pipeline construction disturbed sacred, cultural, and burial sites. It crosses the Missouri River twice, risking contamination of the river and Lake

FIGURE 3.1 Faith Spotted Eagle speaks in opposition to the Keystone XL Pipeline
Source: Associated Press

Oahe, the reservation's primary source of fresh drinking and ceremonial waters.[40] The Standing Rock Sioux, other indigenous tribes, and their allies object to the DAPL project for disregarding tribal sovereignty, breaching US environmental law, and violating fundamental human rights, including indigenous rights. These indigenous rights include: the right to water; the right to land, territories, and resources; the right to self-determination; the right to practice and protect manifestations of indigenous culture; and the right to participate in decision-making in matters that affect indigenous rights.[41]

Standing Rock Sioux leaders, including Faith Spotted Eagle, have adopted a trifold strategy to gain recognition of their rights. First, they raised awareness through protest, prayer, and nonviolent direct action. A historic gathering of tribes and allies to peacefully and spiritually resist construction of the pipeline attracted thousands of people from across the Western Hemisphere, including representatives of 416 indigenous nations, ordinary Americans, and military veterans.[42] Second, tribal leaders and grandmothers lobbied elected officials and testified before Congress, governmental subcommittees, and agencies at every level – local, state, national, and at the UN. Finally, they took the government to court, arguing that members of the tribe were not adequately consulted on the route, that the pipeline is operating without a valid permit, and that the US government is "obligated by law to protect the integrity of the reservation." This includes "protecting the integrity of the water on which the Standing Rock people rely" and respecting the political, social, and cultural rights of indigenous peoples.[43]

Oil flows through the DAPL and litigation to stop the pipeline continues. Yet, the Standing Rock movement is considered a human rights success. The fight against the pipeline grew into a global movement of solidarity, enflaming consciousness around environmental justice, tribal sovereignty, and indigenous rights. Standing Rock showed the value of coalition-building and demonstrated that grassroots organizing can change the course of events and reshape the national conversation, even in the face of governmental and corporate power. Its legal efforts have won recognition from the US government that it has not respected the rights of the Standing Rock Sioux. The movement has trained and inspired a new generation of rights activists who have been quietly leading efforts to stop environmentally destructive projects across the United States. Perhaps most importantly, indigenous peoples and their fight for their rights are now more visible.[44]

Faith Spotted Eagle offers important lessons for human rights advocates. She teaches that allyship means respecting the culture and centering the voices of those who are fighting for their own rights. Supporters of human rights movements, and especially indigenous protest actions, must resist a settler colonial mentality to take charge and try to rescue others. Non-indigenous allies must respect the decisions of indigenous communities. They must stand in their full spirit and be physically and mentally prepared to contribute to the cause, or they risk becoming a burden to those they seek to support. And they should augment rather than reduce the resources of the communities they seek to serve.[45] Abiding by these lessons is essential to ethical human rights allyship.

ISIS and Sexual Violence against Yazidi Women in Northern Iraq

Like the Flint Water Crisis, the use of rape as a weapon against Yazidi women illustrates the interdependent character of rights and the negative interdependence of human rights violations. An estimated 736 million women worldwide have experienced intimate partner violence, non-partner sexual violence, or both at least once in their lifetimes. This amounts to almost one in three women aged 15 and older.[46] Violence negatively affects women's general well-being and their full participation in society. Globally, women are under-represented in political decision-making, over-represented among the world's poor, are more likely than men to face food insecurity, are disproportionately impacted by climate change, and paid significantly less than their male counterparts in the workplace.[47]

A global gender gap exists between women and men on health outcomes, educational attainment, economic opportunity, and political empowerment.[48] Women's political, economic, social, and cultural rights are interconnected and the violation of any particular set of rights jeopardizes the fulfillment of others. These preexisting patterns of discrimination against women are exacerbated during periods of conflict, repression, and civil strife. Gender inequality and discrimination increases the risk of sexual and gender-based violence (SGBV) during conflict. This is particularly true when sexism merges with hatred based on ethnic, racial, or religious identity. SGBV has been used as a tactic of terrorism, strategy of war, and a weapon of genocide. ISIS used sexual violence against Yazidi women in northern Iraq for all three of these purposes.

The Islamic State of Iraq and Syria (ISIS) – also known as the Islamic State, ISIL, or Daesh – began as a local branch of the terrorist organization al Qaeda in Iraq. In 2014, ISIS launched a series of military attacks to capture territory in Iraq and Syria as part of its effort to create an Islamic caliphate. In early August 2014, ISIS fighters attacked the Sinjar region of northern Iraq – home to the majority of the world's Yazidi population. The Yazidi are a distinct religious group of ethnic Kurdish descent.[49] During its military attack, ISIS forced more than 800,000 people from their homes and deliberately destroyed religious and cultural sites. With few military objectives in the region, ISIS fighters targeted the Yazidi people for forced conversion, rape, torture, kidnapping, and murder.[50] Upon capture, ISIS separated the men and older boys from the women and other children. The men and older boys were summarily executed if they refused to convert to Islam. Women and girls as young as nine were enslaved and given or sold to ISIS fighters as wives, domestic servants, or sex slaves. Treated as commodities, many were bought and resold multiple times in public markets or online. Prepubescent children were sold with their mothers and abused to control or punish them. As children aged, they were separated from their mothers. As early as age seven, boys were sent to ISIS training camps to become child soldiers and girls could be enslaved separately from their mothers at age nine.[51]

The threat and use of sexual violence against Yazidi women and making them *sabiyya* – a word that means woman captive – was a key military strategy adopted by ISIS. First, it served several strategic objectives of terrorism. SGBV displaced populations, destabilized social structures, and advanced extremist ideology.[52] ISIS used sexual violence as a recruitment and propaganda tool. They promised fighters they would be rewarded with captured women as spoils of war and offered a distorted religious justification for raping them. The strategy of widespread rape of religious minority women even had a name – *Jihad al nikah* – which translates as sexual intercourse in pursuit of struggle. The capture and sale of Yazidi women also became a lucrative source of finance for the Islamic State. At the height of their rule, it is estimated that ISIS held almost 7,000 Yazidi women and girls in sexual slavery and the slavery market may have contributed $21 million to its economy.[53] The profit potential of trafficking in Yazidi women significantly increased after ISIS began ransoming the women back to their families and the Yazidi community for prices as high as $20,000–$30,000 per captive, creating the potential to generate tens of millions of dollars in additional income.[54]

Second, sexual violence has become an enduring strategy of war, especially in contexts where sexism and inter-ethnic or inter-religious hatred combine. Women biologically and culturally reproduce their nations through childbirth and the socialization of children in cultural and religious traditions. If the goal is to displace and destroy a people, targeting and destroying women – the material and symbolic center of the community – becomes a strategic tactic.[55] SGBV accompanies murder, displacement, enslavement, extortion, and property destruction as war tactics aimed specifically at civilian populations. By attacking Yazidi women, ISIS aimed to reduce the sustainability of the Yazidi community by eliminating its ability to reproduce biologically and culturally through destruction of the family and preventing women's ability to pass down culture. Tactically, rituals of sexual violence also bind perpetrators to the regime. By distorting the language of the Qu'ran and principles of Islamic scholarship to justify rape of Yazidi *sabiyya*, ISIS instrumentalized rape to spread its own "militarized, masculinized, religious and genocidal" form of nationalism.[56]

Third, ISIS used SGBV to commit genocide, alongside crimes against humanity, war crimes, and other human rights violations.[57] ISIS's sexual enslavement of Yazidi women and children and their degrading treatment in captivity were intended to cause physical and mental harm, prevent future Yazidi births, and forcibly sever Yazidi children from their distinct religion and culture.[58] The decision to kill, convert, and enslave Yazidi for the purpose of destroying their identity and religion was the official policy of ISIS. This policy was widely publicized in various statements and documents, including official pamphlets regulating the rules of slavery and its English-language publication, *Dabiq*.[59] While sexual violence perpetrated against Yazidi women by ISIS was part of its military strategy, and a tactic of terrorism and genocide, it was also an extension of the patriarchal power ISIS asserts over women's bodies more generally. Discriminatory gender norms held by the Islamic State limit women's roles and their enjoyment of basic human rights. Women members of the caliphate and women who live under ISIS rule must abide by strict gender codes that regulate women's dress, limit their freedom of movement, and restrict their access to healthcare, employment, and education.[60]

The human rights violations perpetrated by ISIS against the Yazidi people are numerous. According to international human rights law, denying equal rights and dignity to women is fundamentally unjust. ISIS's treatment of women is inconsistent with the UDHR, the ICCPR, the ICESCR, and the Convention on the Elimination of Discrimination Against Women (CEDAW). CEDAW was created to prioritize women's equal legal status and is often described as an international bill of human rights for women.[61] Other ISIS human rights abuses include, violations of the right to life, liberty, and security of the person; the prohibition against torture and other cruel and inhumane acts; the freedom of religion or belief; and the prohibition against slavery. The forced displacement and sale of women and girls further amounts to human trafficking. The fact that the fate of thousands of men and boys remains unknown constitutes the crime of enforced disappearance.[62]

These acts – given their scale, context, systematic character, and underlying motive – also constitute genocide, war crimes, and crimes against humanity (see Chapter 4).

While states have the primary responsibility to respect, protect, and fulfill human rights, everyone including non-governmental actors, rebel groups, and terrorist organizations like ISIS has a legal obligation to respect (i.e., not violate) human rights. When non-state entities act contrary to those obligations it is described as "human rights abuse" and perpetrators can be held criminally accountable for these crimes (see Chapter 5). States, and especially Iraq, have additional human rights responsibilities to protect and fulfill even though they are not the direct perpetrators. This includes protecting Yazidi rights from being violated by ISIS and punishing perpetrators when protection fails. In 2005, the UN also formally adopted the *responsibility to protect* (R2P) – a commitment for the international community to protect populations from mass atrocity crimes when the responsible state is unable or unwilling to do so (see Chapter 4).[63]

Human rights activism to protect the Yazidi has been driven by the Yazidi people themselves with support from human rights NGOs and other allies. Governmental, intergovernmental, and UN action generally has resulted from these individual and collective efforts. Survivors like Nadia Murad (see Box 3.2) and Farida Khalaf who escaped their enslavement became advocates for the Yazidi in captivity. Their accounts of ISIS crimes garnered international attention, raised global consciousness, and mobilized action by individual states and at the UN.[64] Vian Dakhil, the sole Yazidi Kurd member of Iraq's parliament, is credited with mobilizing the Iraqi, Kurdish, and US governments. A dedicated group of Yazidi Americans extensively lobbied the US government to intervene militarily to rescue tens of thousands of Yazidi who were trapped by ISIS on Mt. Sinjar. Baba Sheik, the highest Yazidi spiritual leader, developed a new rebirth ceremony to welcome Yazidi women and girls who had been sexually violated back into the community as full and respected members.[65] International human rights organizations like Human Rights Watch and the Simon-Skjodt Center for the Prevention of Genocide meticulously documented ISIS crimes and called on leaders and governments at all levels to respond. At the request of the Government of Iraq, the Human Rights Council established a fact-finding mission to investigate ISIS crimes. The UN Security Council (UNSC) had already adopted a series of resolutions that address sexual violence against women and children in armed conflict and call for its prevention and punishment.[66] After the Yazidi genocide, the UNSC recognized SGBV as a tactic of terrorism and established the nexus between trafficking, sexual violence, terrorism, and transnational organized crime.[67] The Iraqi government and the UNSC also have authorized the creation of an independent, impartial investigative team to collect and preserve evidence of ISIS crimes for domestic prosecutions.[68] Trials are underway but no prosecutions for sexual enslavement or rape have yet occurred.

ISIS crimes against Yazidi women demonstrate the negative interdependence of human rights whereby the violation of some human rights leads to the violation of others. SGBV against Yazidi captives is an extension of the radicalism and violent extremism that is already entrenched within the Islamic State. There is a direct link between ISIS's treatment of women within its state-building project and its treatment of female captives of war. SGBV against Yazidi women illustrate how the violation of women's human rights manifest in the extreme violation of others such that multiple forms of discrimination are at work simultaneously.

BOX 3.2 DEFENDING HUMAN RIGHTS: NADIA MURAD'S FIGHT AGAINST ISIS

My story, told honestly and matter-of-factly, is the best weapon I have against terrorism, and I plan on using it until those terrorists are put on trial...I want to be the last girl in the world with a story like mine.[69]

Nadia Murad

Nadia Murad had a loving family and dreamed of opening a beauty parlor in her hometown of Kocho, a small farming village in northern Iraq. In August 2014, the terrorist group ISIS launched a military attack against the Yazidi people in the Sinjar district, which included Kocho. Yazidi men who were unable to escape were killed and buried in mass graves. Most Yazidi women and children were enslaved, and subsequently given or sold to ISIS fighters as wives, domestic servants, sex slaves, or trained as child soldiers.[70] Murad lost many family members and friends in the genocide.[71] She was enslaved, sold, and purchased multiple times. Yet Murad never lost her hope or her fight. When she eventually escaped to freedom, she learned her voice was a powerful weapon and she used it to fight for justice for the Yazidi people.

Nadia Murad is a powerful advocate for women in conflict and survivors of wartime sexual violence. She is the UN Goodwill Ambassador for the Dignity of Survivors of Human Trafficking and a 2018 Nobel Peace Prize winner. Murad was selected by the Nobel Committee for her "efforts to end the use of sexual violence as a weapon of war and armed conflict," for refusing to be silent, and her "uncommon courage in recounting her own sufferings and speaking up on behalf of other victims."[72] With her Nobel prize money, she founded *Nadia's Initiative* – a nonprofit organization that works to end the use

FIGURE 3.2 Nadia Murad
Source: Kay Nietfeld/Pool via AP

of women and girls as weapons of war and seeks to redevelop the Yazidi homeland. *Nadia's Initiative* advocates for global gender equality, women's rights, and the prosecution of ISIS militants for crimes against the Yazidi.[73] It provides education, healthcare, water, sanitation, and hygiene services, and supports the rehabilitation of Sinjar's agricultural industry. Murad is also a collaborator in the establishment of the Murad Code – "a global code of conduct for those collecting information from survivors of conflict-related sexual violence."[74] Composed of eight core principles, the goal is to better protect the rights and dignity of sexual violence survivors by training practitioners who interact with them in safer, more ethical, more effective practices that comply with international law and uphold survivor human rights.[75] Nadia Murad is a human rights defender. She invites us to "raise our voices together and say: no to violence, yes to peace, no to slavery, yes to freedom, no to racial discrimination, yes to equality and to human rights for all."[76]

Conclusion

The cases in this chapter illustrate how the 30 articles of the Universal Declaration of Human Rights are interdependent. They show that human beings require protection of all categories of human rights to enjoy the equality and dignity that the UDHR imagines. Political rights can be used to advocate for economic rights, and social and cultural rights can help protect civil rights. It is similarly true that the violation of a single human right can make other rights insecure. If states are willing to violate one right, they often are willing to violate others. The human rights contained in the UDHR were separated for political and instrumental reasons – to encourage states to legally codify them so that they might be better protected. Yet human beings require the protection of both the ICCPR and IESCR to experience freedom, justice, and peace.

Notes

ICCPR & IESCR

1 Daniel Whelan, *Indivisible Rights: A History* (University of Pennsylvania Press, 2010), p. 3.
2 Amartya Sen, "Freedom and Needs," in Robert McCorquodale (ed.), *Human Rights* (Routledge, 2003).
3 James W. Nickel, "Rethinking Indivisibility: Towards a Theory of Supporting Relations between Human Rights," *Human Rights Quarterly*, 30 (2008), p. 988.
4 Craig Scott, "Interdependence and Permeability of Human Rights Norms: Towards a Partial Fusion of the International Covenants on Human Rights," *Osgoode Hall Law Journal*, 27:3 (Fall 1989), p. 780.
5 Nickel, "Rethinking Indivisibility," pp. 988–989.
6 Michael Goodhart, "Revisiting Interdependence in Times and Terms of Crisis," *Journal of Human Rights*, 19:5 (2020), p. 523.
7 Goodhart, "Revisiting Interdependence," p. 524.
8 A series of debates exist within human rights scholarship and practice about whether some rights are essential rights from which other rights are derived, whether there are categories of rights that are more important than others (like subsistence rights), and whether we should consider rights as generations of rights where first generation rights are political and civil rights, second generation rights are economic, social, and cultural rights, and third generation rights are group or solidarity rights like minority rights and the right to development.
9 Scott, "Interdependence and Permeability," pp. 792–794.
10 Scott, "Interdependence and Permeability," p. 794.
11 Scott, "Interdependence and Permeability," p. 793.
12 Whelan, *Indivisible Rights*, p. 208.
13 Whelan, *Indivisible Rights*, p. 208. Notably, there was significant ambivalence about human rights domestically in the US. Supporters saw the treaties as a tool to reckon with America's slave-holding past and continuing racial segregation and discrimination. Detractors opposed US involvement with human rights for these same reasons. In the UK a similar ambivalence existed due to colonialism. Chris Roberts, *The Contentious History of the International Bill of Human Rights* (Cambridge University Press, 2014).
14 Scott, "Interdependence and Permeability," pp. 795–798.
15 Scott, "Interdependence and Permeability," p. 772.
16 Mona Hannah-Attisha, *What the Eyes Don't See: A Story of Crisis, Resistance, and Hope in an American City* (One World Press, 2015); Nadia Gaber, "Mobilizing Health Metrics for the Human Right to Water in Flint and Detroit, Michigan," *Health and Human Rights Journal*, 21:1 (2019), p. 183.
17 The phrase poisoned by policy came from the testimony of Dr. Mona Hannah-Attisha before an independent panel investigating the Flint Water Crisis. See also Hannah-Attisha, *What the Eyes Don't See* and Benjamin J. Pauli, *Flint Fights Back: Environmental Justice and Democracy in the Flint Water Crisis* (MIT Press, 2019).

18 American Civil Liberties Union (ACLU), "Unelected & Unaccountable: Emergency Managers and Public Act 4's Threat to Representative Democracy," July 12, 2012, www.aclumich.org/en/publications/unelected-unaccountable-emergency-managers-a nd-public-act-4s-threat-representative, accessed 9/24/2021, p. 1.
19 The Flint Water Advisory Task Force, an independent commission set up by Michigan Governor Rick Snyder's office, identified the Michigan Department of Environmental Quality, Michigan Department of Health and Human Services, Michigan Governor's Office, and State-Appointed Emergency Managers as primarily responsible for the Flint Water Crisis. The City of Flint Public Works, Genesee County Health Department, and the United States Environmental Protection Agency were also criticized for failures that threatened public health. Flint Water Advisory Task Force, *Final Report*, commissioned by the Office of Governor Rick Snyder, State of Michigan, March 6, 2016, pp. 6–8.
20 See Pauli, *Flint Fights Back*.
21 Paul M. Taylor, "Article 25: Right to Participate in Public Affairs, Electoral Rights and Access to Public Service," in *A Commentary on the International Covenant on Civil and Political Rights* (Cambridge University Press, 2020), p. 693.
22 Taylor, "Article 25," p. 710; OHCHR, "International Covenant on Civil and Political Rights," December 16, 1966, www.ohchr.org/en/professionalinterest/pages/ccpr.aspx, accessed 6/26/2021.
23 ACLU, "Unelected & Unaccountable," p. 9.
24 Pauli, *Flint Fights Back*, p. 103; Hannah-Attisha, *What the Eyes Don't See*, p. 28.
25 Hannah-Attisha, *What the Eyes Don't See*, p. 28.
26 Nina Reiners, "General Comment No. 15 on the Right to Water (2002)," in *Quellen zur Geschichte der Menschenrechte, herausgegeben vom Arbeitskreis Menschenrechte im 20. Jahrhundert, März* (2018), p. 4.
27 Reiners, "General Comment No. 15."
28 Reiners, "General Comment No. 15"; OHCHR, "The Right to Water"; UN Committee on Economic, Social and Cultural Rights, November 2002, adopted January 2003, www2.ohchr.org/english/issues/water/docs/CESCR_GC_15.pdf, accessed 9/24/2021.
29 Reiners, "General Comment No. 15."
30 Daniel Tagliarina and Corinne M. Tagliarini, *Bringing Human Rights Back: Embracing Human Rights as a Mechanism for Addressing Gaps in United States Law* (Lexington Books, 2021), p. 78.
31 Pauli, *Flint Fights Back*, p. 130.
32 Pauli, *Flint Fights Back*, pp. 6, 14.
33 Pauli, *Flint Fights Back*, p. 6; Candy J. Cooper with Marc Aronson, *Poisoned Water: How the Citizens of Flint Michigan, Fought for Their Lives and Warned a Nation* (Bloomsbury Press, 2020).
34 For an in-depth analysis of the opportunities and risks of citizen science see Chapter 7 of Pauli, *Flint Fights Back*. See also Gaber, "Mobilizing Health Metrics"; and Hannah-Attisha, *What the Eyes Don't See*.
35 "Flint Michigan Crisis 'Not Just About Water,' UN Rights Experts Say Ahead of President Obama's Visit," UN News, May 3, 2016, https://news.un.org/en/story/2016/05/528272-flint-michigan-crisis-not-just-about-water-un-rights-experts-say-ahead, accessed 9/24/2021.
36 Julia Conley, "Answering Rights Groups' Call, UN Human Rights Panel Demands Trump Admin Address Water Justice," *Common Dreams*, April 8, 2019, www.commondreams.org/news/2019/04/08/answering-rights-groups-call-un-human-rights-panel-demands-trump-admin-address-water, accessed 9/24/2021.
37 Tagliarina and Tagliarina, *Bringing Human Rights Back*, p. 85.

38 City of Flint website, "Service Line Replacement Program," www.cityofflint.com/gettheleadout/, accessed 5/29/2021.

39 National Resources Defense Council, "Pittsburgh Agrees to Terms for Tackling its Lead-Contaminated Water," February 7, 2019, www.nrdc.org/experts/nrdc/pittsburgh-agrees-terms-tackling-its-lead-contaminated-water, accessed 7/29/2021; UN News, "In Detroit, City-Backed Water Shut-Offs 'Contrary to Human Rights' Says UN Expert," October 20, 2014, https://news.un.org/en/story/2014/10/481542-detroit-city-backed-water-shut-offs-contrary-human-rights-say-un-experts, accessed 7/29/2021.

40 Faith Spotted Eagle, "Pre-filed Rebuttal Testimony of Faith Spotted Eagle," Docket No. HP 14–002, *In the Matter of the Application of Dakota Access, LLC for an Energy Facility Permit to Construct the Dakota Access Pipeline*, p. 5.

41 See the UN Declaration on the Rights of Indigenous Peoples (A/61/L.67 and Add.1), September 13, 2007. The DAPL also threatens women's rights by risking contamination of sacred sites used for sundances, ceremonies, and communal care. Oil pipeline and extractive industry projects in indigenous territories also increase the risk of human trafficking and physical and sexual violence against women. Faith Spotted Eagle, "Pre-filed Rebuttal Testimony," pp. 3 and 5; OHCHR, *End of Mission Statement by the United Nations Special Rapporteur on the rights of indigenous peoples, Victoria Tauli-Corupuz, of her visit to the United States*, March 3, 2017, p. 5; and Earth Justice, "Standing with Standing Rock," https://earthjustice.org/features/teleconference-standing-rock, accessed 6/26/2021.

42 Dan Gunderson, "'I live with Standing Rock in My Heart': Massive Pipeline Protests Resonates 5 Years Later," *Minnesota Public Radio News*, April 1, 2021.

43 Earth Justice; Rebecca Herscher, "Key Moments in the Dakota Access Pipeline Fight," *National Public Radio*, February 22, 2017.

44 Dan Gunderson, "'Not Invisible Anymore': Standing Rock a Year After Pipeline Protests," *MPR News*, September 13, 2017, www.mprnews.org/story/2017/09/13/standing-rock-nd-a-year-after-oil-pipeline-protests, accessed 5/15/2021.

45 Faith Spotted Eagle, "Confronting Settler Colonialism," Longhouse Media, interview recorded at Standing Rock in 2016, https://vimeo.com/198902656, accessed 5/15/2021; Jacki Homan, "A Native American Activist Speaks Candidly About What It's Like," *Repeller*, September 20, 2017, https://repeller.com/faith-spotted-eagle-activist/, accessed 5/13/2021.

46 UN Women, "Facts and Figures: Ending Violence Against Women," www.unwomen.org/en/what-we-do/ending-violence-against-women/facts-and-figures, accessed 6/8/2021.

47 UN Women, "Turning Promises into Action: Gender Equality in the 2030 Agenda for Sustainable Development," www.unwomen.org/en/digital-library/sdg-report, accessed 9/27/2021.

48 World Economic Forum, *Global Gender Gap Report 2020*, www.weforum.org/reports/gender-gap-2020-report-100-years-pay-equality/digest, accessed 6/8/2021.

49 The Yazidi religion is a derivation of the Zoroastrian faith (an ancient pre-Islamic religion of Iran) which combines elements of Islam, Christianity, and Judaism.

50 Naomi Kikoler, *Our Generation is Gone: The Islamic State's Targeting of Iraqi Minorities in Ninewa* (United States Holocaust Memorial Museum, 2015).

51 United Nations Human Rights Council, *They Came to Destroy: ISIS Crimes Against the Yazidis* (A/HRC/32/CRP.2), June 15, 2016.

52 UN Security Council, *Conflict-related Sexual Violence: Report of the Secretary-General* (S/2019/280), March 29, 2018.

53 Susan Hutchinson, "Financing Da'esh with Sexual Slavery: A Case Study in Not Gendering Conflict Analysis and Intervention," *Journal of Global Security Studies*, 5:2 (2020), p. 382.

54 Hutchinson, "Financing Da'esh with Sexual Slavery," p. 384.

55 Ruth Siefert, "The Second Front: The Logic of Sexual Violence in Wars," *Women's Studies International Forum*, 19:1–2 (1996), 35–43; Nira Yuval-Davis, "Women and the Biological Reproduction of 'the Nation'," *Women's Studies International Forum*, 19:1–2 (1996), 17–24.

56 Miriam Cooke, "Murad vs. ISIS: Rape as a Weapon of Genocide," *Journal of Middle East Women's Studies*, 15:3 (November 2019), p. 262.

57 The Convention on the Prevention and Punishment of Genocide defines genocide as the targeting of members of a racial, religious, ethnic, or national group and committing destructive actions with the specific intention to destroy the protected group. The genocidal acts prohibited by the convention include killing members of the group, causing serious bodily or mental harm to members of the group, torture and inhuman and degrading treatment, forcible transfer of group members, deliberately inflicting on the group conditions of life calculated to bring about its physical destruction in whole or in part, imposing measures intended to prevent births within the group, and forcibly transferring children of the group to another group. Expert inquiries by Human Rights Watch, the UN Human Rights Council, and the US Holocaust Memorial Museum have found ISIS satisfies the core elements of the crime of genocide as defined by the Convention.

58 Under Yazidi religious tradition, both parents must be Yazidi for the child to be of the Yazidi faith.

59 Kikoler, *Our Generation is Gone*, pp. 20–21; UN Human Rights Council, *They Came to Destroy*, p. 29. See Cooke, "Murad vs. ISIS" for an analysis of ISIS documents regulating sexual relations between ISIS militants and their female captives.

60 Human Rights Watch, *Iraq: Women Suffer Under ISIS*, April 5, 2016, www.hrw.org/news/2016/04/05/iraq-women-suffer-under-isis, accessed 6/9/2021.

61 OCHCR, "Convention on the Elimination of Discrimination Against Women," December 18, 1979, www.ohchr.org/en/professionalinterest/pages/cedaw.aspx, accessed 12/29/2020.

62 UN Human Rights Council, *They Came to Destroy*, p. 32.

63 UN General Assembly, 2005 World Summit Outcome Document (A/RES/60/1), October 24, 2005, paras 38 and 39.

64 Cooke, "Murad vs. ISIS."

65 Susan Shand, *Sinjar: 14 Days that Saved the Yazidis from Islamic State* (Rowman and Littlefield, 2018).

66 UN Security Council Resolutions 1820 (2008), 1888 (2009), 1960 (2013).

67 UN Security Council Resolution 2242 (S/RES/2242), 2015 and UNSC Resolution 2231 (S/RES/2231), 2016.

68 See Beth Van Schaack, "The Iraq Investigative Team and Prospects for Justice for the Yazidi Genocide," *Journal of International Criminal Justice*, 16 (2018), 113–139.

69 Nadia Murad, *The Last Girl: My Story of Captivity, and My Fight Against the Islamic State* (Tim Duggan Books, 2017), p. 308.

70 Kikoler, *Our Generation is Gone*; Human Rights Watch, Iraq: ISIS Escapees Describe Systematic Rape: Yezidi Survivors in Need of Urgent Care, April 14, 2015, www.hrw.org/news/2015/04/14/iraq-isis-escapees-describe-systematic-rape, accessed 10/7/2021; Human Rights Watch, Submission to the Committee on the Elimination of All Forms of Discrimination against Women on Iraq, October 7, 2019, www.hrw.org/news/2019/10/07/submission-committee-elimination-all-forms-discrimination-against-women-iraq, accessed 10/7/2021.

71 Nadia Murad, *Nobel Lecture*, Oslo, December 10, 2018.

72 The Nobel Prize, "Nadia Murad: Facts," www.nobelprize.org/prizes/peace/2018/murad/facts/, accessed 2/21/2021.

73 Nadia's Initiative, www.nadiasinitiative.org/, accessed 2/21/2021.
74 The Murad Code: Global Code of Conduct for Documenting Conflict-Related Sexual Violence, www.muradcode.com/home, accessed 2/21/2021.
75 The Murad Code, https://muradcode.com/draft-murad-code, accessed 5/30/2021.
76 Murad, *Nobel Lecture*, 2018.

4

INTERNATIONAL CRIMES

In Rwanda, women, children, and men who shelter in a church are methodically murdered by members of the army aided by local militia and civilians using machetes because they belong to the wrong ethnic group. In Syria, government security forces repeatedly open fire on peaceful protesters. Those shot are denied medical care, detained, and tortured. A humanitarian aid convoy delivering food and medical supplies to civilians trapped in a war zone is intentionally bombed despite a United Nations (UN)-brokered ceasefire agreement. Like these wrongdoings, some human rights violations are so egregious and widely condemned that they are categorized as international crimes. International crimes include categories of violations universally recognized as criminal despite cultural difference. International crimes include genocide, crimes against humanity, and war crimes. They are a matter of international concern and punishable internationally, or by any state, regardless of where the crimes take place because of their severity. This chapter explores the Rwandan genocide and crimes against humanity and war crimes in Syria to introduce the core features and underlying dynamics of these international crimes, also called mass atrocity crimes. Despite promises of "Never Again" made by governments in the aftermath of the Holocaust and the creation of an institutional machinery designed to stop them, mass atrocity crimes remain a persistent practice in domestic and international politics. In 2021, they are underway in Afghanistan, Burkina Faso, China, Cameroon, the Democratic Republic of Congo, Ethiopia, Israel and Palestine, Mali, Myanmar, Niger, North Korea, Syria, Venezuela, and Yemen.[1] While not eradicated, the international political context in which mass atrocity crimes take place has changed in recent decades due to strengthened human rights norms. It is no longer permissible for leaders to justify mass atrocity crimes as acceptable state practice. Human rights defenders have developed new forms of response and heightened

DOI: 10.4324/9781003256939-5

the expectation of an international responsibility to protect populations and to punish the perpetrators of these international crimes.

The international crimes discussed in this chapter are a small subset of human rights violations focused primarily on gross and systematic violations of physical integrity rights – rights that protect against the infliction of physical or bodily harm.[2] Their brutality and intentional character attract media attention and generate outrage. Yet once underway they are some of the most challenging human rights violations to stop. They bring into sharp relief the challenge of enforcing human rights designed to transcend the boundaries of the nation-state in an international system organized around state sovereignty. For decades following the creation of the UN, state sovereignty was used as a shield of protection by rights-violating governments. Despite the existence of the Universal Declaration of Human Rights, a Genocide Convention specifically prohibiting genocide, and more than a century of legal tradition prohibiting war crimes, states were seldom held accountable for genocide, crimes against humanity, and war crimes.

The 1994 Rwandan genocide against the Tutsis marked a turning point. The absolute failure of the international community, and especially the UN, to prevent the murder of nearly 1 million people in Rwanda or stop the genocide while it was underway contributed to a reckoning on the meaning of sovereignty. In a world characterized by widespread and growing acceptance of human rights, sovereignty could no longer permit governments to do whatever they wanted to their populations. Since the early 2000s, the meaning of state sovereignty has evolved to emphasize the responsibilities of sovereignty and not just the rights. Known as the responsibility to protect (R2P) norm, it requires states to protect populations from mass atrocity crimes and the international community to protect populations when states are either unable or unwilling to do so. It is harder for states to justify international crimes now than in any other historical period. Yet the case of Syria demonstrates mass atrocity prevention and response remain inconsistent and subject to the political interests of powerful states. Together, the cases of Rwanda and Syria show that the international community is currently more likely to adopt a lower-risk strategy of punishing states for committing international crimes than a higher-risk strategy of stopping them while underway, despite a legal environment that authorizes both. At the start of the 21st century, human rights norms prohibiting international crimes are more developed than the practice of stopping them, yet many organizations and advocates are working tirelessly to end mass atrocity crimes.

The Crime of Genocide

The UN General Assembly declared genocide a crime under international law in 1946. The subsequent UN Convention on the Prevention and Punishment of Genocide (Genocide Convention) was the first human rights treaty adopted by the UN General Assembly, preceding the adoption of the Universal Declaration of Human Rights.[3] The Genocide Convention and its formal definition of genocide was the result of a political compromise brokered at the drafting convention. But laws do not simply emerge. They reflect the agency of the individuals who dream, create, and fight for them. The term "genocide" was created by the Polish lawyer Rafäel Lemkin in 1944. Lemkin was troubled to discover that no law existed under which the leaders of state-directed mass killing could be prosecuted. Indeed, a government's mass killing of its own people was not even considered a crime.[4] A person could be tried for murder of another human being but state-directed murder of the Armenians by the Ottoman Empire and of the Jews by the German Nazi regime were not formally, legally prohibited. Lemkin created the word genocide from the Greek prefix *genos-* meaning race or tribe and combining it with the Latin suffix *-cide* meaning killing. He used the word "genocide" to describe the destruction of a nation or ethnic group.[5] He then led the effort to develop a treaty and its eventual adoption was due in large part to his campaigning efforts.

The Genocide Convention defines genocide as a crime committed with the intent to destroy a national, ethnical, racial, or religious group. The formal definition contains both a physical (substantive) element and a mental element (intent). The physical element of genocide can include any of the following acts: killing or causing serious bodily or mental harm to members of the group; deliberately inflicting life conditions intended to physically destroy the group (in whole or in part); preventing births within the group or forcibly transferring children out of the group. To be genocide, these acts must be committed with a specific purpose – the intention on the part of the perpetrator(s) to physically destroy the targeted group. Committing these acts for another purpose, like removing a group of people from a specific territory to gain control of it or committing these acts in an indiscriminate manner against all people, regardless of their group membership, would not be genocide. They would be other crimes like ethnic cleansing, crimes against humanity, or war crimes (see Table 4.1). It is the intent behind these acts – to eliminate a people based on their identity – that makes genocide distinctly abhorrent. Importantly, perpetrators do not have to succeed at eliminating the group for their crime to be genocide; but it does require for their violent actions to be undertaken with this eliminationist intent. Examples include the Armenian Genocide, the Holocaust, and the Rwandan Genocide. The crimes recently committed against the Yazidi and ongoing against the Rohingya in Myanmar also meet the definition of genocide. Genocide can occur during peacetime or in the context of war – the prohibition against genocide always applies.

States have three core obligations under the Genocide Convention: 1) the obligation to not commit genocide; 2) the obligation to prevent genocide; and 3) the obligation to punish genocide. Notably, genocide is punishable by any state regardless of where the crimes occurred. The Genocide Convention is binding on everyone. The International Court of Justice (ICJ) has ruled that the Genocide

TABLE 4.1 International Crimes

Genocide	Criminal acts committed with the intent to destroy a national, ethnical, racial, or religious group	Can occur during armed conflict or in times of peace
Crimes Against Humanity	Widespread, large-scale, or systematic attacks directed against a civilian population	Can occur during armed conflict or in times of peace
War Crimes	Serious violations of international humanitarian law – the laws and customs of war; and grave breaches of the Geneva Conventions	Occur during armed conflict
Ethnic Cleansing★	Planned, deliberate, and forceful removal of persons of a particular ethnic group from a specific territory to make the area ethnically homogenous	Can occur during armed conflict or in times of peace

Note: ★ethnic cleansing is a political concept that is not formally defined in international law. The crimes that lead to ethnic cleansing are typically prosecuted as crimes against humanity or war crimes if they occur during armed conflict.

Convention embodies principles that are part of customary international law. This means that all states "are bound as a matter of law by the principle that genocide is prohibited under international law" even if they have not formally ratified the treaty.[6] The definition of genocide contained in the Genocide Convention has been widely adopted both nationally by governments into their domestic law and internationally by courts and tribunals, including the ad hoc International Criminal Tribunal for Rwanda (ICTR) and the International Criminal Court (ICC).

The Rwandan Genocide

The war that started in Rwanda in 1990 was deeply rooted in a legacy of colonial exploitation and a long tradition of domestic political leaders manipulating fears of ethnic violence to maximize their own power and defeat political rivals. Rwanda was comprised of three ethnic groups: the Hutu comprised nearly 85% of the population, the Tutsi at 15%, and the Twa made up less than 1%. President Juvenal Habyarimana, a Hutu, had taken power in a 1973 coup. The Rwandan Patriotic Front (RPF) – a nationalist organization composed primarily of Tutsis living in exile in Uganda – invaded Rwanda in October 1990. They justified their invasion as an effort to solve the Tutsi refugee crisis, stop political persecution of Tutsis in Rwanda, and to replace Habyarimana's authoritarian rule with democracy.[7] Habyarimana characterized the invasion as an attempt to impose Tutsi-dominated rule and install a system of ethnic apartheid against the Hutus.

The Rwandan Armed Forces (FAR) and the RPF fought each other for nearly three years. The civil war intensified preexisting political instability, heightened inter-ethnic mistrust, and brought the country close to economic collapse.[8] Habyarimana used the threat posed by the RPF to tighten his grip on power and undermine internal challenges to his rule by arbitrarily arresting members of the political opposition and demonizing members of the Tutsi minority as accomplices of the RPF and enemies of the Hutu. Battles between the FAR and RPF were followed by massacres of Tutsi civilians by government troops.[9] Indeed, several independent human rights experts and international human rights nongovernmental organizations (HROs) had warned as early as March 1993 that Rwandan government leaders had organized the killings of thousands of Tutsis who remained at risk.[10]

The UN got involved in Rwanda in October 1993. The Security Council had authorized a peacekeeping mission to monitor a cease-fire agreement between the parties in Rwanda's civil war in preparation for democratic elections. The Arusha Accords, which ended the conflict between the Rwandan Armed Forces and the Rwanda Patriotic Front, instituted political, military, and constitutional reforms including a power-sharing agreement, transfer of political power to a transitional government, a protocol on the repatriation of Tutsi refugees, and an armed forces integration agreement.[11] Unhappy with the loss of power, President Habyarimana and his government had been stalling on implementing the agreement. By April 1994, the UN was losing patience. At a regional meeting of heads of state in Dar-es-Salaam, Habyarimana faced significant pressure from other African leaders to honor the accords. On April 5, Habyarimana publicly agreed to the immediate transfer of political authority to the interim transitional government upon his return to Rwanda the next day.[12]

The Rwandan genocide of the Tutsi people began on April 6, 1994 with the assassination of Rwanda's President Habyarimana when his plane was shot down on its approach to Kigali airport. Within the hour, members of the Presidential Guard and military and civilian militias composed of Hutu extremists set up roadblocks throughout Kigali. They began killing Tutsis, identifying them by their identity cards at roadblocks and by using prepared lists to hunt those targeted for extermination at their homes. In their quest to secure power, Hutu extremists also murdered members of opposition political parties and members of the interim transitional government who were authorized to take power by the Arusha peace agreement.[13] Over a period of 100 days, nearly 1 million Rwandans were killed by their government, military, local militias, and neighbors. Presidential Guard troops and the *Interahamwe* militia (the militant youth wing of Habyarimana's political party) led the massacres. With organized assistance in local communities throughout the country, they massacred Tutsi civilians on the streets, in their homes, and in schools, orphanages, and churches.[14] They used machetes, clubs, and farming tools where guns were not available. Not even children were spared. All Tutsis were targeted for death based on their ethnicity, and Tutsi women were consistently raped as a precursor to death or as a means of murder. Hutus in the political opposition, and those Hutus who opposed the genocide, or who resembled, sought to protect, or protected Tutsis, were also among the murdered.[15] General Roméo Dallaire, force commander of the UN peacekeeping mission in Rwanda and eyewitness to the genocide, reported that the massacres were methodical rather than spontaneous, involving a "well-executed operation involving the army, *Gendarmerie, Interahamwe* and civil service."[16]

According to Scott Straus, the three dynamics of war, race, and power drove the genocide. Extremist Hutus who sought to hold on to power captured control of the Rwandan state by eliminating the moderate opposition. They authorized the killing of Tutsis who they categorized as the enemy due to their identity. They used the material power of the state and its legitimacy to make killing Tutsis a mandatory, state-sanctioned project. The context of war (e.g. fear, insecurity, and anger) created a rationale for the killing. The murder of Tutsis was characterized by extremists as self-defense: all Tutsis were the enemy who had to be attacked first before they killed the Hutu.[17] The crimes committed in Rwanda were genocide. Rwandan Tutsis were raped, physically attacked, and killed because of their membership in an ethnical or racial group – the Tutsi. The perpetrators sought to eliminate the Tutsis from Rwanda. In addition to murder and physical violence against group members, perpetrators sought to prevent future births and murdered Tutsi children.

The international community failed to stop the genocide. A peacekeeping operation was on the ground when the genocide started but the UN specifically ordered it to remain impartial and prohibited the use of force to defend civilians. Permanent members of the Security Council, including France, the United Kingdom, and the United States, rescued their own nationals within days of the start of the genocide but refused to reinforce UN troops or to protect Rwandan civilians. The genocide ended in July when the RPF won the war and gained control of the Rwandan government. The backlash against the UN and democratic members of the Security Council from domestic and international publics was immense – they had failed to live up to the promises of international human rights and the rules of a law governed international society. The failure of the international community to protect the people of Rwanda undermined the legitimacy of the UN and contradicted its core values. Although it failed to prevent the genocide or stop it while underway, the UN Security Council established an independent commission of inquiry to investigate the crimes and an international tribunal to prosecute the perpetrators responsible.[18] The International Criminal Tribunal for Rwanda helped establish the facts of the genocide, held more than 60 high-level perpetrators criminally accountable for their participation and planning, and strengthened international law. It was the first international tribunal to enforce the Genocide Convention, to convict a former head of state for the crime of genocide, and to recognize rape as a tool of genocide.[19]

The failure to protect Rwandans from genocide marked a turning point in thinking about how the international community should respond to mass atrocity crimes. The Rwandan genocide represented a dramatic failure of human rights and reflected limited political will to restrict state sovereignty. A second UN failure to respond effectively to international crimes in Kosovo in 1999 compounded the dilemma. In a speech to the General Assembly, Secretary-General Kofi Annan argued that respecting sovereignty all the time meant accepting a world where more Rwandan genocides would happen. Alternatively, permitting states to intervene militarily in the domestic affairs of other states without Security Council authorization like happened in Kosovo threatened to undermine the UN Charter and upend international order. He warned "traditional notions of sovereignty can no longer do justice to aspirations of peoples everywhere to attain their fundamental freedoms."[20] Annan urged UN members to find a way to reconcile sovereignty with human rights. The response to Annan's challenge came not from within the UN but from the International Commission on Intervention and State Sovereignty (ICISS) – a high-level panel of independent experts from all regions of the world. The ICISS argued that sovereignty entails state responsibility for protecting the rights and dignity of the people within its borders. And in a world with international human rights, state responsibility for protection was shared by the international community.[21] The UN codified the responsibility to protect (R2P) in 2005. Individual states have a responsibility to protect their populations from genocide, war crimes, crimes against humanity, and ethnic cleansing. The international community should help states meet their responsibility. When states fail, the international community must provide protection collectively through measures consistent with the UN Charter.[22] Multiple high impact developments on international crimes were influenced by the Rwandan genocide, including the adoption of R2P, the creation of an ad hoc international criminal tribunal to punish genocide – the ICTR, and in 1998 the establishment of a permanent International Criminal Court to prosecute genocide, crimes against humanity, war crimes, and the crime of aggression.

BOX 4.1 DEFENDING HUMAN RIGHTS: THE GLOBAL CENTRE FOR THE RESPONSIBILITY TO PROTECT

"If not now, when?"[23]
Dr. Simon Adams, Executive Director of the Global Centre for the Responsibility to Protect

The responsibility to protect (R2P) is a norm that protects populations from genocide, war crimes, crimes against humanity, and ethnic cleansing.[24] Formally affirmed by the UN in 2005, R2P encompasses three pillars of responsibility: 1) states have a responsibility to protect the populations within their borders from mass atrocity crimes; 2) the international community has a responsibility to help states protect populations; and 3) when states are unwilling or unable to do so, the international community must protect populations from mass atrocity crimes through collective action consistent with the UN Charter.[25] The Global Centre for the Responsibility to Protect (GCR2P) exists to make R2P a reality.[26]

Established in 2008, the GCR2P is a human rights organization that conducts research to increase understanding of R2P and provides policy advice to states, UN bodies, and other organizations on how to implement it. The Centre works in three main areas. First, it seeks to clarify R2P by publishing briefing papers for policy makers, reaching out to the UN, and providing media commentary on crises where R2P applies.[27] The GCR2P also advocates for R2P implementation where populations are at risk. The R2P Monitor is a quarterly bulletin that sounds the alarm when mass atrocities are happening but also spotlights situations of serious concern or imminent risk. It puts usable information into the hands of decision-makers – background information, policy analyses, actionable data, and policy recommendations.[28] Countries in crisis demanding an urgent response in 2021 include: Afghanistan, Ethiopia, Myanmar, Venezuela, and Yemen. Countries where atrocity prevention is still possible include Central African Republic, Mozambique, Nigeria, South Sudan, and Sudan.[29] Creating politically usable information and directing it to where it will have the most impact is an important tool of human rights change.

Finally, the GCR2P helps strengthen and institutionalize R2P. This means building support for it among member states and within regional and international organizations, growing networks and partnerships, and building the atrocity prevention and response capacity of first responders – governments, international organizations, and peacekeepers.[30] It is working. More than 90 Security Council resolutions and nearly 50 Human Rights Council resolutions reference R2P. The GCR2P facilitates a global network of national, regional, and institutional "R2P Focal Points" that analyze crises through an atrocity prevention lens, challenge militaries to rethink their strategies and tactics for responding to mass atrocity cases, and help them strengthen their institutional capacity to do so. While there are still too many failures – in Syria, Myanmar, Sudan, and Yemen – there are also successes where R2P stopped the recurrence of violence in Kenya, Sierra Leone, Liberia, Guinea, Côte d'Ivoire, the Gambia, and Kyrgyzstan.[31] Ultimately, the goal is to save lives by mobilizing the international community to prevent international crimes before the mass graves are dug.[32] The GCR2P has been part of helping R2P achieve the purpose it was created for: to change norms and reform institutions to prevent mass atrocity crimes and to prompt an effective reaction when prevention fails.[33]

Crimes Against Humanity

Crimes against humanity are widespread and systematic attacks directed at a civilian population. Like genocide, crimes against humanity can occur during peacetime or be connected to armed conflict. What defines crimes against humanity is violence against civilians. This violence may include: murder; extermination; enslavement; forcible population transfer; imprisonment; torture; grave forms of sexual violence; persecution; enforced disappearance; apartheid; and other inhumane acts. Any of these acts can be a crime against humanity if: 1) they are committed as part of a geographically widespread, large-scale (in terms of number of victims), or systematic attack against any civilian population; and 2) if they are planned or committed to advance state or organizational policy.[34] Unlike genocide, crimes against humanity are not identity-specific. As an example, the Revolutionary United Front (RUF) rebel group in Sierra Leone (1991–2002) engaged in widespread crimes against humanity against civilians. The RUF attacked and looted villages, amputated the body parts of villagers (including hands to keep them from voting), raped women, and abducted children to serve as rebel soldiers and wives to fighters. Captured children often were forced to commit atrocities against their own family members to prevent them from escaping to return home.[35] The crimes in Sierra Leone were systematic, large-scale, and geographically widespread. They were directed at civilians as part of RUF strategy to supply, reinforce, and reward its troops, diminish support for the government, and gain control of territory.

BOX 4.2 DEFENDING HUMAN RIGHTS: THE INTERNATIONAL CRIMINAL COURT

In July 1998, 120 states signed the Rome Statute establishing the first permanent treaty-based international criminal court. The International Criminal Court (ICC) investigates and, where warranted, prosecutes individuals charged with grave international crimes: genocide, war crimes, crimes against humanity, and the crime of aggression. As a court of last resort, it seeks to complement, not replace, national Courts. This means that it investigates and prosecutes cases only when the domestic courts of its member states, called States Parties, are unable or unwilling to do so. The goal of the ICC is to end impunity for international crimes by holding those responsible for them criminally accountable, and by doing so, helping to prevent these crimes from happening again. The ICC is based on the belief that individuals, regardless of their official positions, should be criminally prosecuted for genocide, war crimes, crimes against humanity, and aggression – all crimes that can never be legitimate acts of state power. Since it began operation in July 2002, there have been 30 cases before the ICC including ten convictions and four acquittals. In 2021, there are 123 States Parties to the ICC including: 33 African states, 19 Asian-Pacific states, 18 Eastern European, 28 Latin American and Caribbean, 25 Western European and other states.

The idea of crimes against humanity developed through customary international law, the domestic law of states, and through the jurisdiction of international courts and tribunals like the International Criminal Tribunal for Yugoslavia (ICTY), the ICTR, and the International Criminal Court. Like other international crimes (e.g. genocide and war crimes) the prohibition on crimes against humanity is a peremptory norm, meaning a norm accepted by the international community that must always be followed without exception. The consensus definition for crimes against humanity can be found in Article 7 of the Rome Statute of the International Criminal Court.[36]

War Crimes

Wars have rules. Warring parties cannot do whatever they want. They must obey international human rights law (which always applies) and international humanitarian law, which regulates how wars are fought and who must be protected during armed conflict. The Geneva Conventions and their additional optional protocols protect people not participating in hostilities, along with other rules considered part of customary international law and binding on all states. War crimes refer to a wide variety of violent acts that become criminal when they are committed against people who should be protected during armed conflict. These acts include, but are not limited to, killing, torture, causing serious injury or bodily harm, and sexual violence. War crimes, by definition, occur only during armed conflict and do not need to be large scale or widespread. A comprehensive list of war crimes is found in Article 8 of the Rome Statute of the International Criminal Court. While protections vary slightly for international and non-international conflict, the intentional attack of civilians, medical personnel, humanitarian aid workers, or others involved in humanitarian assistance or peacekeeping operations is prohibited. Anyone not participating in fighting must also be protected from inhumane treatment including combatants who have surrendered, are sick, or detained. Attacks can only be directed against military objectives. Parties to war must distinguish between civilians and combatants and must spare the civilian population, their property, and those things upon which civilian life depends, like access to food and water. Due to this requirement for distinction, armed forces cannot use methods or means of warfare that are indiscriminate (and could harm protected people) or cause unnecessary and excessive suffering like poisonous gases or chemical weapons. The intentional bombing of schools, hospitals, and humanitarian aid convoys, for example, are war crimes. In short, armed forces may not intentionally use violence against any civilians and must take due care to spare them from hostilities.

Crimes Against Humanity and War Crimes in Syria

The war in Syria is marked by crimes against humanity and war crimes. This section illustrates in detail the defining features and underlying dynamics of crimes against humanity and war crimes, offering two examples of each. The Syrian case demonstrates the persistence of international crimes and the lack of an effective international response shows how challenging it remains to protect fundamental human rights in an international system designed around state sovereignty. Like Rwanda before it, the failure to prevent mass atrocity crimes in Syria or to stop them has undermined the international human rights project and delegitimized rule-based international order and institutions like the UN Security Council who are charged with protecting it. The norm of R2P is only effective when decision-makers and practitioners implement it. The problem lies not with the idea of R2P, which has gained widespread support, but with those that fail to honor it and those who fail to punish its violators.

The conflict in Syria began in March 2011 when 15 school children in Daraa were detained and tortured for writing antigovernment graffiti criticizing President Bashir al-Assad on the wall of their school. The government response to the nonviolent street protests that followed was violent and disproportionate. Unarmed community members and families protesting the inhumane treatment of their children and calling for their release from detention were met with artillery fire, which generated greater outrage among the population. As protests multiplied in cities across Syria, government security forces responded with deadly force and violent repression. By June, Human Rights Watch had released a detailed report describing crimes against humanity in Daraa.[37] Security forces used lethal force against peaceful protesters and bystanders, often without warning. Snipers positioned on rooftops deliberately shot unarmed protesters in the head, neck, and chest after receiving "shoot-to-kill" orders from commanders. Human Rights Watch also reported a large-scale military operation in which security forces occupied every Daraa neighborhood, ordering residents to stay indoors or be shot. Security forces cut electricity and communications and imposed a blockade on the community that caused shortages of food, water, and medicine.[38] Human Rights Watch documented a similar pattern of unlawful killings and occupation of neighborhoods in Homs. By November, thousands in Homs also had been subjected to arbitrary arrest, enforced disappearance, and torture.[39] Syrian government actions in Daraa and Homs qualify as crimes against humanity because the violence was methodically directed at civilians on a large scale. The Syrian government blamed this violence on armed terrorist gangs sponsored from abroad. But Human Rights Watch investigators found protesters were unarmed in most cases. In cases where armed protesters and defectors from the security forces fought back after being fired upon, the disproportionate response was unjustified.[40] Growing government repression provoked armed self-defense and eventually the organization of the Free Syrian Army (FSA), composed mainly of armed civilians and defectors from the Syrian security forces. By 2012, Syria had descended into civil war.

The war in Syria continues in 2021 – a decade after its start – but the war has changed character multiple times as the political context has evolved and new parties to the conflict emerged, gaining and losing control of territory. These parties have variously included several armed political opposition groups, sectarian fighters, foreign governments, and terrorist groups who thrive in disorder like the self-proclaimed Islamic State of Iraq and Syria (ISIS). To date, more than 580,000 people have died, more than 13 million are displaced, and approximately 130,000 have been arbitrarily detained, abducted, or disappeared.[41] Throughout the ten-year period of war, the Syrian government has engaged in war crimes. The chemical weapon attack on Ghouta in 2013 and the joint Syrian and Russian airstrikes on civilian infrastructure in Idlib province in 2020 are snapshots of the war that provide representative examples of persistent war crimes.

In August 2013, the Syrian government launched two chemical weapons attacks on eastern and western Ghouta, killing hundreds of civilians, including large numbers of children. Although the Syrian government denied responsibility, two separate independent investigations by Human Rights Watch and the United Nations proved that Bashar al-Assad's government launched rockets containing weaponized sarin into the two residential areas in the suburbs of Damascus, killing an estimated 1,400 people.[42] The images of the children – the rows of bodies of the children who died and the hospitalized toddlers in diapers clinging to life wearing oxygen masks – elicited international outrage. The use of chemical weapons is a war crime. They are indiscriminate, inhumane, and illegal. In response, the UN Security Council authorized the Organisation for the Prohibition of Chemical Weapons to oversee the destruction of Syria's chemical weapons stockpile. Under pressure from the Security Council and both Russia and the US, Syria joined the convention banning chemical weapons in October 2013.[43] Nonetheless, emboldened by a general lack of punishment for its war crimes, the Syrian government continued to use chemical weapons against civilians at least 32 times between August 2013 and March 2021 including weaponized sarin, chlorine, and sulfur mustard gas.[44]

Russia began militarily intervening in the civil war on Syria's behalf in 2015. Since then, Russian and Syrian forces have been accused of targeting hospitals, schools, and UN and humanitarian aid convoys.[45] As an example, an October 2020 Human Rights Watch report, "Targeting Life in Idlib," documented dozens of unlawful air and ground strikes against civilian targets by Syrian and Russian armed forces between April 2019 and March 2020. The 46 air and ground attacks on Idlib displaced 1.4 million people, killed hundreds of people, and damaged 12 healthcare facilities, ten schools, five markets, four displaced people's camps, and four neighborhoods along with commercial areas, a prison, church, stadium, and NGO office. These attacks occurred without warning and with no evidence of military objectives, personnel, or military in the vicinity of the attacks.[46] The deliberate destruction of civilian infrastructure is a war crime. Unlawful attacks on hospitals, schools, markets, and neighborhoods also threaten the human rights to health, education, food, water, and shelter.[47]

BOX 4.3 DEFENDING HUMAN RIGHTS: THE WHITE HELMETS AND HUMANITARIAN RESCUE IN SYRIA

As barrel bombs rain down on the civilian population in parts of Syria under rebel control, members of the Syrian Civil Defence Forces, also known as the White Helmets, run toward the flames rather than away from them. This volunteer corps of former tradesmen, teachers, professionals, and students have responded to the absence of core government services by becoming first responders, acting to save the Syrian people and themselves because no one else will. In a country ravaged by civil war, they risk their lives to help anyone in need regardless of religion or politics.

The White Helmets started organically through dozens of grassroots voluntary initiatives to help civilians cope with continuous aerial bombardment and the destruction of core civilian infrastructure including water and electricity networks, homes, hospitals, and schools. By 2020, the Syrian Civil Defence had more than 4,300 volunteers including 450 women, who have adopted a code of conduct to adhere to principles of neutrality, impartiality, and humanity as they fulfill their duties to: 1) provide disaster and war response in Syria; 2) carry out search and rescue operations; and 3) work to save as many lives as possible.[53] The White Helmets have adopted as their slogan a verse from the Holy Qu'ran, "to save one life is to save all of humanity." In a war characterized by war crimes and crimes against humanity, they recognize the human dignity of all Syrians and commit to abiding by all international conventions and charters that safeguard and protect civilians and their human rights,[54] even as the Syrian regime aided by the Russian government do not.[55]

White Helmet volunteers engage in search and rescue – digging the living and the dead out from the rubble, rushing the injured to hospitals, and responding to chemical attacks. They work to restore electricity, water, and sewage services, remove unexploded ordinance, help the displaced by establishing camps, open blocked roads to connect cities and towns, and provide basic medical services and community education through women's centers. The White Helmets are credited with saving more than 100,000 lives in the five-year period 2015–2020. The coronavirus pandemic has heightened the risk to Syrian civilians displaced by the war. Years of deliberate attacks on medical personnel, hospitals, and health centers by the Bashar Al-Assad regime has destroyed health infrastructure, making civilians in rebel areas particularly vulnerable to coronavirus. With many civilians living in overcrowded refugee camps where physical distancing is impossible and with little access to running water, soap, and cleaning products, the White Helmets are raising awareness about the risks of COVID-19 and providing medical and preventive equipment.

The White Helmets are also on the frontlines of human rights protection. White Helmet teams have provided vital data, eyewitness testimony, and photographic evidence to international investigations into war crimes by the United Nations, the Organization for the Prohibition of Chemical Weapons, and human rights groups.

The international response to conflict in Syria has been hampered by division among Security Council members. The UN Security Council has consistently failed in its responsibility to protect the Syrian people. Russia alone has vetoed 14 resolutions designed to protect the Syrian population and punish perpetrators of crimes against humanity and war crimes, including a referral of Syria to the International Criminal Court. China has vetoed eight of these resolutions alongside Russia.[48] Historically, Russia and the US have been the most frequent users of the Security Council veto but the use of the veto has dramatically increased by Russia and China since 2011, disrupting the Security Council's ability to consistently exercise R2P. Small and medium-sized states have organized to improve Security Council methods in response, establishing a cross-regional group called Accountability, Coherence and Transparency (ACT). The ACT code of conduct urges members of the Security Council to voluntarily refrain from using the veto in situations involving mass atrocity crimes. As of January 2020, 120 states supported the code of conduct including the permanent Security Council members of France and the United Kingdom.[49] France and Mexico have advocated for a similar veto restraint initiative at the ministerial level. With the Security Council blocked, the General Assembly established the International, Impartial and Independent Mechanism (IIIM) to help investigate and prosecute perpetrators of atrocity crimes in Syria.[50] Some governments, including Germany, the Netherlands, and Canada, have initiated domestic legal proceedings to prosecute some of Syria's perpetrators.[51] Responding to the failure of Syria and the UN to protect Syrians, Simon Adams, director of the Global Centre for the Responsibility to Protect says,

> the Responsibility to Protect is an international norm, but it does not possess independent agency. The failure to end atrocities and protect civilians in Syria is not a failure of R2P, but of the imperfect actors and institutions charged with its implementation.[52]

BOX 4.4 DEFENDING HUMAN RIGHTS: ANAS AL-DYAB DOCUMENTS WAR CRIMES AND CRIMES AGAINST HUMANITY

Anas al-Dyab, a White Helmets volunteer, spent years documenting the horrors of the civil war through his photography at search and rescue sites. A former college student whose studies were interrupted by the war, al-Dyab's photography captured the terrible destruction of the war while also illustrating the humanity and courage of the people affected by it.[56] His heartbreaking and dramatic photographs, which have been published internationally, expose the human cost of war and shine a light on violations of international humanitarian

FIGURE 4.1 Anas al-Dyab
Source: White Helmets (Syria Civil Defence)

law happening in Syria. One of the worst chemical attacks against civilians in Syria occurred on July 4, 2017 in Idlib Province.[57] Al-Dyab took the pictures.

In July 2019, al-Dyab was tragically killed in a Russian airstrike while documenting the bombardment of his hometown, Khan Sheikhun. He was 23 years old. Anas al-Dyab is one of nearly 300 White Helmet volunteers who have been killed by direct targeting or double tap strikes while doing life-saving humanitarian work.[58] He has been described by his friends and colleagues as loved by everyone and someone who wanted to show the world what was happening in Syria. He was frequently seen talking with young children, showing them how to operate his camera, and sharing the photographs he had taken of them. The White Helmets said in a statement, "Anas will always be remembered as the one who chose to stay behind the scenes and fight with his camera. May you rest in peace, brother."[59] In testimony recorded before his death al-Dyab said, "Maybe if my camera fails, the minds and memories of millions of Syrians who have lived through this war and have experienced this Syrian reality, will not fail or lie."[60] When so many chose to pick up a gun or flee, al-Dyab picked up his camera to document violations of international human rights and international humanitarian law committed against the people of Syria. He dedicated his life to an ideal – that all people are equally deserving of dignity and rights. Anas al-Dyab made the ultimate sacrifice. Like many of his White Helmet brothers and sisters, he lost his own life while protecting the rights and lives of others.

Conclusion

International crimes like genocide, crimes against humanity, and war crimes are so egregious that no state openly defends them. Even those states that commit mass atrocity crimes deny their existence, argue the violence is being misinterpreted, assign responsibility for them to others, or defend them not as crimes but as legitimate acts of self-defense against genocidal or terrorist enemies that threaten them. While these crimes persist despite the creation of an international human rights architecture designed to stop them, the environment in which they take place has changed in important ways thanks to the hard work of human rights defenders. Before 1948, a state's decision to systematically murder its own people was not even formally recognized as a crime. Genocide, crimes against humanity, and war crimes are now expressly prohibited. The international community recognizes that states and the international community itself both have a responsibility to protect populations from mass atrocity; it has become a requirement of state sovereignty. Governments have adopted consequential practices to respond to late 20th and early 21st century mass atrocity cases. These include developing early warning systems and undertaking preventive measures to stop international crimes from recurring in places like Kenya and the Gambia. In rare cases, like Libya in 2011, the international community has used military force to disrupt mass atrocity as it starts. More frequently, in cases including Rwanda, Sierra Leone, Timor Leste, the former Yugoslavia, the Democratic Republic of Congo, Iraq, and even Syria, the international community has punished perpetrators of international crimes using existing judicial mechanisms or creating new ones. Protecting international human rights in an international system designed around state sovereignty poses significant challenges for enforcement, even against international crimes that are so egregious that they are universally prohibited. The commitment to protect populations from genocide, crimes against humanity, and war crimes has grown alongside the human rights project; but norms of protection remain far ahead of practice.

Notes

1 Global Centre for the Responsibility to Protect (GCR2P), "Populations at Risk," www.globalr2p.org/populations-at-risk/, accessed 6/30/2021.

2 Violations of physical integrity rights include acts like extrajudicial killing, enforced disappearance, torture, arbitrary imprisonment, rape and sexual violence, and other forms of physical force or violations of bodily integrity.

3 ICC, "Rome Statute of the International Criminal Court," 2011, www.icc-cpi.int/resource-library/documents/rs-eng.pdf, accessed 10/6/2021

4 Kristina E. Thalhammer, Paula O'Loughlin, Myron Peretz Glazer, and Nathan Stoltzfus, *Courageous Resistance: The Power of Ordinary People* (Palgrave Macmillan, 2007), pp. 125–126.

5 Thalhammer et al., *Courageous Resistance*, p. 127; United Nations Office on Genocide Prevention and the Responsibility to Protect, "Genocide," www.un.org/en/genocideprevention/genocide.shtml, accessed 6/30/2021.

6 UN Office on Genocide Prevention and the Responsibility to Protect, "Genocide."

7 Human Rights Watch, "Rwanda: Human Rights Developments 1994," *Human Rights Watch Annual Report*, www.hrw.org/reports/1994/WR94/Africa-06.htm#P258_112461, accessed 9/27/2021.

8 Linda R. Melvern, *A People Betrayed: The Role of the West in Rwanda's Genocide* (St Martin's Press, 2000), pp. 43–44.

9 International Commission of Investigation on Human Rights Violations in Rwanda, *Report of the International Commission of Investigation on Human Rights Violations in Rwanda since October 1, 1990* (Human Rights Watch and Africa Watch, 1993).

10 These included the International Federation of Human Rights, the Inter-African Union of Human Rights, Africa Watch, International Centre of Rights of the Person and of Democratic Development, and the UN Special Rapporteur for the Commission on Human Rights.

11 Carrie Booth Walling, *All Necessary Measures: The United Nations and Humanitarian Intervention* (University of Pennsylvania Press, 2013), p. 125. For information on the Arusha Accords see Gérard Prunier, *The Rwanda Crisis: History of a Genocide* (Colombia University Press, 1995), pp. 159–197 and Melvern, *A People Betrayed*, pp. 59–67.

12 Alison Des Forges, *"Leave None to Tell the Story": Genocide in Rwanda* (Human Rights Watch, 1999), p. 81.

13 Scott Straus, *The Order of Genocide: Race, Power, and War in Rwanda* (Cornell University Press, 2007), p. 49.

14 Des Forges, *"Leave None to Tell the Story"*, pp. 4–10.

15 For a detailed analysis of the genocide and its causes see Des Forges, *"Leave None to Tell the Story"*; Straus, *The Order of Genocide*; and Melvern, *A People Betrayed*.

16 Roméo Dallaire, *Shake Hands with the Devil: The Failure of Humanity in Rwanda* (Random House, 2003), pp. 280–281, Gendarmerie refers to a force of gendarmes who are a military force with law enforcement duties among the civilian population.

17 Straus, *The Order of Genocide*, pp. 173–174.

18 UN Security Council, Resolution 955 (S/RES/955), 1994.

19 Carrie Booth Walling, "Responses" in Deborah Mayersen (ed.) *The Cultural History of Genocide in the Modern World* (Bloomsbury Press, 2021), p. 127; United Nations International Residual Mechanism for Criminal Tribunals, "The ICTR in Brief," https://unictr.irmct.org/en/tribunal, accessed 10/7/2021.

20 Kofi Annan, "Speech to the UN General Assembly," September 20, 1999, www.un.org/press/en/1999/19990920.sgsm7136.html, accessed 7/1/2021.

21 International Commission on Intervention and State Sovereignty (ICISS), *The Responsibility to Protect* (International Development Research Center, 2001), pp. 7–8.

22 UN General Assembly, *2005 World Summit Outcome* (A/RES/60/1), September 16, 2005, www.un.org/en/development/desa/population/migration/generalassembly/docs/globalcompact/A_RES_60_1.pdf, accessed 7/1/2021.

23 Simon Adams, *Mass Atrocities, the Responsibility to Protect and the Future of Human Rights* (Routledge, 2021).

24 International Commission on Intervention and State Sovereignty, *The Responsibility to Protect* (International Development Research Centre, December 2001), https://idl-bnc-idrc.dspacedirect.org/bitstream/handle/10625/18432/IDL-18432.pdf?sequence=6&isAllowed=y, accessed 9/27/2021.

25 United Nations General Assembly, 2005 World Summit Outcome (A/RES/60/1), September 16, 2005, paras 138 and 139.

26 Global Centre for the Responsibility to Protect (GCR2P), "About Us," www.globalr2p.org/about/, accessed 6/26/2021.

27 GCR2P, "About Us."

28 GCR2P, "Populations at Risk," www.globalr2p.org/populations-at-risk/, accessed 6/26/2021.

29 Additional countries where mass atrocities are occurring include Cameroon, Central Sahel, China, Democratic Republic of Congo, Israel and the Occupied Territories/Palestine, and Syria. R2P Monitor, Issue 57, June 1, 2021, www.globalr2p.org/publica tions/r2p-monitor-issue-57-1-june-2021/, accessed 6/26/2021.

30 GCR2P, "About Us."

31 Gareth Evans, "The Responsibility to Protect: The Dream and The Reality," European Centre for the Responsibility to Protect 2020 Lecture, Leeds University, November 2020, https://ecr2p.leeds.ac.uk/ecr2p-annual-lectures/2020-annual-lec ture-professor-gareth-evans/, accessed 7/1/2021.

32 See Simon Adams, *Mass Atrocities, The Responsibility to Protect and The Future of Human Rights: 'If Not Now, When?'* (Routledge Press, 2021).

33 Gareth Evans, "R2P: The Dream and the Reality," speech delivered virtually at the European Centre for the Responsibility to Protect's Annual Lecture, Leeds University, November 26, 2020, https://ecr2p.leeds.ac.uk/ecr2p-annual-lectures/2020-annual-lec ture-professor-gareth-evans/, accessed 6/26/2021.

34 UN Office on Genocide Prevention and the Responsibility to Protect, "Crimes Against Humanity," www.un.org/en/genocideprevention/crimes-against-humanity. shtml, accessed 6/30/2021.

35 Lansana Gberis, "Fighting for Peace: The United Nations, Sierra Leone and Human Security," *UN Chronicle*, 2 (2000), p. 52; Chris Coulter, *Bush Wives and Girl Soldiers: Women's Lives Through War and Peace in Sierra Leone* (Cornell University Press, 2009); Ishmael Baeh, *A Long Way Gone: Memoirs of a Boy Soldier* (Sarah Crichton Books, 2008).

36 Rome Statute of the International Criminal Court, www.icc-cpi.int/resource-library/documents/rs-eng.pdf, accessed 6/30/2021.

37 Human Rights Watch, "'We've Never Seen Such Horror': Crimes against Humanity by Syrian Security Forces," 2011, www.hrw.org/sites/default/files/reports/syria 0611webwcover.pdf, accessed 7/1/2021.

38 Human Rights Watch, "Syria: Crimes Against Humanity in Daraa: Killings, Torture in a Locked-Down City Under Siege," June 1, 2011, www.hrw.org/report/2011/06/01/weve-never-seen-such-horror/crimes-against-humanity-syrian-security-forces, accessed 9/27/2021.

39 Human Rights Watch, "Syria: Crimes Against Humanity in Homs: Arab League Should Suspend Syria," November 11, 2011, www.hrw.org/news/2011/11/11/syria -crimes-against-humanity-homs, 9/27/2021.

40 HRW, "Syria: Crimes Against Humanity in Homs."

41 Global Centre for the Responsibility to Protect, "A Decade of Atrocities and International Failure in Syria," March 15, 2021, www.globalr2p.org/publications/a-deca de-of-atrocities-and-international-failure-in-syria/, accessed 9/27/2021.

42 Adams, *Mass Atrocities*, p. 50; Human Rights Watch, "Attacks on Ghouta: Analysis of Alleged Use of Chemical Weapons in Syria," September 10, 2013, www.hrw.org/rep ort/2013/09/10/attacks-ghouta/analysis-alleged-use-chemical-weapons-syria, accessed 7/1/2021; UN, "Secretary-General's remarks to the Security Council on the report of the United Nations Mission to Investigate Allegations of the Use of Chemical Weap-ons on the incident that occurred on 21 August 2013 in the Ghouta area of Damas-cus," September 16, 2013, www.un.org/sg/en/content/sg/statement/2013-09-16/secretary-generals-remarks-security-council-report-united-nations, accessed 7/1/2021.

43 UN Security Council Resolution 2118 (S/RES/2118), September 27, 2013. The formal name of the treaty is the Convention on the Prohibition of the Development, Production, Stockpiling and Use of Chemical Weapons and on their Destruction.

44 GCR2P, "A Decade of Atrocities and International Failure in Syria."

45 Adams, *Mass Atrocities*, p. 54.

46 Human Rights Watch, "Syria/Russia: Strategy Targeted Civilian Infrastructure: Unlawful Attacks on Hospitals, Schools, Markets Forced Idlib Population Out,"

October 15, 2020, www.hrw.org/news/2020/10/15/syria/russia-strategy-targeted-ci vilian-infrastructure, accessed 9/27/2021; Human Rights Watch, "Targeting Life in Idlib," October 15, 2020, www.hrw.org/report/2020/10/15/targeting-life-idlib/syria n-and-russian-strikes-civilian-infrastructure, accessed 7/1/2021.

47 HRW, "Syria/Russia: Strategy Targeted Civilian Infrastructure."
48 Global Centre for the Responsibility to Protect, "Syria: Nine Years of Atrocities, Impunity and Inaction," March 14, 2020, www.globalr2p.org/publications/syria -nine-years-of-atrocities-impunity-and-inaction/, accessed 9/27/2021.
49 Security Council Report, "UN Security Council Working Methods: The Veto," December 16, 2020, www.securitycouncilreport.org/un-security-council-working-m ethods/the-veto.php, accessed 7/2/2021.
50 On Syria see Beth Van Schaack, *Imagining Justice for Syria* (Oxford University Press, 2020).
51 GCR2P, "A Decade of Atrocities and International Failure in Syria."
52 Simon Adams, *Failure to Protect: Syria and the UN Security Council*, Occasional Paper Series No. 5, March 5, 2015, p. 3.
53 Syria Civil Defence, "The Volunteer Code of Conduct," www.wyriacivildefence.org/ en/who-we-are/code-conduct/, accessed 11/19/2020.
54 Syria Civil Defence, "The Volunteer Code of Conduct."
55 Adams, *Mass Atrocities*.
56 Dakin Andone, Mohammad Elshamy, and Bernadette Tuazon, "Remembering Pho-tographer Anas al-Dyab," CNN digital, July 21, 209, www.cnn.com/2019/07/21/ world/gallery/syrian-photographer-anas-al-dyab/index.html, accessed 11/18/2020.
57 Anne Barnard and Michael R. Gordon, "Worst Chemical Attack in Years in Syria; U.S. Blames Assad," *The New York Times*, April 4, 2017, www.nytimes.com/2017/04/04/ world/middleeast/syria-gas-attack.html, accessed 12/5/2020.
58 A double tap strike is the practice of following an airstrike with a second strike shortly after to target first responders rushing to the site to help. This practice is commonly employed by the Syrian and Russian governments in Syria.
59 Andone et al., "Remembering Photographer Anas al-Dyab"; author correspondence with the White Helmets, November 26, 2000; Facebook testimony of Anas al-Dyab, www.facebook.com/watch/?v=653477961786124m, accessed 7/25/2021.
60 Facebook Syrian Civil Defense, www.facebook.com/SyriaCivilDefense/videos/ 653477961786124/, accessed 12/5/2020.

5

JUSTICE AND RECONCILIATION AFTER ATROCITY

Human rights violations are the result of decisions made by people with power, the ordinary people who participate in them, and the bystanders who choose not to intervene. After systematic human rights violations end, how do perpetrators, victims, and bystanders learn to live together? How can survivors trust a government that harmed or failed to protect them? The set of practices that can be taken to help society move from a period of human rights violations to one in which human rights are respected is referred to as transitional justice. After periods of conflict or repression, human rights violations can be so widespread or so systematic that the normal justice system cannot provide an adequate response.[1] Transitional justice processes recognize the suffering of victims and aim to promote truth, justice, peace, and reconciliation. While there is no single formula, and goals and processes will vary by context, the aim is to provide some measure of justice and prevent the violations from happening again.

This chapter explores how societies use both judicial and non-judicial measures to redress the legacies of past human rights violations. It focuses on the two most prevalent transitional justice mechanisms – criminal prosecutions and truth commissions. The cases that follow challenge conventional wisdom by showing how human rights ideas and practices flow from the global south to the global north and not simply the reverse. Human rights trials in Argentina helped shape the justice norm – the norm of individual criminal accountability – now championed by the United Nations (UN) and replicated globally by other states. The South African Truth and Reconciliation Commission (SATRC) has become a global model for truth-telling bodies, illustrating the importance of truth for both restorative and retributive forms of justice. While most effective at achieving their aims when adopted by governments, civil society actors can adopt transitional justice processes when states are unable or unwilling to do so. The Greensboro

DOI: 10.4324/9781003256939-6

Truth and Reconciliation Commission – the first truth commission in the United States – demonstrates that truth processes can be an effective means for strengthening human rights practices even in the absence of government support and when faced with official opposition to their creation.

Since the 1980s, democratic states are increasingly using a variety of transitional justice mechanisms to address past human rights violations. These include human rights trials, truth commissions, official apologies, memorialization processes, and reparations (see Table 5.1). Human rights trials aim to hold individuals criminally accountable for human rights violations. Whether conducted at the national or international level, human rights trials underscore that violations of fundamental human rights are not legitimate state acts. The individuals who commit them should be held criminally accountable because no one is above the law. And the free and fair trial rights of the accused must be respected throughout the judicial process.[2] Truth commissions are temporary fact-finding bodies authorized to investigate, document, and publicize past human rights violations. They directly engage victims in the fact-finding process, clarify institutional responsibility for past abuses, and promote reforms through an official report of their findings.[3] Memorialization is the process of creating public memorials, historic sites, monuments, or museums. Memorialization can contribute to a culture of justice by teaching lessons of the past.[4] Official government apologies acknowledge that human rights violations have occurred, admit responsibility for harm caused, and accept responsibility for wrongdoing. Effective apologies address the future as well as the past and are accompanied by material forms of reparations.[5] Reparations refer to an official state policy of granting material compensation or restitution to victims, family members, or victim communities for past human rights violations. Reparations can be individual or collective and range from individual monetary compensation to societal programs or institutional reforms. These transitional justice processes are not alternatives. Commonly, states pursue multiple processes simultaneously or adapt their strategies as political opportunities change.[6]

TABLE 5.1 Transitional Justice Processes

Human Rights Trials	Prosecutions to hold individuals criminally accountable for human rights violations
Truth Commissions	Temporary fact-finding bodies that investigate, document, and publicize past human rights violations
Apology	Public acknowledgment and acceptance of responsibility for past human rights violations and the harm caused by them
Memorialization	Creation of public memorials, historic sites, monuments, memorials, or museums that honor the memory and struggle of victims and survivors of human rights violations
Reparations	Official state policy of granting individual or collective compensation or restitution to those harmed by human rights violations

These practices are adopted by states after they transition to a democratic or semi-democratic regime. Because they follow periods of political transition (e.g. repression, conflict, or civil strife) and seek to provide some measure of accountability for past violations of human rights or humanitarian law, they are termed transitional justice.[7] But transitions can cover a period of decades and not simply the immediate aftermath of political change. Choices made in the earliest stages of a transition may not be enduring as shifts in the domestic and international political context open and close new possibilities for achieving justice and reconciliation. It matters, for example, whether the previous regime was defeated by the new one or if the transition was negotiated with former leaders who continue to hold political or military power. Human rights trials might be possible in the former but not the latter. The transitional justice mechanisms that a society adopts are goal dependent, context specific, and can change over time.

Understandings of justice also can vary by purpose, culture, and context. The wide variety of transitional justice mechanisms are often categorized as either retributive or restorative. Retributive justice focuses on the punishment of offenders and reinforcing the rule of law and norms of society that have been broken by the offense committed. The goal is to rebalance the scales of justice. Ideally, penalty removes the undeserved benefit the perpetrator gained through commission of their crime. Retributive justice is distinguished from vengeance when punishment is proportional to the offense committed and consistent among perpetrators. Human rights trials are primarily a form of retributive justice. They are offender-centered, focused on punishment, and prioritize re-establishing the rule of law. Restorative justice prioritizes victims and emphasizes restoring the offender to a law-abiding life. It involves all stakeholders – perpetrators, victims, and affected communities – in a justice process focused on healing. The goal is to repair the harm done to victims and communities by acknowledging their pain and creating an opportunity for the offender to: 1) understand the harm caused; 2) take responsibility for it; and 3) take action to repair damage done.[8] Truth commissions are primarily restorative. They focus on victims – their experiences and need for acknowledgement. Their primary purpose is to uncover and expose the truth about past violations and how and why they happened with a view to preventing them from happening again. Some truth commissions aim specifically to achieve communal reconciliation. Those that do, encourage perpetrators to acknowledge their victims, promote apology and forgiveness, and address underlying systems of repression as well as individual rights violations.

While conceptually distinct, the boundaries between retributive and restorative justice are permeable in practice. Human rights trials can serve a reparative function by empowering victims, affirming their right to justice, and changing the way they are perceived by society.[9] Truth commissions can contain elements of retributive justice – they hold perpetrators accountable by publicly recounting their crimes and they construct an evidence base that may, in some cases, be used for future prosecutions. Many transitioning countries, like Argentina, have pursued both trials and truth commissions in their pursuit of accountability and reconciliation.[10] Some countries, like South Africa, have found ways to combine mechanisms in creative ways. Collectively, the purpose of transitional justice is to acknowledge the dignity of victims, ascertain and publicize the truth about human rights violations, hold perpetrators accountable for their crimes, offer restitution, reconcile broken communities, and reform institutions to prevent repetition. There are a variety of pathways that countries pursue as they seek to balance ethical imperatives for justice and truth with political constraints, international human rights norms with local needs, and the very meaning of justice within that cultural context.[11]

Human Rights Trials and Argentina

Historically, government officials who violated the human rights of their populations were seldom held accountable for doing so. While impunity for human rights abuse continues to persist, democratizing states are increasingly holding individuals, including government leaders, criminally accountable for past violations through trials – a trend called the "justice cascade."[12] Human rights trials can take many forms. Domestic human rights trials refer to judicial proceedings held in response to past human rights violations committed by government officials or state agents in democratizing states. These trials have the most potential for achieving transitional justice goals because they occur within the society where the crimes have occurred. Sometimes, societies emerging from repression or conflict lack the institutional capacity or political will to prosecute past crimes. In those cases, international assistance may be required. Human rights prosecutions have occurred in the domestic judicial systems of foreign countries like trials held in Spain for crimes committed in Argentina (foreign trials), in international courtrooms like the International Criminal Tribunal for the Former Yugoslavia or the International Criminal Court (international trials), or in criminal bodies that combine international and national law and staff like the Special Court for Sierra Leone or the Extraordinary Chambers in the Courts of Cambodia (hybrid trials).[13] Latin American countries, and especially Argentina, were early innovators of human rights trials and have served as an influential example for other states.

Survivors of human rights violations and the families of victims want those who are responsible to be held accountable for the harm they have caused. This is especially true when their own government is responsible for their victimization, whether by action or omission. Human rights trials serve many purposes. They can restore the dignity of victims by acknowledging that what was done to them was a crime and identifying those responsible for their victimhood. Human rights prosecutions benefit societies as well. The adversarial format of a trial and the ability to cross-examine evidence produces a verdict that is difficult to contest, convincing other members of society that perpetrators deserve to be punished.[14] Human rights trials help citizens discover the truth. Trials create a common

understanding of the past. Because they focus on individual criminal accountability, they remove the stigma of collective guilt from innocent members of the
community, making it easier for people to live together again. Human rights trials
also help citizens discover the law.[15] Trials re-establish the legitimacy of the rule
of law by demonstrating that no one, not even government officials, are above
the law. Human rights (and democracy) need the rule of law to flourish (see
Chapter 1). Conversely, impunity – the refusal to investigate and prosecute
crimes – encourages future human rights violations. When violations are widespread and its impractical to prosecute all perpetrators, trials target the leaders
most responsible for organizing the crimes.

Argentina is a global human rights protagonist and leader in the use of human
rights trials.[16] In the process, Argentina has shown that it is possible to go from
human rights violator to human rights innovator. A military junta ruled Argentina
between 1976–1983 during a period that came to be known as the dirty war.
The junta suspended democracy, eliminated basic rights, and systematically
repressed those opposed to its rule. Using a system of clandestine detention centers and death squads, the military junta curbed dissent by abducting, disappear-
ing, torturing, and sometimes killing its political opponents. By the time the
military regime collapsed, an estimated 30,000 people had been victimized and up
to 10,000 people had been killed or remained disappeared. The democratic
government that replaced the junta initiated a truth commission to investigate
human rights violations followed by prosecutions. In 1985, nine former commanders in chief of the armed forces were put on trial for human rights violations
in Argentina, including kidnapping, torture, forced disappearance, and murder.
Five were convicted. The two most powerful leaders – General Jorge Videla and
Admiral Emilio Massera – were sentenced to life in prison while the other three
received sentences ranging from four to 17 years. The trial of the military juntas
was the first prosecution of a former head of state in Latin America and the first
major human rights trial held since the successor trials of World War II.[17] The
trial put into practice the right to justice which Latin American countries had
fought to include in both the American Convention on Human Rights and the
Universal Declaration of Human Rights decades before.[18] The trial captured the
attention of the entire country, forging a new national understanding of the past
including recognition that the junta was guilty of crimes. The trial emboldened
survivors to increase their demands for justice in Argentina and elsewhere,
sometimes before the rest of society was ready. Charges against hundreds of
lower-level officers soon followed but were interrupted by the passage of two
amnesty laws that significantly limited how trials could proceed going forward.
Argentina was a fragile democracy with a deeply divided society. Short-term fears
that too much justice could provoke a military coup won out over victims'
demands for it.

The trial of the juntas changed peoples' expectations about what was politically
possible in the aftermath of systematic human rights violations. With human

rights trials blocked by the amnesty laws, Argentina innovated again. Human rights organizations gathered evidence and testimony related to a crime excluded from the amnesty law – the kidnapping of the babies of disappeared women. Between 1985 and 2005, 38 defendants were indicted for kidnapping children and falsifying public documents to change their identities. Defendants were found guilty and sentenced in 84% of those cases, including some leaders of the military junta.[19] Family members of the disappeared and human rights NGOs also petitioned Argentine courts to permit judicial investigations designed to discover the truth about the disappeared. They argued that even though perpetrators could not be criminally prosecuted for their crimes, families still had a right to the truth about what happened to their loved ones. What followed was a judicial process that came to be known as "truth trials." Truth trials allowed Argentine courts to solicit and analyze information and testimony to discover the fate of victims without imposing criminal penalties against the accused who were compelled to testify.[20] Truth trials contained elements of both trials and truth commissions and kept the possibility of future prosecutions alive in the minds of survivors and victims' families. When Argentine courts overturned the amnesty laws in 2005, criminal prosecutions for past human rights violations resumed. Between 2006 and 2016, Argentina convicted more than 800 individuals for past human rights violations.[21]

BOX 5.1 DEFENDING HUMAN RIGHTS: DR. ŞEBNEM KORUR FINCANCI

Achieving human rights and justice for all requires obtaining, documenting, and disseminating credible information about human rights violations. Dr. Şebnem Korur Fincancı is an internationally recognized forensic physician who uses science, medicine, and the law to defend human rights. Forensic expertise has become an invaluable tool in support of transitional justice processes like human rights trials and truth commissions. An incontrovertible, fact-based record of abuse can corroborate and supplement the testimony of survivors or produce a reliable account of events when the violence is so horrendous and complete that no survivors remain.[27] The facts that scientific investigations uncover can be used by human rights defenders to expose patterns of abuse, advocate for government reparation, and promote institutional reforms.

A founding member of the Forensic Doctors' Association, Dr. Fincancı is one of the authors of the United Nations' *Manual on the Effective Investigation and Documentation of Torture and Other Cruel, Inhuman or Degrading Treatment or Punishment* (also known as the Istanbul Protocol). The Istanbul Protocol is the international standard for forensic investigation and documentation of the crime of torture.[28] Effective documentation brings evidence of torture to light so that institutionalized patterns of abuse can be eliminated and perpetrators can be held accountable for their actions.[29] It has become an effective tool for ending impunity.

FIGURE 5.1 Şebnem Korur Fincancı
Source: Marius Becker/dpa/Alamy Live News

Dr. Fincancı fights for human rights at home and abroad. She is President of the Human Rights Foundation of Turkey, a non-governmental organization dedicated to the treatment and rehabilitation of torture survivors. The organization investigates and documents cases of abuse and advocates for the eradication of torture and other forms of ill-treatment.[30] While Dr. Fincancı has investigated allegations of torture, sexual violence, deaths in detention, and mass graves in places like South Africa, Bahrain, Israel, the Philippines, and Bosnia, she is most well known for her anti-torture and anti-impunity work in her native Turkey. An outspoken advocate for human rights, Dr. Fincancı has been persecuted and wrongfully imprisoned by the Turkish government for speaking out against policies that violate the human rights of Turkish citizens (including members of the Kurdish minority) and for accusing the Turkish state of violating international law.[31] In 2016, Dr. Fincancı was among 700 academics charged with "propagandizing for a terrorist organization," after she signed a petition that called for the end of "deliberate massacre and deportation of Kurdish and other peoples" in south-east Turkey.[32] After a series of trials, Dr. Fincancı was acquitted in 2019. That acquittal verdict was overturned in 2020 and her legal fight is ongoing.[33] Dr. Fincancı has witnessed and documented numerous human rights violations, making her a target of state repression. Nonetheless, Dr. Fincancı refuses to be afraid of revealing the truth. She urges, "you have to influence the world the way you want it to be."[34]

Argentina is credited with helping to initiate the dramatic increase in human rights trials – a trend that is regionally concentrated in the Americas and Europe but internationally diffuse. The Transitional Justice Research Collaborative presents data on human rights trials, truth commissions, and amnesties for 109 democratic transitions in 86 countries from 1970–2012. The data shows that Latin America leads the world in domestic human rights prosecutions, truth commissions, and the use and reversal of amnesties.[22] Data also shows that the trial of the juntas in Argentina contributed significantly to this broader trend of seeking legal accountability for human rights crimes.[23] The Argentine case demonstrates that choices about transitional justice are not fixed. They change in response to the political and legal context. Domestic trials in Argentina were preceded by a truth commission and followed by amnesties and pardons which were followed by additional trials. The choices states make are influenced by the level and nature of the crimes, the character of the transition and who holds political power, the support of civil society, the structure of the judicial system, and which transitional justice goals (e.g. truth, accountability, or reconciliation) are prioritized. States often employ multiple transitional justice mechanisms. Trials alone cannot address the deep wounds inflicted by widespread human rights violations and they cannot establish a full and accurate record of a country's past.

Critics of human rights often claim that human rights norms and practices reflect the interests of the most powerful states who dominate international politics and impose them on less powerful states. The global trend on human rights trials shows the reverse. Human rights innovation can emerge from the periphery of international politics and set normative standards that even powerful states are pressured to adopt. It is now widely accepted that states have a duty to investigate, prosecute, and punish human rights violations. The reciprocal idea that victims and their families have a "right to truth" and "right to justice" also emerged in the Americas and gained prominence through a series of decisions within the Inter-American human rights system.[24] These state duties and victim rights have been codified by the UN.[25] The UN also has adopted a formal policy on amnesty and prosecution which is designed to create "a space for justice" so that the door to criminal accountability for past human rights crimes remains open even if conditions for prosecutions are not immediately conducive.[26]

South Africa's Truth and Reconciliation Commission

Victims, their families, and societies have a right to know the truth about what happened to their loved ones. Human rights trials can prove that specific legal violations were committed against the victim by the accused and provide criminal accountability for those violations. But trials are ill-suited to examine the broader political and societal context that made those crimes probable. And trials cannot help families whose loved ones have disappeared without evidence of who is responsible. Truth commissions are the preferred mechanism for unearthing hidden, denied, or forgotten truth. They are investigative bodies that publicly document past human rights violations, identify their underlying causes and societal consequences, and aim to increase acceptance of this shared history by society's members. But truth commissions are not just about the past. They explain past violations so they can be prevented in the future by making changes to the policies, practices, and relationships that encouraged them.[35] Truth commissions have several defining features: 1) they are focused on past events; 2) they investigate a pattern of human rights violations that occurred over a period of time; 3) they engage directly with victims, survivors, and populations affected by these violations; 4) they are temporary bodies that report their findings and usually make recommendations for reform; and 5) they are official bodies authorized by the state.[36] The first major truth commission was Argentina's National Commission on the Disappeared (CONADEP), but the truth commission that captured the global imagination and inspired their widespread use is the South African Truth and Reconciliation Commission (TRC). Yet the South African TRC teaches that there is no blueprint. States adopt approaches that address their specific needs. In Argentina, the removal of former leaders from power (called a ruptured transition) created a political context in which trials initially were possible. South Africa's transition from authoritarian regime to democracy was negotiated between government officials who still held power and those seeking racial equality and democratization (called a pacted transition) making a truth commission a preferred approach politically to trials of the former leaders whose cooperation was necessary to replace apartheid with democracy.

South Africa adopted a truth commission to deal with apartheid – a system of institutionalized racial segregation. Apartheid was the official state policy of South Africa between 1948 and 1994. The white South African government created a racial caste system that codified and legitimized white minority rule over all other racial groups. People categorized as African (Black), Coloured (of mixed racial heritage), and Indian (descended from South Asian immigrants) were variously disenfranchised, denied fundamental human rights, and intentionally oppressed. The government maintained this system of racial oppression by developing laws and policies aimed at the social exclusion and economic marginalization of other racial groups and policed it through violence. Those subjected to its rule opposed it, sometimes with revolutionary violence. Apartheid violates core international human rights treaties and is recognized as a crime against humanity under international law. The UN passed a treaty to suppress and punish apartheid in 1973. It describes apartheid as "inhuman acts committed for the purpose of establishing and maintaining domination by one racial group of persons over any other racial group of persons and systematically oppressing them."[37] These inhuman acts include murder, torture or inhumane treatment, arbitrary arrest, enforced disappearance, rape, persecution, the deliberate imposition of living conditions on a racial group intended to cause their physical destruction, or the adoption of legislative measures designed to exclude racial groups or deny them their rights.

The end of apartheid in South Africa was secured through a negotiated settlement after decades of armed struggle. Both the white apartheid government and the African National Congress (ANC), the main liberation movement, possessed real power but had reached an impasse where one side could not impose its will on the other. The new Constitution established South Africa as a multiracial democracy. It included in its epilogue a commitment to pursue transitional justice guided by the African principle of *ubuntu* – the idea that all of humanity is connected.[38] The decision was to pursue a plan of national reconciliation. South Africa did not set out to develop a truth commission from the start. Rather, it turned out to be the mechanism best suited to meet societal goals within the limitations of the political context. Originally, non-white South Africans preferred trials with criminal accountability while white South Africans preferred unconditional amnesty. South Africa chose a third way – a truth commission which would grant amnesty to perpetrators in exchange for full disclosure of their crimes complemented by trials and the risk of conviction for perpetrators who refused to participate in good faith.[39]

The South African TRC illustrates the importance of pursuing a transitional justice pathway that is context specific. Trials had posed a challenge for several reasons. The judicial system needed reform – it had never been fair for non-whites under apartheid. Indeed, it was the legal system itself that enforced apartheid and legitimized its existence. The law had been abused in South Africa to protect the interests of the powerful and to persecute those the powerful deemed undeserving of their rights. Further, there was insufficient evidence to gain convictions if trials were held. Sometimes the only living witnesses to crimes were the perpetrators themselves, many who could use the resources of the state to cover up or destroy evidence.[40] In these circumstances, trials risked limiting truth and threatened to keep families ignorant about the fate of their loved ones.[41] Given the long duration and widespread nature of the crimes, prosecutions would impose serious judicial strain and financial cost, limiting resources available to address competing priorities in education, health, and housing. Amnesties were strongly opposed by apartheid's victims. To victims, amnesty meant forgetting the past. Amnesties would have revictimized survivors and the families of those killed by ignoring their needs and silencing their voices.[42] Practically, human rights violations cannot be ignored. To do so is to continually renew the injustice of the past in the present. Victims' families never forget. They never stop fighting for the truth or for justice. Finally, impunity increases the likelihood that those who committed crimes in the past will do so in the future. Through its unique design, the South African TRC decided to prioritize truth and reconciliation. Trials and amnesties would be used only narrowly in pursuit of these goals. Amnesty would be limited and come at the cost of public admission of the crime. The hope was that perpetrators would acknowledge victims, reveal the truth, and be willing to apologize for the harm they caused. In return, those harmed might be willing to forgive, producing a more reconciled society.

The Government of National Unity set up the Truth and Reconciliation Commission (1996–2003) to address crimes committed during the period of apartheid and to advance reconciliation between racial groups. The TRC's founding act created three interconnected committees. The Human Rights Violations Committee collected testimony from victims and witnesses; the Amnesty Committee processed applications for amnesty made by perpetrators; and the Reparations and Rehabilitation Committee produced recommendations for reparation and reform.[43] Over a period of more than six years, the TRC collected testimony from more than 21,000 people in private and public hearings held throughout the country. In addition to victim hearings, dozens of special hearings focused on key institutions and societal groups were also held. Many hearings were broadcast live on national radio and were covered extensively by print and television media. The TRC processed more than 7,000 applications for amnesty, denying those that did not meet the requirements.[44] The final report, which was made publicly available, filled seven volumes.

The TRC is among the most well-known and influential truth commissions for its successes. It affirmed the dignity of thousands of victims and acknowledged their suffering. For many, it was the first time that a government entity had demonstrated any concern for what had happened to them or admitted it was unjust. The TRC provided a forum for victims and perpetrators from all sides to face one another and discover the other's humanity in an environment designed to foster truth and forgiveness. It helped families discover the fate of the disappeared. This could resuscitate a damaged reputation, reunite loved ones, or in many cases give families a body to bury with dignity. Sometimes, remorse was expressed by perpetrators and it produced forgiveness at the interpersonal level. In other cases, perpetrators simply responded to a subpoena and were motivated by fear of prosecution, not regret or remorse. This lack of sincerity caused additional pain for families of victims. "The reality is that, when you trade amnesty for truth, murderers get away with murder."[45] Yet in an environment where crimes were covered up, the truth itself was a form of justice. And in cases where forgiveness was not possible, the ability to live together in the same society might count as a form of success. Importantly, the TRC established a collective memory for the country, preventing denialism.[46] The human rights violations revealed were more barbarous and widespread than many people in the country had understood. Almost a decade post-apartheid, a large majority of South Africans agreed that apartheid was a crime against humanity and that the state must be held to certain legal standards, and a portion of South African society reported being somewhat reconciled.[47] Perhaps most striking to the outside world, South

Africa made a relatively peaceful and unexpected transition from an apartheid dictatorship to a peaceful, stable, multiracial democracy. More than 1,000 other truth and reconciliation commissions have been established worldwide since its creation.[48]

BOX 5.2 DEFENDING HUMAN RIGHTS: THE SREBRENICA GENOCIDE MEMORIAL

Public memorialization is an important part of transitional justice processes. Public memorials honor the memory of victims and the struggle of survivors, acknowledging the injustices done to them. Memorials also play an important role in truth-telling. They reveal the scars of an ugly past that perpetrators and bystanders would prefer communities forget. In this way, memorials are an antidote to misinformation and denial, and can make an important contribution to the fight against impunity. Public memorials can also contribute to a culture of democracy by generating conversations within communities and across generations about the lessons of the past and the ways those past crimes continue to shape the present.[57]

In July 1995, Srebrenica became the site of the largest massacre in Europe since the end of World War II. Over a period of several days, Bosnian Serb

FIGURE 5.2 A woman prays during the funerals of nine massacre victims, Srebrenica, Bosnia
Source: Associated Press

military forces led by General Ratko Mladić, Commander of the Bosnian Serb Army, murdered more than 8,000 Muslim men and boys, burying them in mass graves. The Bosnian Serb military and police forces also forcibly deported over 25,000 Bosniak women, children, and elderly, many of whom were subjected to physical abuse and rape.[58] These crimes were part of a systematic attempt to eradicate the Bosniak people and to destroy the nascent multi-ethnic state of Bosnia-Herzegovina.[59] The International Court of Justice (ICJ) and the International Criminal Tribunal for the former Yugoslavia (ICTY) ruled that the crimes committed in Srebrenica were genocide.[60]

The Srebrenica-Potočari Memorial and Cemetery for the Victims of the 1995 Genocide (Srebrenica Memorial) was established to honor the memory of the victims of the Srebrenica genocide. The work of the Srebrenica Memorial Center is multi-faceted. With the assistance of the International Commission on Missing Persons, the Srebrenica Memorial has assisted in the identification and reburial of over 6,900 victims in a process that respects their dignity. More than 1,700 victims remain missing after the exhumation of 94 mass gravesites.[61] The Srebrenica Memorial Center preserves the truth about what happened in Srebrenica. The Center contains public exhibitions and research archives. Visitors learn about the Srebrenica genocide and the prosecutions that followed by listening to oral testimonies, watching educational films, examining material evidence, and reviewing court documents.[62] Finally, the Srebrenica Memorial Center promotes tolerance. It fights the hatred that gives rise to genocide and genocide denial by promoting evidence-based genocide research and encouraging inter-faith and inter-ethnic dialogue.[63]

The Srebrenica Memorial and other sites-of-conscience are important because they prevent societies from forgetting the past. Denying past human rights violations actively renews the hatred and societal divisions that gave rise to the original crimes. Remembering atrocity crimes and addressing their painful legacy is essential for a peaceful (and just) present and future.

While the achievements of the TRC are important, it has also been marked by disappointments and failures. Decades later some of its work remains unfinished. Many of the cases referred by the TRC for further investigation and possible prosecution remain before the National Prosecution Authority; and many of its recommendations for reparation and reform were never fulfilled. The TRC did not adequately address the gendered experiences of apartheid, including gender-specific crimes. While the TRC held women's hearings, it failed to recognize sexual abuse as a politically motivated and systemic tool of state repression.[49] And the TRC did not address the structural impacts of apartheid and preceding colonial exploitation. South Africa's apartheid legacy includes widespread poverty, severe economic inequality, and high levels of social and criminal violence.[50] The people who had suffered the most during decades of apartheid continued to subsist in poor neighborhoods while the security officials who enforced apartheid remained wealthy.[51] Yet it's important to recognize that the TRC is only part of what should be a wider political and societal transition process. It was not designed to address systemic, institutionalized, and structural injustice. It was designed to address specific atrocities – the violation of physical integrity rights which are a sub-category of political and civil rights.[52] While it might not be fair to expect the TRC to accomplish tasks it was not designed to do, the TRC process offers an important lesson: to achieve societal reconciliation, justice should address economic, social, and cultural rights, as well as political and civil rights. If human rights and justice advocates focus exclusively on political and civil rights, the socio-economic effects of human rights violations, like apartheid, will remain largely intact.[53] And if transitional justice processes focus only on individual rights violations, the collective character of injustices like forced displacement, unequal education, and economic exclusion will be neglected.[54] The South African TRC, like all mechanisms of transitional justice, was an imperfect response to the irreparable harms caused by human rights violations.[55] It may take multiple processes over an extended period to meet a society's transitional justice needs. As South African scholar and human rights activist Yazier Henry says, "Human rights, democracy, and the systematic creation and construction of atrocity takes place over time. They don't just occur, and they don't just end."[56]

The South Africa case offers another example of how human rights norms can develop in, and travel from, the global south and become internationalized. The TRC was designed to respond to the specific needs of the local context, producing an innovative transitional justice mechanism that incorporated the limited use of trials and amnesties within the framework of a truth commission. South Africa's TRC promoted both restorative and retributive forms of justice but prioritized reconciliation as its highest goal. The legacy of apartheid still plagues South Africa and the TRC was unable to heal all wounds. But the TRC created a collective memory of apartheid in South Africa – one that is known throughout the world – and in the process offered the gift of truth to victims and their families as a form of justice. In a country that the world expected to erupt into racial war, the TRC helped birth an imperfect multiracial democracy characterized by a stable peace.

The Greensboro Truth and Reconciliation Commission

In the absence of government leadership, civil society actors have formed "unofficial" truth commissions. Unlike the official transitional justice processes in Argentina and South Africa, the Greensboro Truth and Reconciliation Commission (GTRC) was a citizen-initiated truth-finding project with a mandate to examine the context, causes, sequence, and consequences of a massacre that took place in Greensboro, North Carolina on November 3, 1979. It was the first truth commission in the United States and was greatly influenced by the South African TRC, illustrating how ideas about human rights travel across borders.[64] The

Greensboro case demonstrates that a well-organized, grassroots-driven, community-led truth commission can achieve transitional justice goals in the absence of state support, even when faced with government opposition. Yet there are limits to what an unofficial truth commission can achieve in terms of victim acknowledgement and community healing when the government was a source of the original harm.

On November 3, 1979 the Communist Workers Party (CWP) then known as the Workers Viewpoint Organization (WVO) organized a "Death to the Klan" rally in Greensboro's Black Morningside Homes public housing community.[65] A caravan of armed white supremacists composed of Nazis and Ku Klux Klan members – an American white supremacist hate group – fired into the crowd of mostly unarmed demonstrators as they assembled. Five anti-Klan demonstrators were killed, and eight demonstrators were wounded along with one Klansman and one news photographer. Neighbors and witnesses were traumatized by the massacre unfolding on their lawns. The violence was not unforeseen. The WVO and the Klan had a history of confrontation. The Klan sought to disrupt the WVO's efforts to unionize poor Black mill workers and the WVO taunted the Klan with violent rhetoric in the press and at counter-protests outside Klan events. The rally had been publicly advertised. Members of the press were on-site, but no police were present. The Greensboro Police Department (GPD) provided a permit for the protest but did not provide security despite the tension between the groups. They failed to warn the WVO or community members of the risk, despite evidence suggesting that armed Klansmen intended to violently disrupt the rally. The GPD and city officials characterized the event not as a massacre or crime, but as a shootout between two hate groups led by agitators from outside the community. In the two criminal trials that followed, the white defendants (Klansmen and Nazis) were acquitted of all charges by all white juries, despite video evidence clearly identifying them as the perpetrators. A 1985 civil lawsuit found members of the GPD, an FBI informant, and six Klansmen and Nazis jointly liable for the wrongful death of one of the demonstrators.

Almost 25 years later, an alliance of Black and white citizens, who believed that justice for the Greensboro Massacre had never been served, initiated the truth and reconciliation process. The Greensboro Truth and Reconciliation Commission (GTRC) was established in 2004 and its seven Commissioners selected through a democratic process with meaningful community participation.[66] Its goals included: reclaiming the humanity of those who died on November 3 and that of their spouses and friends who survived; bringing hidden facts to light through a public process that would nurture democracy and build social trust; and changing future patterns of interaction among social classes and races, and between institutions and the people.[67] The GTRC pursued its objectives through research and a program of civic engagement. The research component focused on establishing an accurate public record of what occurred on November 3 and reconciling multiple perspectives of how the event was caused and should be interpreted, as well as clarifying what the consequences had been for the community.[68] To accomplish this, Commissioners reviewed documents, consulted experts, conducted interviews, and gathered written and oral testimony from witnesses. Seventy-eight people provided written statements and 54 people testified at public hearings, including one of the Klansmen.[69] The civic engagement part of the GTRC process sought "to educate, inform, and involve the public in the truth-seeking, truth-telling, and reconciliations processes."[70] The idea was to reexamine the past, not for the purpose of retribution, but as a process of restorative justice that could lay the foundation for future community healing. It would be up to the community, not the GTRC, to achieve reconciliation.[71] Thus, the GTRC sought to strengthen democratic participation, amplify previously silenced voices, and "establish a new tradition of compassionate listening and reasoning in the struggle for justice."[72] The GTRC understood that reconciliation is an unfolding process and not a singular event.

The GTRC succeeded in several respects. It revealed a more accurate and complex picture of what happened in 1979. The Commission identified the Klansmen and Nazis as bearing the heaviest responsibility for the massacre. They came armed to the rally location intending to break the law. The Commissioners criticized the WVO for underestimating the risks of provoking the Klan with their violent rhetoric and for disregarding the safety of marchers and neighborhood residents. The GTRC identified the absence of police as the single most important factor that contributed to the violent confrontation. They noted that this police absence was the result of some intentionality on behalf of at least some police officers who failed to provide equal protection to all residents.[73] A majority of Commissioners also found that the GPD and key city leaders deliberately misled the public about what happened to shift responsibility away from the police department, protect the city's image, and discourage additional protests.[74] By publicly stating that WVO members did not deserve to be killed and were not responsible for their own deaths, the Commissioners rehumanized the victims and acknowledged their suffering. The GTRC found that the effects of November 3 were far-reaching, extending beyond the individual deaths, psychological trauma, and physical injuries. The GTRC increased community awareness of underlying structures of division and exclusion in their community by revealing how the events "were woven through with issues of race and class" and encouraged community dialogue about them.[75] Community silence about the events of November 3 exacerbated race and class tensions in the community, caused a spike in racist violence and hate group activity, and heightened distrust of police, the justice system, elected officials, and the media.[76] Finally, the GTRC process itself increased community capacity for democratic participation and renewed the long tradition of activism that pre-existed in Greensboro.[77]

The GTRC offers two important lessons about transitional justice. First, unofficial truth commissions can be an effective truth-seeking tool, but lack of government participation limits their reconciliation potential. The GTRC faced strong opposition from city officials and local police who sought to undermine its efforts by disseminating misinformation, discouraging residents from participating, and intimidating people associated with the GTRC. The City Council voted 6–3 along racial lines to oppose the truth commission. The mayor described the process as "unappetizing" for its focus on poverty and race. None of the white members of the city council attended any of the hearings or the report release ceremony.[78] These actions hampered reconciliation by revealing how the institutionalized racism identified in the GTRC report persisted in Greensboro, and that local officials were unwilling to address it.[79] Yet government opposition also demonstrated that the process mattered, had the potential to foster change, and could not be ignored, warranting their effort to delegitimize it.[80] The GTRC successfully completed its mandate, demonstrating that mobilized people can have an impact in absence of political power even when powerful people work against them.

Second, unpopular minority groups risk having violations of their human rights ignored by democratic societies when the majority disapproves of their viewpoints or conduct. For this reason, transitional justice advocates must protect the rights of, and seek justice for, those marginalized by democracy. The GTRC argued that the police had a duty to protect all people, including the demonstrators who had espoused anti-police rhetoric and communist views that were not widely accepted. The requirements of human rights are clear – everyone is equally deserving of dignity and rights. In the words of the GTRC, "Indeed, civil and human rights do not derive their meaning from their protection for the universally adored and cooperative. Rights only have meaning when they apply to everyone, even those whose views may be seen as threatening."[81] For many people in Greensboro, the GTRC was an important tool for truth and reconciliation. Its success suggests that unofficial truth commissions might be an effective mechanism for other communities in the United States and elsewhere seeking to address racial injustices of the past when national efforts to do so are blocked.

Conclusion

Transitional justice processes will always fall short of some of the expectations of them. No amount of truth or justice brings murdered loved ones back to life or compensates for the harm caused by human rights violations. Like all political processes, they emerge from compromise and operate in the difficult circumstances of past conflict and ongoing injustice. For these reasons, the success of transitional justice should be measured against the alternative of letting injustice continue rather than the ideal of a fully reconciled society. Historically, governments that abused the human rights of their people did so with impunity. Most governments, even democratic ones, have been content to forget the past and focus on the future. But denying the past renews the harm in the present and failing to address human rights violations makes them likely to recur. Transitional justice processes disrupt this pattern by bringing some measure of accountability, however limited. The trend toward acknowledgment, truth-seeking, and accountability for human rights violations has strengthened alongside human rights norms; yet transitional justice efforts are persistently challenged by those who hold power.

Argentina and South Africa were early adopters of transitional justice mechanisms. Argentina's willingness to criminally prosecute former military leaders showed that it was possible and initiated a modern cascade of human rights trials, including the creation of international courts to prosecute perpetrators when states are unable to do so. South Africa's innovative Truth and Reconciliation Commission triggered a wave of truth commissions across the world. Both are cases where human rights innovation emerged from the global south and diffused internationally. And in both countries, the political and social context shaped the processes adopted and goals pursued. The Greensboro case shows that communities can recover history and strengthen democracy even in the absence of government participation in transitional justice processes. While official processes are more meaningful for victims and have greater potential for institutional reform, unofficial truth commissions also empower people to acknowledge the past and participate in building a new future.[82]

Notes

1 International Center for Transitional Justice, "What is Transitional Justice?" www.ictj. org/about/transitional-justice, accessed 5/31/2021.

2 On human rights trials and the trend toward prosecution see Kathryn Sikkink, *The Justice Cascade: How Human Rights Prosecutions are Changing the World* (WW Norton & Company, 2011).

3 For a comprehensive introduction to truth commissions see Priscilla B. Hayner, *Unspeakable Truths: Transitional Justice and the Challenge of Truth Commissions*, Second edition (Routledge, 2011).

4 Sebastian Brett, Louis Bickford, Liz Ševčenko, and Marcela Rios, *Memorialization and Democracy: State Policy and Civic Action* (International Center for Transitional Justice, 2007).

5 Ruben Carranza, Cristián Correa, and Elena Naughton, *More Than Words: Apologies as a Form of Reparation* (International Center for Transitional Justice, 2015), pp. 5–6.

6 Kathryn Sikkink and Carrie Booth Walling, "The Impact of Human Rights Trials in Latin America," *Journal of Peace Research*, 44:4 (2007), 427–455; Tricia D. Olsen, Leigh A. Payne, and Andrew G. Reiter, *Transitional Justice in Balance: Comparing Processes, Weighing Efficacy* (United States Institute of Peace, 2010).

7 Naomi Roht-Arriaza, "The New Landscape of Transitional Justice," in Naomi Roht-Arriaza and Javier Mariezcurrena (eds.), *Transitional Justice in the Twenty-First Century: Beyond Truth versus Justice* (Cambridge University Press, 2006), p. 2.

8 For a thoughtful discussion on the differences between retributive and restorative justice see Michelle Maiese, "Retributive Justice," and "Restorative Justice," *Beyond Intractability* originally published in 2003, updated in 2013 by Heidi Burgess and Sarah Cast with current implications added by Heidi Burgess in 2020, www.beyondintracta bility.org/essay/retributive.justice and www.beyondintractability.org/essay/restorative-justice, accessed 6/1/2021.

9 Rosario Figari Layús, *The Reparative Effects of Human Rights Trials: Lessons from Argentina* (Routledge Press, 2018), p. 4.

10 Kathryn Sikkink and Carrie Booth Walling, "Argentina's Contribution to Global Trends in Transitional Justice," in Naomi Roht-Arriaza and Javier Mariezcurrena (eds.), *Transitional Justice in the Twenty-First Century: Beyond Truth versus Justice* (Cambridge University Press, 2006), p. 310.

11 Jose Zalaquett, "Balancing Ethical Imperatives and Political Constraints: The Dilemma of New Democracies Confronting Past Human Rights Violations," *Hastings Law Journal*, 43 (1992).

12 Ellen Lutz and Kathryn Sikkink, "The Justice Cascade: The Evolution and Impact for Foreign Human Rights Trials in Latin America," *Chicago Journal of International Law*, 2:1 (2001); Sikkink and Walling, "The Impact of Human Rights Trials in Latin America"; Sikkink, *The Justice Cascade*.

13 Examples of foreign trials include Spanish prosecution of Argentine nationals for human rights crimes committed in Argentina. International courts include the ad hoc courts created by the UN Security Council to prosecute human rights violations in the former Yugoslavia (ICTY) and Rwanda (ICTR). The International Criminal Court has jurisdiction over only a small subset of human rights related crimes – genocide, war crimes, and crimes against humanity. Hybrid courts have been created for Sierra Leone, Kosovo, Bosnia, Timor-Leste, and Cambodia.

14 Sikkink, *The Justice Cascade*, p. 75.

15 On the idea of "discovery of law" see Catalina Smulovitz, "The Discovery of Law: Political Consequences in the Argentine Case," in Yves Dezalay and Bryant G. Garth (eds.), *Global Prescriptions: The Production, Exportation, and Importation of a New Legal Orthodoxy* (University of Michigan Press, 2002). See also Sikkink and Walling, "The Impact of Human Rights Trials in Latin America," p. 441.

16 See Kathryn Sikkink, "Latin American Countries as Norms Protagonists of the Idea of International Human Rights," *Global Governance*, 20 (2014), 389–404. The section that follows draws on Sikkink and Walling, "Argentina's Contribution to Global Trends."

17 The only precedents to the Latin America trials were the successor trials held after World War II and the 1974 trial of the Greek colonels in Greece but neither precedent shaped Argentine decision-making.

18 Sikkink, "Latin American Countries," p. 398.

19 Layús, *The Reparative Effects of Human Rights Trials*, p. 81.

20 Sikkink and Walling, "Argentina's Contribution to Global Trends."

21 Layús, *The Reparative Effects of Human Rights Trials*, pp. 115–116.

22 Geoff Dancey, Francesca Lessa, Bridget Marchesi, Leigh A. Payne, Gabriel Pereira, and Kathryn Sikkink, "The Transitional Justice Research Collaborative: Bridging the Qualitative-Quantitative Divide with New Data," 2014, www.transitionaljusticedata. com, accessed 6/5/2021.

23 Ellen L. Lutz and Caitlin Reiger, *Prosecuting Heads of State* (Cambridge University Press, 2009); Sikkink, *The Justice Cascade*.

24 Carrie Booth Walling, "Insight on Victim Testimony and Transitional Justice," *Journal of Human Rights*, 17:3 (2018), p. 384; Juan E. Méndez, "Accountability for Past Abuses," *Human Rights Quarterly*, 19:2 (1997), p. 259.

25 Walling, "Insight on Victim Testimony," p. 384; UN Security Council Resolution 1674 (S/RES/1674), 2006; S/PRST/2006/28, June 22, 2006; A/RES/60147, March 2006.

26 OHCHR, *Rule-of-Law Tools for Post-Conflict States: Amnesties* (United Nations, 2009), www.ohchr.org/Documents/Publications/Amnesties_en.pdf, accessed 9/28/2021, p. 3; see also OHCHR, *Rule-of-Law Tools for Post-Conflict States: Prosecution Initiatives* (United Nations, 2006), www.ohchr.org/Documents/Publications/RuleoflawProsecu tionsen.pdf, accessed 9/28/2021, which identifies domestic prosecutions as crucial for transitional justice.

27 Carrie Booth Walling and Susan Waltz, "Forensic Evidence and Human Rights Reporting," Human Rights Advocacy and the History of International Human Rights

Standards, http://humanrightshistory.umich.edu/research-and-advocacy/forensic-evi dence-and-human-rights-reporting/, accessed 11/24/2020.

28 Physicians for Human Rights, "Advisory Council: Sebnem Korur Fincancı," https://p hr.org/people/sebnem-korur-fincanci/, accessed 11/24/2020.

29 Physicians for Human Rights, "Focus Areas: The Istanbul Protocol," https://phr.org/ issues/istanbul-protocol/, accessed 11/24/2020.

30 Human Rights Foundation of Turkey, "About HRFT," https://en.tihv.org.tr/a bout-hrft/, accessed 11/24/2020.

31 International Federation for Human Rights, "Turkey: Acquittal of Ms. Şebnem Korur Fincancı, Mr. Erol Önderoğlu and Mr. Ahmet Nesin," July 18, 2019, www.fidh.org/ en/issues/human-rights-defenders/turkey-acquittal-of-ms-sebnem-korur-fincanci-m r-erol-onderoglu-and-mr, accessed 9/28/2021; Physicians for Human Rights, "Perse- cution in Turkey: Dr. Şebnem Korur Fincancı," https://phr.org/issues/health-under-a ttack/persecution-of-health-professionals/persecution-in-turkey/dr-sebnem-korur-finca nci/, accessed 9/28/2021.

32 Elizabeth Redden, "Peace Petition Signatories Face Continued Prosecution," *Inside Higher Ed*, July 1, 2019, www.insidehighered.com/news/2019/07/01/about-700-aca demics-have-been-criminally-charged-turkey-their-signatures-petition, accessed 11/ 24/2020.

33 Frontline Defenders, "Acquittal Verdict of Şebnem Korur Fincancı Overturned," www.frontlinedefenders.org/en/case/case-history-sebnem-korur-fincanci, accessed 11/24/2020.

34 Physicians for Human Rights, "PHR Honors Dr. Sebnem Korur Fincancı," https://p hr.org/issues/health-under-attack/persecution-of-health-professionals/persecution-in- turkey/dr-sebnem-korur-fincanci/, accessed 11/24/2020.

35 Hayner, *Unspeakable Truths*, p. 11.

36 Hayner, *Unspeakable Truths*, p. 11.

37 Convention on the Suppression and Punishment of the Crime of Apartheid in November 1973, http://hrlibrary.umn.edu/instree/apartheid-supp.html, accessed 10/ 7/2021.

38 Archbishop Desmond Tutu, chair of the South Africa TRC, defines *ubuntu* as the idea that "my humanity is caught up, is inextricably bound up, in yours" or "a person is a person through other persons" in *No Future Without Forgiveness* (Image Press, 2000), p. 31.

39 Tutu, *No Future Without Forgiveness*.

40 Tutu, *No Future Without Forgiveness*, pp. 22–23.

41 Tutu, *No Future Without Forgiveness*, pp. 25–26.

42 Tutu, *No Future Without Forgiveness*, p. 29.

43 Paul Gready, *The Era of Transitional Justice: The Aftermath of the Truth and Reconciliation Commission in South Africa and Beyond* (Routledge, 2011), p. 4; Hayner, *Unspeakable Truths*, p. 28.

44 Hayner, *Unspeakable Truths*, p. 29.

45 Michael Ignatieff, "Digging Up the Dead," *The New Yorker*, November 10, 1997, p. 93.

46 Albie Sachs, "Meeting the Man who Organised a Bomb in My Car," in Mia Stewart and Karin van Marle (eds.), *The Limits of Transition: The South African Truth and Reconciliation Commission 20 Years On* (Brill, 2017), p. 32.

47 James L. Gibson, "Overcoming Apartheid? Can Truth Reconcile a Divided Nation?" *Annals of the American Academy of Political and Social Science*, 603 (2006), pp. 95–97.

48 Sisonke Msimang, "All is Not Forgiven: South Africa and the Scars of Apartheid," *Foreign Affairs*, (January/February 2018), p. 32.

49 Hayner, *Unspeakable Truths*, p. 88. See also Rina Kashyap, "Narrative and Truth: A Feminist Critique of the South African Truth and Reconciliation Commission," *Con- temporary Justice Review*, 12:4 (2009), 449–467.

50 Gready, *The Era of Transitional Justice*, p. 1.
51 Sachs, "Meeting the Man who Organised a Bomb in My Car," p. 34.
52 Physical integrity rights protect against the infliction of physical bodily harm and include acts like extrajudicial killing, torture, enforced disappearance, and arbitrary imprisonment.
53 Msimang, "All is Not Forgiven"; Gready, *The Era of Transitional Justice*.
54 Msimang, "All is Not Forgiven," p. 32.
55 See Richard A. Wilson, *The Politics of Truth and Reconciliation in South Africa: Legitimizing the Post-Apartheid State* (Cambridge University Press, 2009).
56 Yazier Henry in "Yazier Henry on Transcending South Africa's Violent, Lingering Landscape of Inequality," *State & Hill*, April 26, 2016, https://fordschool.umich.edu/news/2016/toward-language-greater-equality-and-peace, accessed 6/3/2021.
57 Sebastian Brett, Louis Bickford, Liz Ševœnko, and Marcela Rios. *Memorialization and Democracy: State Policy and Civil Action* (International Center for Transitional Justice, 2011), p. 2.
58 The term Bosniak refers to the Bosnian Muslim population of Bosnia and Herzegovina. Both terms are regularly used interchangeably.
59 Carrie Booth Walling, *All Necessary Measures: The United Nations and Humanitarian Intervention* (University of Pennsylvania Press, 2013); Monica Hanson Green, *Srebrenica Genocide Denial Report 2020* (Srebrenica Memorial, 2020), p. 14; For a detailed examination of post-war attempts to address the Srebrenica Genocide see Lara J. Nettlefield and Sarah E. Wagner, *Srebrenica in the Aftermath of Genocide* (Cambridge University Press, 2013).
60 International Court of Justice, "Application of the Convention on the Prevention and Punishment of the Crime of Genocide (Bosnia and Herzegovina vs. Serbia and Montenegro)," www.icj-cij.org/en/case/91, accessed 11/21/2020; International Criminal Tribunal for Yugoslavia (ICTY), "Srebrenica Genocide: No Room for Denial," www.icty.org/en/outreach/documentaries/srebrenica-genocide-no-room-for-denial, accessed 11/21/20.
61 International Commission on Missing Persons, "Srebrenica Figures as of 28 June 2019," www.icmp.int/wp-content/uploads/2017/06/srebrenica-english-2019.pdf in Green, *Srebrenica Genocide Denial Report 2020*, p. 21.
62 Srebrenica Memorial Center, "About Us," www.srebrenicamemorial.org/bs/article/209/o-nama, accessed 11/21/2020.
63 Srebrenica Memorial Center, www.srebrenicamemorial.org, accessed 11/21/2020.
64 Three prominent figures of the South African TRC consulted with members of the GTRC and the Greensboro community at various stages of the truth-finding and reconciliation process. These were Reverend Richard Storey, Archbishop Desmond Tutu, and Alex Boraine.
65 Information in this section comes from the Greensboro Truth & Reconciliation Commission Report, May 25, 2006, https://greensborotrc.org/, accessed 6/22/2021.
66 GTRC, "Frequently Asked Questions," https://greensborotrc.org/, accessed 6/22/2021.
67 Spoma Javanović, *Democracy, Dialogue, and Community Action: Truth and Reconciliation in Greensboro* (University of Arkansas Press, 2012), pp. 15, 70–74.
68 GTRC, "About," https://greensborotrc.org/, accessed 6/22/2021.
69 Javanović, *Democracy, Dialogue, and Community Action*, p. 83. An excellent documentary film about the GTRC is Adam Zucker's *Greensboro: Closer to the Truth* produced by Longnook Pictures in 2007, https://greensborothemovie.com/, accessed 6/27/2021.
70 GTRC, "About," https://greensborotrc.org/, accessed 6/22/2021.
71 Javanović, *Democracy, Dialogue, and Community Action*, p. 92.
72 Javanović, *Democracy, Dialogue, and Community Action*, p. 80; Lisa Magarrell and Joya Wesley, *Learning from Greensboro: Truth and Reconciliation in the United States* (University of Pennsylvania Press, 2008).

73 Greensboro Truth & Reconciliation Commission Report, p. 12.
74 Greensboro Truth & Reconciliation Commission Report, pp. 18–19.
75 Greensboro Truth & Reconciliation Commission Report, p. 18; Magarrell and Wesley, *Learning from Greensboro*, pp. 208–210.
76 Greensboro Truth & Reconciliation Commission Report, p. 24.
77 Javanović, *Democracy, Dialogue, and Community Action*, pp. 138, 154.
78 Greensboro Truth & Reconciliation Commission Report, p. 25; Magarrell and Wesley, *Learning from Greensboro*, p. 172.
79 Greensboro Truth & Reconciliation Commission Report, p. 23.
80 Magarrell and Wesley, *Learning from Greensboro*, pp. 174–175.
81 Greensboro Truth & Reconciliation Commission Report, p. 12.
82 See Signe Waller Foxworth, "Greensboro's Radical Experiment in Democracy," *Poverty & Race*, 17:6 (2008), p. 26.

6

MAKING HUMAN RIGHTS CHANGE

Human rights belong to all people, but they are not equally respected, protected, or fulfilled in different communities and countries. Achieving a world in which all humans are equal in dignity and rights requires challenging the people and power structures that perpetuate oppression, inequality, discrimination, and injustice. This chapter explores the people, processes, and places of human rights change. Human rights practitioners confront those in power who benefit from rights violations and demand radical transformation of the political and legal practices that cause them.[1] Often, it takes the concerted effort of a broad-based coalition of actors who use the power of the human rights idea and credible evidence of rights violations to generate human rights change. The goal is the adoption of equitable policies that respect human dignity and the realization of justice. If this cannot be achieved by changing hearts and minds, rights advocates aim to increase the costs of committing human rights violations for perpetrators through material or social sanction. Human rights, then, are intensely political everywhere.

While human rights are political, they are intended to be non-partisan in the broadest sense. Human rights are not designed to privilege any specific person, group, government, or political party.[2] Instead, human rights action is motivated by a commitment to equal human dignity. Human rights practitioners should strive to be "equal opportunity antagonist[s] of all human rights violating governments."[3] This means that advocates should condemn human rights violations whether they happen in a democracy like the United States or under an authoritarian regime like Myanmar. While human rights are principally designed to protect people from the overbearing power of the modern nation-state, human rights practitioners also investigate abuses committed by rebel groups, multinational corporations, terrorist organizations, and other private actors. The Universal Declaration of Human Rights (UDHR) promotes equality and justice for

DOI: 10.4324/9781003256939-7

all human beings without distinction and promotes the realization of all types of human rights. Human rights practitioners commit to protecting them.

Indeed, one of the simple yet radical requirements of human rights change is that its defenders also must respect rights in their research, advocacy, and policy work. This might seem like a simple requirement when fighting for the rights of a repressed group whose empowerment you support. It is much more challenging to protect the rights and dignity of those you fundamentally disagree with, including the very perpetrators who are responsible for human rights violations. Yet, that is exactly what the human rights framework requires. No human being is authorized to judge which other human beings are worthy of dignity and rights – *all must be*. Human rights change may require confrontation and political contestation. Yet it is also a principled, law-driven approach where the means matter as well as the ends. Within the human rights framework, the ends alone cannot justify the means.

This chapter explores how human rights change happens. It explores "best practices" of human rights advocacy and investigates the strengths and weaknesses of existing mechanisms of human rights monitoring and enforcement. These findings are based on impact rather than success – it is difficult to label the reduction of human rights violations a success when victims still suffer. Driving up the political costs of committing human rights violations for governments, however, can be measured as impact. And this cost increase can be measured in stages. It often starts by galvanizing public debate, or starting a new one, against an egregious and harmful practice like torture or enforced disappearance; then gaining enough support for its prohibition to define it as a norm. Another step is to develop a monitoring mechanism like the creation of a United Nations (UN) Special Rapporteur – an independent expert to report on its use and advise steps to increase protection. The next stage focuses on prevention by creating a legal instrument that formally codifies the norm, like the Convention Against Torture and Other Cruel, Inhuman or Degrading Treatment or Punishment or the International Convention on the Protection of All People from Enforced Disappearance. Punishment is the cost at the next level. The idea is to create a mechanism of enforcement (e.g. an international court or tribunal or sanctions regime). The final stage of impact we might also consider success – the creation of a system of protection whereby the right is universally fulfilled.[4] At every stage of impact, people are the drivers of human rights change. People assert the claim to rights, mobilize support for it, develop the monitoring practices, create the treaties and instruments designed to prevent violations, and build institutions and mechanisms of enforcement.

Human Rights Defenders

Human rights defenders, like the many featured throughout this book, are people who promote human rights through nonviolent actions, individually and collectively with others.[5] Defenders like Beatrice Mtetwe in Zimbabwe highlight injustices and empower victims. Like Anas al-Dayab in Syria they use information strategically to change attitudes and advocate for inclusive policies and practices that protect the rights and dignity of others. Importantly, human rights defenders like Iraq's Nadia Murad support victims and work to secure accountability and end impunity for human rights violations. And like Cédric Herrou in France, they encourage everyone who has the power to do so (e.g. individuals, corporations, organizations, governments) to respect rights and dignity for all. People who advocate for human rights at the national and international level, like Wai Wai Nu from Myanmar and Şebnem Korur Fincancı in Turkey, are frequently harassed and have their own rights violated by governments and other actors whose rights abuses they criticize. But all human beings are entitled to their human rights and have the right to defend human rights. The United Nations (UN) Declaration on Human Rights Defenders protects human rights defenders by clarifying their rights:

- to conduct human rights work individually or collectively, including having the occupation of "human rights defender" and forming associations;
- to seek, obtain, receive, and hold information relating to human rights;
- to develop new human rights ideas and advocate for their acceptance;
- to complain about official policies relating to human rights and have those complaints reviewed;
- to provide advice and assistance in defense of human rights, including professionally qualified legal aid;
- to attend public hearings, proceedings, and trials to monitor their compliance with national law and international human rights obligations;
- to unhindered access to and communication with NGOs and inter-governmental organizations;
- to solicit, receive, and use resources for the purpose of protecting human rights, including receipt of funds from abroad; and
- to peacefully oppose acts or omissions by the government that result in violations of human rights.[6]

The rights of human rights defenders are supported at the UN by the Special Rapporteur on the situation of Human Rights Defenders who encourages governments to implement the declaration, monitors the situation of human rights defenders at risk, and recommends strategies to better protect them.[7] Human rights defenders also are protected by Non-Governmental Organizations (NGOs) like Frontline Defenders and the MesoAmerican Initiative of Women Human Rights Defenders.[8]

Human Rights Organizations (HROs) and Human Rights Advocacy

Defending human rights is a collective endeavor and defenders rarely work alone. Instead, they build networks of support and work collaboratively with others

BOX 6.1 DEFENDING HUMAN RIGHTS: THE COALITION OF IMMOKALEE WORKERS

Immokalee, Florida is frequently referred to as "the winter tomato capitol" of the United States (US). More than 90% of the fresh tomatoes consumed in the US between December and May are picked by farmworkers in the fields of Immokalee.[9] Previously known for terrible abuses – dangerous work conditions, unfair wages, sexual exploitation, forced labor, violence, wage theft, and human enslavement – Immokalee has become internationally recognized as one of the best working environments in American agriculture.[10] The reason: Immokalee is home to the Coalition of Immokalee Workers.

The Coalition of Immokalee Workers (CIW) is a farmworker community and worker-based human rights organization. Founded in 1993, CIW mobilizes farmworkers through popular education on labor history and social justice and teaches organizing, speaking, and leadership. CIW operates three programs that have helped transform one of the poorest, disenfranchised communities in the US into the political base for an effective worker movement with global human rights impact. The Campaign for Fair Food educates consumers on farm worker exploitation and forges alliances between farmworkers, consumers, and corporate buyers to increase wages and raise labor

FIGURE 6.1 The Coalition of Immokalee Workers stages a protest over wages and working conditions for tomato pickers in Florida
Source: L. Kragt Bakker / Shutterstock.com

standards for workers. The Anti-Slavery Campaign uncovers and investigates human rights abuses and assists in the federal prosecution of slavery rings that prey on farmworkers. CIW has participated in seven major investigations that liberated more than 1,200 workers from captivity and forced labor. CIW contributed to the formation of the US Department of Justice Anti-Trafficking Unit, the passage of the landmark federal Trafficking Victims Protection Act in 2000, and the inclusion of the United States in the rankings of the State Departments annual Trafficking in Persons report.[11]

The Fair Food Program (FFP) is a worker-led, market-enforced approach to human rights protection using corporate supply chains. The centerpiece is a penny per pound program where big companies (e.g. Taco Bell, McDonald's, and Walmart) pledge to only buy produce from growers who follow the FFP code of conduct and pay an extra penny for each pound they purchase which goes directly to the pickers.[12] These companies also pledge to stop working with suppliers who violate the standards. The program covers over 35,000 farmworkers. It is effective, according to Greg Asbed (one of CIW's founders), because it harnesses the market power of big corporations to eliminate worker abuses.[13] Organizer Gerardo Reyes Chavez describes this partnership as a "win-win-win" proposition. "For farmworkers, it protects their fundamental human rights. For farmers it stabilizes their labor supply and increases productivity. And for retail brands with global supply chains it eliminates public relations risks."[14]

The FFP's worker-driven social responsibility model is considered the "gold standard" due to its mechanisms for "empowering rights holders to know and exercise their rights."[15] It sets human rights standards drafted by workers themselves, mandates a health and safety program, and monitors grower compliance with these measures. The Fair Standards Council, an independent monitoring body, investigates complaints of sexual harassment, wage disputes, and other code violations.[16] It eliminates purchases to growers that violate human rights and gives workers an effective complaint resolution mechanism, making it one of the best workplace-monitoring systems in the United States. The UN Human Rights Council calls the FFP "an international benchmark" in the fight against modern slavery.[17] The program has become a global model of worker empowerment, bettering the lives of tens of thousands of agricultural workers.[18] The Coalition of Immokalee Workers is internationally recognized for its achievements in empowering workers, fighting human trafficking, reducing gender-based violence at work, and eliminating slavery in much of Florida's agricultural industry. Through a transformative model of worker-driven social responsibility, these farmworkers are leading a 21st century human rights revolution in agriculture.[19]

who share their interests and values (see Box 6.1). Sometimes, they create institutions to advance their human rights mission like the Srebrenica Genocide Memorial in Bosnia and Herzegovina or the Global Centre for the Responsibility to Protect. The international human rights movement entails a loose coalition of international organizations, national organizations, and international networks that include thousands of domestic and international NGOs alongside individual human rights defenders. The defining feature of Domestic and International Human Rights NGOs (also called Human Rights Organizations or HROs) and their civil society partners is their independence from governments and their willingness to confront and challenge them when persuasion fails, making them credible advocates for human rights change. Effective human rights change often relies on the interaction of multiple actors, mechanisms, and approaches operating at local, national, and international levels.

Human rights organizations call attention to human rights concerns by publicizing violations and developing new norms when existing human rights law fails to fully protect human dignity. While HROs use human rights law as a tool, they are not limited by the gaps and silences in the law. Instead, they use facts to generate consensus that a human rights problem exists and then collaborate with networks of activists, like-minded states, and intergovernmental bodies to establish new human rights standards. Finally, they urge states to implement these standards and monitor state compliance with them. As an example, the *Abuelas de Plaza de Mayo* (Grandmothers of the Plaza de Mayo), a domestic organization in Argentina comprised of family members of the disappeared, was legally unable to bring cases on behalf of their kidnapped grandchildren before Argentine courts. During the dirty war, hundreds of young children had been disappeared along with their parents or had been born to pregnant mothers in captivity. Kidnapped children were frequently adopted into military families or by supporters of the regime using false identity papers. Consequently, the Grandmothers became active in the international drafting process for the UN Convention on the Rights of the Child (CRC). During negotiations, they lobbied Argentina and other governments to include provisions that would protect children's right to identity. They succeeded and Articles 7 and 8 of the CRC are referred to as the "Argentine articles."[20] Article 7 requires children to be registered immediately after birth and establishes their right to acquire a nationality and know their parents. Article 8 requires states to respect the right of the child to preserve their identity, including nationality and family relations. It also requires governments to assist in re-establishing identity where a child has been illegally deprived of it.[21] When the CRC was ratified by Argentina, these provisions became binding domestically as well and the Grandmothers had legal standing to bring court cases to uncover the fate of their missing grandchildren. The Grandmothers found a gap in the law, helped establish new human rights standards to bridge that gap, and then used those standards to pursue justice and recover the identities of their missing grandchildren.

HROs like Human Rights Watch investigate allegations and document crimes using evidence-based research methods to establish a fact-based record of human rights abuses. They publicize the findings in reports and engage in strategic advocacy using both traditional and social media to mobilize people to claim their rights, publicly name and shame perpetrators, and pressure decision-makers at all levels to strengthen human rights protection. The typical human rights report targets three audiences simultaneously: 1) perpetrator and observer governments, 2) national and international mass media, and 3) members of the public in the target state and democracies. It combines the personal testimony of witnesses with forensic truths – the essential facts of what happened.[22] Paul Gready describes this practice as "the craft of bringing together legal norms and human stories in the service of justice."[23] It works. The ability to obtain, verify, and disseminate reliable information is the cornerstone of effective human rights advocacy. In the absence of material forms of power, HROs use their expertise as leverage to persuade or pressure perpetrator and observer governments to use their power to end violations and protect human rights. Said differently, HROs drive up the costs of committing human rights violations for perpetrators. Other international HROs well known for the rigorous quality of their research and reporting methods include Amnesty International, Human Rights First, International Federation for Human Rights, International Commission of Jurists, and Physicians for Human Rights.

Human rights scholar Alison Brysk highlights the importance of information, symbolism, and storytelling to human rights advocacy. Brysk argues that the struggle for human rights depends on the ability of advocates to "speak rights to power" – the ability to effectively deploy persuasive rhetoric in support of human rights.[24] Put simply, advocates need to tell a persuasive story. "Rights talk" contains several elements that work together to secure the recognition of rights, generate solidarity among peoples, and foster political reform.[25]

> Human rights campaigns succeed when they follow the same rhetorical strategies of successful political campaigns: employing charismatic or authoritative speakers, compelling narratives, plots performed in public space, well-framed messages, skillful use of appropriate media, and targeting audiences. Although not every successful campaign will have all of these elements, under comparable conditions those appeals that embody more of these qualities, will secure greater recognition of human rights.[26]

Think back to the example of the Grandmothers of the Plaza de Mayo. As grandmothers of the missing, they were authoritative speakers. They were viewed as loving caregivers. Their demand to know the truth about what happened to their missing grandchildren who had been kidnapped by the military regime or born to dissident mothers in captivity created a heartbreaking and compelling narrative. Their public appeals for truth and accountability garnered extensive media attention and generated widespread empathy domestically and abroad, increasing pressure on the Argentine state.[27]

Jo Becker, Advocacy Director for the Children's Rights Division of Human Rights Watch, also argues that a compelling narrative is an important component of an effective human rights campaign, especially when those most affected by violations speak directly to their own experiences.[28] There is also power in numbers. Diverse and broad-based alliances organized around a unified message can magnify the strength and credibility of an advocacy campaign. Information and its skillful deployment are the main currency of human rights movements. Advocacy campaigns should be built around credible research and documentation that spotlight patterns of abuse, making it hard for policy makers to ignore violations. Effective rights advocates should also prepare for unique (and often unexpected) opportunities to make progress – moments when they can deploy their information strategically and at multiple points of pressure. For example, when the International Olympic Committee selected Beijing to host the 2008 summer Olympics, Students for a Free Tibet suddenly had an opportunity to turn the Olympic spotlight on human rights violations in Tibet.[29] Though no one formula works for every context or issue, human rights advocates who operate within these fundamental principles are often successful even as their specific tools and tactics vary to match the needs of a specific situation.[30]

Networks of activists are significant domestically and internationally. They put human rights ideas on the agenda, shape the terms of debate on human rights, and influence policy outcomes. When they are effective, they can change the behavior of states and international organizations.[31] These networks of activists who work collaboratively together and with other sympathetic actors, who share common values, a common discourse, and engage in dense exchanges of information and support, are called advocacy networks. When these networks form across borders, they are what Margaret Keck and Kathryn Sikkink have termed, "transnational advocacy networks."[32] Transnational advocacy networks are typically composed of domestic and international NGOs, social movements, financial donors and foundations, members of the media, churches, trade unions, intellectuals, and parts of governments or regional and international organizations that share the network's values.[33] These groups exchange information, resources, and services, and work collaboratively to identify human rights problems, frame them in ways that demonstrate they can be solved, use their expert information and victim testimony to promote solutions, pressure rights-violators to implement solutions and monitor compliance with human rights standards. Human rights defenders engage in transnational advocacy when they believe that networking with their like-minded peers will further their goals. It is a common strategy used by domestic groups when they are unable to directly persuade or pressure their own governments and believe that external pressure from international allies can help further their cause.[34]

Transnational advocacy had a profound effect on human rights in Argentina.[35] While individual activists and domestic NGOs like the Grandmothers and other human rights groups including the Mothers of the Plaza de Mayo (*Madres de Plaza de Mayo*) pressured their government directly, they also built and activated a network of supporters abroad. Group members traveled to the US and Europe where they shared information and strategized with international human rights organizations, condemned government abuses in the press, and met with government officials. Sympathetic foundations and individual donors contributed funds to support domestic NGO efforts. External partners in the network began to pressure Argentina from the outside. When both Amnesty International and the InterAmerican Commission on Human Rights publicly disclosed and condemned the junta's human rights practices, it became embarrassing and politically costly for democracies to be seen supporting Argentina. For example, the United States, France, and Sweden all denounced the junta's rights violations and either imposed sanctions or cut military aid. A confluence of factors eventually led to the improved human rights situation in Argentina and the fall of the military junta, but the transnational human rights advocacy network played a pivotal role.

Keck and Sikkink have identified four network tactics that are effective for promoting human rights change. These include: 1) generating politically usable information and directing it strategically to where it will have the most impact (information politics); 2) employing symbols and stories to make sense of human rights problems for external audiences (symbolic politics); 3) leveraging the influence of powerful allies against the target state (leverage politics); and 4) holding powerful actors accountable to previously stated policies, principles, and promises (accountability politics).[36] Combined, these four tactics can be used by network partners to pressure and persuade rights-violating governments to make concessions toward human rights protection. A common feature of all human rights advocacy is that it is human-centered. This means placing people at the center of concern, empowering victims, and uplifting their voices, and respecting human dignity. Achieving human rights change requires painstaking effort, persistent organizing, and long-term commitment. It does not come easy and often has limited impact, but the world has experienced profound human rights change in the decades following the adoption of the Universal Declaration of Human Rights.

International Human Rights, National Implementation

One of the great paradoxes of human rights is that governments are both the primary violators of human rights and the primary duty bearers of human rights enforcement. In a world of sovereign states, international law is negotiated by and for states. International human rights treaties reflect promises states have made about how they will protect their own people. This means that the enforcement of states' human rights obligations largely falls to states themselves. The world's governments have designed a system of international human rights that adopts a common standard of rights and dignity that apply universally to all people and all nations but it gives enforcement authority to the very governments whose behavior human rights law seeks to regulate. It is no surprise then that an international human rights framework built to complement state sovereignty struggles to protect people against state perpetrators. A national-level system of human rights enforcement works if, and when, your national government recognizes and protects your human rights. It fails when your national government violates your human rights or the human rights of others within or outside its national borders. Indeed, as Eric Weitz aptly notes, the modern territorial nation-state lives on inclusion and exclusion – defining the boundaries of who has the right to have rights.[37] And as cases in this text have shown, even states that profess commitment to human rights often can protect the rights of some while limiting rights for others. When a state fails to respect, protect, and fulfill the human rights of its people, victims and advocates must appeal for recognition of rights from the very government denying them or appeal to external actors with political, economic, or military leverage to pressure state officials to honor their human rights commitments. What follows is a brief overview of how governments and the international human rights machinery created through the United Nations engage human rights, typically in response to the activism of defenders, HROs, and advocacy networks.

Governments with a professed commitment to human rights may adopt, or are pressured by their populations to adopt, a human rights foreign policy. Human rights practitioners encourage states to pursue a foreign policy approach that is consistent with their domestic human rights obligations. This means: 1) respecting the human rights of non-citizens in their own practices at home and abroad; 2) encouraging allies, trade partners, aid recipients, and strategic partners to fulfill their human rights obligations; and 3) punishing rights-violating governments for their violations. States that have adopted a human rights foreign policy typically have good human rights records themselves. They use a combination of incentives and disincentives to encourage other states to comply with human rights standards or stop human rights violations. Incentives may include promises of greater political engagement, technical assistance, economic partnerships, financial investment, or military cooperation. Disincentives can include exertion of political pressure, reduction of foreign aid, limiting trade and investment, economic sanctions, reducing or eliminating security assistance, or the disruption of diplomatic relations.

Foreign policy pressure works most effectively with two types of governments: 1) governments that care about their reputations; and 2) governments that are vulnerable to material incentives or sanctions from external actors. Importantly, the vulnerability of the *target state* – whose rights-violating behavior defenders want to change – must be matched with the political will of an *enforcer state* committed to elevating human rights as a core foreign policy priority. In practice, this means that developing states are more frequent targets of human rights enforcement than developed states because wealthy and powerful states can evade human rights enforcement in ways that economically and militarily vulnerable states cannot. Democracies, like France or Germany, are more susceptible to public shaming and political pressure from their domestic populations than non-democracies, making them more responsive to external human rights pressure. This means that rights-violating states that are resource-rich (like China), militarily powerful (like Russia), or that do not care about their reputations (like North Korea) are largely invulnerable to external human rights pressure through peer government foreign policy. The result is profoundly unequal for the world's people whose level of human rights protection should not be dictated by the accident of their birth.

In reality, governments like the United States, that have an official human rights foreign policy, have a mixed record when it comes to practice.[38] For example, the US emphasizes political rights and civil rights above others, is more concerned with the human rights violations of its enemies than its friends, and does not always adhere to the human rights principles it upholds for other countries. Nonetheless, the US has a robust official human rights foreign policy. Since the early 1960s the US Congress has required US foreign and trade policy to consider a state's human rights and worker's rights record.[39] Each year, the US State Department publishes and submits to Congress its *Country Reports on Human Rights Practices,* which examines the actions of foreign governments against internationally recognized human rights. These findings are used to shape government decisions on trade, security, and development assistance.[40] For example, in May 2020 the US Congress authorized sanctions on persons responsible for human rights violations committed against Muslim minority groups in China and elsewhere. Nonetheless, the US Congress has the power to disregard the human rights record of a foreign state if it has the votes to do so. For example, US aid to Saudi Arabia has continued without interruption despite a dismal women's human rights record, its participation in crimes against humanity in Yemen, and its horrific murder of journalist Jamal Khashoggi in a Saudi embassy in Turkey in October 2018. Other countries with significant human rights foreign policy practices include, among others, Costa Rica, France, Japan, Norway, the Netherlands, New Zealand, South Africa, and Sweden, and the European Union as whole.[41] In December 2020, the European Union adopted the EU Global Human Rights Sanctions Regime. Individuals, entities, and states designated for sanctions are subject to an asset freeze and travel ban in the EU and are prohibited from receiving funds directly or indirectly from any persons or entities residing within EU borders.[42]

BOX 6.2 DEFENDING HUMAN RIGHTS: GAMBIA TAKES MYANMAR TO COURT

In November 2019, Gambia – the smallest country on continental Africa and one of the smallest in the world – took historic action to defend human rights. Acting with the support of the 57 members of the Organization of Islamic Cooperation (OIC), Gambia filed a case before the UN's highest court alleging that Myanmar's atrocities against Rohingya in Rakhine State violated the Genocide Convention. The case is the first time that a country who is not directly connected to the alleged crimes has brought a case of genocide before the International Court of Justice (ICJ).[43] While any of the 149 countries that have ratified the Genocide Convention could have initiated legal proceedings, it was Gambia that did so. According to former Gambian Justice Minister Aboubacarr Tambadou, all states large and small have a legal obligation and moral responsibility to respond to genocide and seek justice for its victims.[44]

The Rohingya have been persecuted in Myanmar for decades but in late 2017 a "military clearance operation" initiated by government authorities forced more than 740,000 Rohingya to flee to neighboring Bangladesh for safety. The UN Independent International Fact-Finding Mission on Myanmar determined that Myanmar's military committed extensive atrocities against

FIGURE 6.2 Gambia's Justice Minister Aboubacarr Tambadou at the International Court of Justice

Source: Associated Press

the Rohingya including deliberately targeting civilians, mass killing, torture, arson, rape, gang rape, and forced deportation – grave violations under international law. The investigation found evidence suggesting genocidal intent. Similar conclusions were reached by the Special Rapporteur of the United Nations to Myanmar and the Special Adviser of the Secretary-General on the Prevention of Genocide.[45]

When these reports reached the desk of Gambia's former attorney general and justice minister, he was reminded of the atrocities committed during the Rwandan genocide. Tambadou had prosecuted Rwandan *genocidaires* at the International Criminal Tribunal for Rwanda and he is the architect of Gambia's own far-reaching transitional justice processes which include a truth commission, a draft constitution that protects human rights, a plan to rejoin the International Criminal Court, and the ratification of several core human rights treaties.[46] Tambadou visited Cox's Bazar, a Rohingya refugee camp in Bangladesh, as part of an OIC mission in May 2018. After listening to the stories of survivors, Tambadou was determined that the world must not abandon the Rohingya the way it abandoned Rwanda in 1994 and his own country during its 22 years of repressive rule.[47] In January 2020, Tambadou scored an early victory for the Rohingya when the ICJ ordered Myanmar to take concrete steps to prevent the genocide of the Rohingya remaining in the country and to preserve evidence relating to the underlying genocide case. While it may take years for the final verdict to be issued, these provisional measures are legally binding and the first formal recognition that the Rohingya people have received from a court of justice.

Myanmar is more than 7,000 miles from Gambia and the two countries have few economic, cultural, or diplomatic connections. Yet to those who ask, "Why Gambia?" Tambadou responds, "Well, why not Gambia?"[48] Tambadou says that international law is a formidable tool in the hands of all responsible countries, not just rich and powerful ones:

> The Gambia is demonstrating quite clearly that you do not have to have military power or economic power to stand for justice, to stand for what is right. We are doing this in the name of humanity. We are doing this because we want the Rohingya to be recognized as human beings, for their rights to be recognized in their own country of Myanmar.[49]

Gambia's bold move in defense of human rights illustrates the power of solidarity. International human rights leadership belongs to any state willing to exercise its voice to defend human dignity. If human rights are universal, then the responsibility to safeguard human rights should be universal too.[50] Tambadou and the country of Gambia have set an example that might encourage other states to struggle for justice, accountability, and protection of human rights within and across borders.

The International Human Rights Machinery

National implementation of human rights is backed up by an international human rights regime that clarifies human rights standards and monitors state compliance with them. The primary challenge facing the United Nations (UN) human rights machinery, however, is state sovereignty. Debra DeLaet argues, "State sovereignty serves as an obstacle to the promotion of universal human rights because, by definition, universal human rights represent an attempt to create a set of rights that transcend state borders."[51] This means that UN human rights machinery generally adopts a cooperative, constructive, and non-confrontational approach to human rights change. International human rights policy has been developed by states working through a variety of international processes and institutions, but the UN remains at the center. Three core UN treaties comprise the International Bill of Human Rights – the UDHR, the International Covenant on Civil and Political Rights (ICCPR), and the International Covenant on Economic, Social and Cultural Rights (ICESCR).[52] Together they form the foundation of international human rights law and are the authoritative source for human rights standards and state obligations. The United Nations has developed three primary mechanisms for promoting and protecting human rights: 1) the Office of the High Commissioner for Human Rights; 2) the Human Rights Council; and 3) Treaty Bodies – committees of independent experts that monitor the core international human rights treaties. Notably, as an intergovernmental organization made up of sovereign state members, UN human rights mechanisms work through a process of peer review and lack coercive enforcement power, except in the rare cases of Security Council action. Designed to reveal the egregious rights violations of states by exposing them to public scrutiny, these mechanisms rely on a form of peer pressure, socialization, and the provision of technical assistance to persuade states to reform themselves with little power to punish or force non-consensual behavioral change.[53] It is important to remember, however, it was through the actions of people working individually and collectively in defense of human rights that these UN mechanisms and processes were created.

Office of the High Commissioner of Human Rights/UN Human Rights

> To recover from the most wide-reaching and severe cascade of human rights setbacks in our lifetimes, we need a life-changing vision, and concerted action.
> *Michelle Bachelet, High Commissioner for Human Rights, June 21, 2021*

For Michelle Bachelet, the UN High Commissioner of Human Rights, the fight for human rights is deeply personal. In her youth, Bachelet was imprisoned and tortured along with her parents after they opposed Augusto Pinochet's 1973 military coup overthrowing Chile's democratic government. The experience shaped Bachelet, strengthening her commitment to human rights and the value of democracy.[54] As the

UN's human rights chief, Bachelet's job is to promote and protect the enjoyment of all human rights within the UN system and among member states – a job that became more complicated by the COVID-19 pandemic which exacerbated and accelerated inequalities within and between states. Bachelet's office, the Office of the High Commissioner of Human Rights (also called OHCHR or UN Human Rights), is the lead entity on human rights for the entire UN system. Composed of the UN High Commissioner for Human Rights and an international staff of more than 1,300 people working in more than 70 countries, the goal of UN Human Rights is to "make human rights a reality for everyone, everywhere."[55] UN Human Rights describes itself as the embodiment of "the world's commitment to the promotion and protection of the full range of human rights and freedoms set forth in the Universal Declaration of Human Rights."[56] Its main task is mainstreaming human rights into the work of the United Nations. This means making sure that all UN programs incorporate a human rights perspective and that the three core pillars of the UN are interlinked and mutually reinforcing – peace and security, development, and human rights.[57]

The OHCHR has many responsibilities. UN Human Rights upholds human rights standards. It elaborates the existing standards used to evaluate global progress on human rights and encourages states to ratify human rights treaties. Another goal is to get governments to comply with the human rights standards to which they have already committed; essentially to convert those promises into practice. UN Human Rights works collaboratively with governments to help them fulfill their human rights obligations by sharing expertise, technical training, and legal advice; supporting the establishment of national human rights institutions; and preventing abuses and defusing situations that could lead to conflict through an active field presence.[58] Its regional offices focus on cross-cutting regional concerns and support human rights implementation at the national level. Country offices are established by joint agreement between UN Human Rights and the host government. These aim to strengthen national capacity through technical assistance and human rights monitoring. Human rights advisers can be deployed to assist UN agencies and states integrate human rights programming and develop protection capacity; and to integrate human rights into UN Peace Operations and Political Missions.

UN Human Rights also empowers people to claim their rights. The Office's research, education, and advocacy activities increase human rights awareness and public engagement in all regions of the world, growing support for human rights. The Office informs people of their rights, amplifies their voices when their rights are denied, and works toward the protection of human rights defenders. UN Human Rights monitors and reports on human rights abuses. This includes speaking out publicly to condemn violations, appealing to governments to increase human rights protection, offering recommendations for reform, and serving as a forum for identifying and developing responses to human rights challenges. In June 2021, for example, UN Human Rights released a report on racial justice and equality. Bachelet, the UN human rights chief, stated, "I am calling on all states to stop denying, and start dismantling, racism; to end impunity and build trust; to listen to the voices of people of African descent; and to confront past legacies and deliver redress."[59] Drawing on evidence from more than 60 states, UN Human Rights called for the creation of an independent commission or other fact-finding body to evaluate and monitor racial discrimination in law enforcement globally.[60] Finally, UN Human Rights also provides substantive expertise and secretariat support to the other UN human rights bodies, including the Human Rights Council, independent thematic and country experts (known as special procedures), and each core human rights Treaty Body.

The Human Rights Council

Deference to state sovereignty is most apparent in the Human Rights Council. The HRC is an intergovernmental body within the UN system, meaning that its members are UN member states.[61] The 47 HRC members are elected by the UN General Assembly based on equitable geographic distribution. They are responsible for the promotion and protection of all human rights around the globe. An advisory committee provides the HRC with expertise and advice on pressing human rights concerns like the right to water or the prohibition on torture; or countries requiring special scrutiny of their rights records like the Democratic People's Republic of Korea (North Korea) for unlawful detention, forced labor, and inhumane treatment in its network of prison camps. The HRC has a complaints procedure which allows individuals and organizations to bring systematic human rights violations to the Council's attention.[62] The Council holds a minimum of three regular sessions a year but in response to a request by one-third of member states, the HRC can hold a special session to address emergencies like the urgent debate convened in June 2020 on "racially inspired human rights violations, systemic racism, police brutality and violence against peaceful protesters" in the aftermath of the police murder of George Floyd in the United States.

Every UN member must have its human rights record periodically examined relative to its human rights commitments by the Human Rights Council. Designed to ensure equal treatment for every country, this Universal Periodic Review process requires each UN member to publicly disclose its progress on human rights practices and have its human rights practices reviewed by other UN members who are encouraged to acknowledge positive achievements, vocalize concerns, and pose recommendations. In practice, however, the process can be highly politicized when governments support their friends and weaponize human rights against their enemies, independent of their actual human rights records. Independent NGO submissions, however, must be formally incorporated into the review process forcing the HRC to synthesize NGO comments, which then become part of the formal record and the official review process. The participation of civil society members offers a counterbalance to strict government peer review. The goal of this peer review process is to ensure that human rights receive focused attention *wherever violations occur* and to improve state compliance with human rights obligations by *all countries*. [63] Former Secretary-General Kofi Annan has said that the HRC's peer review function gives "concrete expression to the principle that human rights are universal and indivisible."[64] The HRC has been credited for being the most representative and legitimate governmental body monitoring human rights because of its broad state membership but criticized for mirroring the political interests of those members and falling victim to geopolitical manipulation and ideological bias by state members.[65] For example, the US withdrew from the Human Rights Council in 2018 citing bias against Israel but coming after receiving a sharp rebuke for its inhumane treatment of immigrant children. And China and Russia were elected to the HRC for terms beginning in 2021 despite high levels of domestic human rights violations.

The Human Rights Council has the authority to establish international commissions of inquiry, fact-finding missions, and conduct other investigations into serious violations of international human rights and humanitarian law. It also provides expertise and support to commissions and missions established by other UN bodies like the UN Security Council. These investigatory bodies allow the UN to examine allegations of abuse, gather evidence, and, where possible, determine responsibility with a view to future accountability, as well as formulate steps to be taken by the UN and rights-violating states. Between 2006 and 2020, the Human Rights Council mandated 32 commissions of inquiry and fact-finding bodies including those in Burundi, Libya, Myanmar, South Sudan, Syria, Venezuela, and Yemen.[66] The Independent International Commission of Inquiry on the Syrian Arab Republic, for example, has a general mandate to investigate alleged violations of international human rights law in Syria since March 2011 and to identify the perpetrators so they can be held accountable. It also has been given special mandates to investigate specific events like indiscriminate aerial bombing in Aleppo in 2016 and the use of chemical weapons against civilians in eastern Ghouta in 2018.

Special Procedures

Special Procedures mandate holders are independent human rights experts who are appointed by the Human Rights Council but serve in their personal capacity, meaning they do not represent any government. Former Secretary-General Kofi Annan once called them the "crown jewel" of the UN human rights system because their independence and deep expertise allow them to produce some of the most far-reaching analyses and recommendations. These were the independent experts that offered the most frank and direct critiques of human rights violations in the Flint Water Crisis (Philip Alston, the UN Special Rapporteur on Extreme Poverty) and in the George Floyd case (E. Tendayi Achiume, the UN Special Rapporteur on Contemporary Forms of Racism, Racial Discrimination, Xenophobia and Related Intolerance). Their mandate is to report and advise the

HRC on human rights from a thematic or country-specific perspective and to recommend ways to protect human rights. Examples of thematic mandates include the Working Group of Experts on people of African Descent, the Special Rapporteur on the Right to Food, and the Independent Expert on Protection against Violence and Discrimination based on Sexual Orientation and Gender Identity. Country-specific mandates include the human rights situation in Belarus, Cambodia, Eritrea, and the Palestinian territories, among others.[67] With support from the OHCHR, special procedures mandate holders undertake country visits, respond to reported violations, conduct annual studies, convene expert consultations, contribute to the development of international human rights standards, engage in advocacy, raise public awareness and provide expert advice.[68] They report their findings and recommendations to the HRC and the General Assembly at least once a year. While these independent experts lack the authority to change the human rights practices of states, an in-depth study undertaken by the Brookings Institution found that special procedures were effective in prompting human rights change. Calling them "catalysts for rights," the Brookings report credited special procedures with "shaping the content of international human rights norms, shining a light on a states' compliance with these norms, and influencing the behavior of states."[69] On their own, elements of the UN human rights machinery, including special procedures, may not have the power to force states to change their rights-violating behavior but when complemented by the activities of other actors (fact-finding bodies, NGOs, survivors, transnational advocacy networks) and forums (OHCHR and HRC) they lay the groundwork for meaningful reform.[70]

Treaty Bodies

Today there are nine core international human rights treaties. Each of these treaties has at least one committee of independent experts charged with monitoring and implementing the treaty, known as treaty bodies (see Table 6.1).[71] These experts from around the world are globally recognized for their competence in human rights and are elected to serve fixed renewable four-year terms by states. Experts work together on committees that gather human rights information from many sources including governments, civil society organizations, and sometimes individuals.[72] The treaty body then questions governments about their human rights records, publicly reports their findings, and makes recommendations for action. Some treaty bodies also have optional protocols which enhance their enforceability by allowing impromptu visits and making expert decisions binding. Domestic and international actors can use these recommendations to encourage governments to better protect human rights.[73] All people have the right to claim their rights. Treaty body reports and recommendations are publicly accessible on the United Nations' website and social media. They can be used by anyone wishing to hold their government accountable.

TABLE 6.1 United Nations Treaty Bodies

Treaty	Treaty Body
International Convention on the Elimination of All Forms of Racial Discrimination (ICERD)	Committee on the Elimination of Racial Discrimination
International Covenant on Economic, Social and Cultural Rights (ICESCR)	Committee on Economic, Social and Cultural Rights
International Covenant on Civil and Political Rights (ICCPR)	Human Rights Committee
Convention on the Elimination of Discrimination against Women (CEDAW)	Committee on the Elimination of Discrimination Against Women
Convention against Torture and Other Cruel, Inhuman or Degrading Treatment (CAT)	Committee on Torture Subcommittee on Prevention of Torture and other Cruel, Inhuman or Degrading Treatment or Punishment
Convention on the Rights of the Child (CRC)	Committee on the Rights of the Child
International Convention on the Protection of the Rights of All Migrant Workers and Members of their Families	Committee on Migrant Workers
International Convention on the Rights of Persons with Disabilities (ICRPD)	Committee on the Rights of Persons with Disabilities
International Convention for the Protection of All Persons from Enforced Disappearance (ICED)	Committee on Enforced Disappearances

Conclusion

Because the UN is an intergovernmental organization comprised of state members that jealously guard their sovereignty, UN human rights mechanisms can only do what its state members empower it to do. Even though human rights work at the UN is supported by independent experts who have the freedom to speak truth to power, their recommendations rely on UN bodies and member states for implementation. Conversely, the defining feature of domestic and international human rights NGOs (often called HROs) and their civil society partners is their independence from governments and their willingness to confront and challenge them when persuasion fails. In practice, effective human rights change often relies on the interaction of multiple actors, mechanisms, and approaches operating at the local, national, regional, and international levels. The international human rights movement is a loose coalition of individual rights advocates, domestic and international NGOs and HROs, regional organizations, like-minded states and parts of governments, the UN human rights machinery, and other intergovernmental organizations. Each has a role to play in making human rights change.

This book has explored human rights as a framework for analyzing situations of inequality and injustice; as a language for making claims to what is required for a life of dignity; and as tools for making equitable and just political, economic, and social change. The human rights detailed in the UDHR and other human rights treaties may not be implemented as completely envisioned by their drafters and human rights practitioners continue to experience opposition from powerful political opponents. Yet human rights remain a powerful affirmation of our equal human dignity and one of the best means we have in the fight for equality. This chapter is followed by a human rights toolkit for building inclusive communities and responding to injustice so that each of us can defend human rights in our own communities.

Notes

1 Jack Donnelly and Daniel Whelan, *International Human Rights* (New York: Routledge, 2018), p. 158.
2 Donnelly and Whelan, *International Human Rights*, p. 158.
3 David Malone and Adam Day, "The UN at 75: How Today's Challenges Will Shape the Next 25 Years," *Global Governance: A Review of Multilateralism and International Organizations*, 26:2 (2020).
4 David Petrasek, in Carrie Booth Walling and Susan Waltz (eds.), *Human Rights: From Practice to Policy* (University of Michigan, 2011), p. 55.
5 OHCHR, "About Human Rights Defenders," www.ohchr.org/EN/Issues/SRHRDe fenders/Pages/Defender.aspx, accessed 6/28/2021.
6 OHCHR, "Declaration on Human Rights Defenders," www.ohchr.org/EN/Issues/ SRHRDefenders/Pages/Declaration.aspx, accessed 12/20/2020; OHCHR, "Declaration on the Right and Responsibility of Individuals, Groups and Organs of Society to Promote and Protect Universally Recognized Human Rights and Fundamental Freedoms," Adopted by General Assembly resolution 53/144 of December 9, 1998, www. ohchr.org/EN/Issues/SRHRDefenders/Pages/Declaration.aspx, 9/29/2021.
7 OHCHR, "Special Rapporteur on the Situation of Human Rights Defenders," www. ohchr.org/en/issues/srhrdefenders/pages/srhrdefendersindex.aspx, accessed 6/28/2021.
8 Frontline Defenders, www.frontlinedefenders.org/en; MesoAmerican Initiative of Women Human Rights Defenders, http://im-defensoras.org/, accessed 6/29/2021.
9 Steven Greenhouse, *Beaten Down, Worked Up: The Past, Present, and Future of American Labor* (Alfred A. Knopf Publishers, 2019), p. 253.
10 Greenhouse, *Beaten Down, Worked Up*, p. 263.
11 Coalition of Immokalee Workers, "Slavery in the Fields and the Foods We Eat," http s://ciw-online.org/slavery.html, accessed 5/8/2021.
12 As of this writing, 14 major retailers are members of the Fair Food Program including Yum Brands (operator of Taco Bell, KFC, and Pizza Hut), McDonald's, Burger King, Whole Foods Market, Subway, Bon Appetit Management Company, Compass Group, Aramark, Sodexo, Trader Joe's, Chipotle Mexican Grill, Walmart, Fresh Market, and Ahold USA: www.fairfoodprogram.org/partners/, accessed 5/12/2021.
13 Steven Greenhouse, "In Florida Tomato Fields, a Penny Buys Progress," *The New York Times*, April 24, 2014, www.nytimes.com/2014/04/25/business/in-florida-tomato-fields-a-penny-buys-progress.html, accessed 5/8/2021.
14 Gerardo Reyes and Greg Asbed, "How Farmworkers Are Leading a 21st Century Human Rights Revolution," TEDMED, February 8, 2019, www.youtube.com/wa tch?v=6rtUy1apCWU&t=2s, accessed 5/12/2021.

15 Fair Food Program, www.fairfoodprogram.org, accessed 5/11/2021.

16 Fair Food Standards Council, www.fairfoodstandards.org/, accessed 5/12/2021.

17 OHCHR, End of visit statement, USA by Maria Grazia Giammarinaro, UN Special Rapporteur in Trafficking in Persons, especially women and children, December 19, 2016, www.ohchr.org/EN/NewsEvents/Pages/DisplayNews.aspx?NewsID=21049&LangID=E, accessed 5/11/2021.

18 Coalition of Immokalee Workers, "About Us," https://ciw-online.org/about/, accessed 5/11/2021.

19 Reyes and Asbed, "How Farmworkers Are Leading a 21st Century Human Rights Revolution."

20 Kathryn Sikkink and Carrie Booth Walling, "Argentina and Global Trends in Transitional Justice," in Naomi Roht-Arriaza and Javier Mariezcurrena (eds.), *Transitional Justice in the Twenty-First Century: Beyond Truth versus Justice* (Cambridge University Press, 2006), p. 319.

21 OHCHR, "Convention on the Rights of the Child," November 20, 1989. www.ohchr.org/en/professionalinterest/pages/crc.aspx, accessed 6/29/2021.

22 Shari Eppel, "A Tale of Three Dinner Plates: Truth and the Challenges of Human Rights Research in Zimbabwe," *Journal of Southern African Studies*, 35:4 (2009), p. 967.

23 Paul Gready, "Introduction-Responsibility to the Story," *Journal of Human Rights Practice*, 2:2 (2010), pp. 177–178.

24 Alison Brysk, *Speaking Rights to Power: Constructing Political Will* (Oxford University Press, 2013), p. 1. DOI: 10.1353/hrq.2014.0041

25 Alison Brysk, "Speaking Rights to Power," *PS: Political Science and Politics*, October 2017, p. 1008. DOI: https://doi.org/10.1017/S1049096517001172

26 Brysk, *Speaking Rights to Power*, p. 3.

27 To learn more on the advocacy impact of the Grandmothers of the Plaza de Mayo and the Mothers of the Plaza de Mayo see Brysk, *Speaking Rights to Power*, pp. 63–65; Margaret E. Keck and Kathryn Sikkink, *Activists Beyond Borders: Advocacy Networks in International Politics* (Cornell University Press, 1998).

28 Jo Becker, *Campaigning for Justice: Human Rights Advocacy in Practice* (Stanford University Press, 2012), p. 248.

29 Becker, *Campaigning for Justice*, pp. 250–251.

30 Becker, *Campaigning for Justice*, pp. 258–259.

31 Keck and Sikkink, *Activists Beyond Borders*, pp. 1–2.

32 Keck and Sikkink, *Activists Beyond Borders*, p. 2.

33 Keck and Sikkink, *Activists Beyond Borders*, p. 9.

34 Keck and Sikkink, *Activists Beyond Borders*, p. 12.

35 See Chapter 3 "Human Rights Advocacy Networks in Latin America," in Keck and Sikkink, *Activists Beyond Borders*.

36 Keck and Sikkink, *Activists Beyond Borders*, pp. 18–25.

37 Eric Weitz, *A World Divided: The Global Struggle for Human Rights in the Age of Nation-States* (Princeton University Press, 2019).

38 Julie A. Mertus, *Bait and Switch: Human Rights and U.S. Foreign Policy* (Taylor & Francis Books, 2004), DOI: https://doi.org/10.1017/S1537592705490155; Kathryn Sikkink, *Mixed Signals: U.S. Human Rights Policy and Latin America* (The Century Foundation, 2004), DOI: https://doi.org/10.1017/S1537592705930491.

39 The US Foreign Assistance Act of 1961 prohibits security and development assistance to countries with poor human rights records. The Trade Act of 1974 links US trade policy to government human rights records. Other examples of Congressional legislation and Executive action on human rights include, among others, the Maginsky Act, the Atrocities Prevention Board, and the Elie Wiesel Act.

40 The United States has not ratified the International Covenant on Economic, Social and Cultural Rights and does not monitor compliance with these categories of human rights.

41 Donnelly and Whelan, *International Human Rights*, pp. 144–145.

42 Council of the European Union, "EU Adopts a Global Human Rights Sanctions Regime," December 7, 2020, www.consilium.europa.eu/en/press/press-releases/2020/12/07/eu-adopts-a-global-human-rights-sanctions-regime/, accessed 6/29/2021.

43 Human Rights Watch, "Questions and Answers on Gambia's Genocide Case Against Myanmar before the International Court of Justice," December 5, 2019, www.hrw.org/news/2019/12/05/questions-and-answers-gambias-genocide-case-against-myanmar-international-court, accessed 12/18/2020; Ryan Lenora Brown, "Rohingya Ruling: How a Tiny African Country Brought Myanmar to Court," *The Christian Science Monitor*, February 13, 2020, www.csmonitor.com/World/Africa/2020/0213/Rohingya-ruling-How-a-tiny-African-country-brought-Myanmar-to-court, accessed 9/29/2021.

44 "Rohingya Crisis: The Gambian Who Took Aung San Suu Kyi to the World Court," BBC News, 23 January 2020, www.bbc.co.uk/news/world-africa-51183521, accessed 9/29/2021.

45 Human Rights Council, *Report of the Independent International Fact-Finding Mission on Myanmar* (A/HRC/39/64), September 12, 2018; United Nations, "Statement by Adama Dieng, United Nations Special Adviser on the Prevention of Genocide, on His Visit to Bangladesh to Assess the Situation of the Rohingya Refugees from Myanmar," March 12, 2018, www.un.org/sg/en/content/sg/note-correspondents/2018-03-12/note-correspondents-statement-adama-dieng-united-nations accessed 12/19/2020. For numerous independent reports, see OHCHR, "Special Rapporteur on the Situation of Human Rights in Myanmar," www.ohchr.org/en/hrbodies/sp/countriesmandates/mm/pages/srmyanmar.aspx, accessed 12//19/2020.

46 Reed Brody, "Giving Gambia a Big Voice on Human Rights: Abubacarr Tambadou Pushed for Justice at Home and Abroad," *Human Rights Watch*, June 26, 2020, www.hrw.org/news/2020/06/26/giving-gambia-big-voice-human-rights, accessed 12/19/2020.

47 Danielle Paquette, "Why a Tiny African Country is Taking the Rohingya's Case to the World Court," *The Washington Post*, November 12, 2019, www.washingtonpost.com/world/africa/why-a-tiny-african-country-is-taking-the-rohingyas-case-to-the-world-court/2019/11/12/f491d5a4-04cd-11ea-9118-25d6bd37dfb1_story.html, accessed 9/29/2021; The World Staff, "Gambian Minister Brought Myanmar to the Hague 'In the Name of Humanity,'" *The World*, December 12, 2019, www.pri.org/stories/2019-12-12/gambian-minister-brought-myanmar-hague-name-humanity, accessed 9/29/2021

48 The World Staff, "Gambian Minister."

49 The World Staff, "Gambian Minister."

50 Brown, "Rohingya Ruling."

51 Debra DeLaet, *The Struggle for Human Rights: Universal Principles in World Politics*, Second edition (Cengage Learning, 2015), p. 3.

52 The International Bill of Human Rights also includes the two optional protocols to the International Covenant on Civil and Political Rights leading some legal scholars to describe the international bill of human rights as containing five rather than three core documents.

53 See Daniel P.L. Chong, *Debating Human Rights* (Lynne Rienner Publishers, 2014), pp. 53–64 for a detailed discussion of the strengths and weaknesses of the UN's model of human rights protection and especially the Human Rights Council.

54 Janina Semenova and Oxana Evdokimova, "Michelle Bachelet: Her Lifelong Fight Against Sexism and for Women's Rights," DW Media, May 1, 2021, www.dw.com/en/michelle-bachelet-her-lifelong-fight-against-sexism-and-for-womens-rights/a-57395259, accessed 6/29/2021.

55 OHCHR, "Make Human Rights a Reality for All," www.ohchr.org/Documents/Publications/UNHumanRights_CfS_cmyk_online.pdf, accessed 9/29/2021, p. 9.

56 OHCRH, "Who We Are: An Overview," www.ohchr.org/EN/AboutUs/Pages/Who WeAre.aspx, accessed 11/30/2020.

57 OHCHR, "What We Do: An Overview," www.ohchr.org/EN/AboutUs/Pages/ WhatWeDo.aspx, accessed 11/30/2020.

58 OHCHR, "OCHCR in the World: Making Human Rights a Reality on the Ground," www.ohchr.org/en/countries/pages/workinfield.aspx, accessed 6/29/2021.

59 Stephani Nebehay, "'Stop Denying Racism, Start Dismantling It,' UN Rights Chief Says," *Reuters*, June 28, 2021, www.reuters.com/world/us/un-rights-chief-calls-system ic-racism-be-dismantled-2021-06-28/, accessed 6/29/2021.

60 Nick Cumming-Bruce, "U.N. Report Calls for Sweeping Action to Root Out Racism," *The New York Times*, June 28, 2021, www.nytimes.com/2021/06/28/world/ united-nations-human-rights.html, accessed 6/29/2021.

61 The Human Rights Council replaced the previous Commission on Human Rights which had been created in 1947 to set international human rights standards but beset by repeated criticism of incapacity, increasing politicization, and declining legitimacy.

62 United Nations Human Rights Council, "Welcome to the Human Rights Council," www.ohchr.org/EN/HRBodies/HRC/Pages/AboutCouncil.aspx, accessed 12/2/2020.

63 OHCHR, United Nations Human Rights Council, www.ohchr.org/hrc, accessed 12/ 1/2020.

64 United Nations General Assembly, *In Larger Freedom: Toward Development, Security and Human Rights for All, Report of the Secretary-General, Addendum: Human Rights Council*, A/59/2005/Add.1, May 23, 3005, p. 3.

65 Chong, *Debating Human Rights*, pp. 56, 58–59.

66 United Nations Human Rights Council, "List of HRC-Mandated Commissions of Inquiries/Fact-Finding Missions & Other Bodies," www.ohchr.org/EN/HRBodies/ HRC/Pages/ListHRCMandat.aspx, accessed 12/1/2020.

67 A complete list of thematic and country-specific mandates can be found on the United Nations Human Rights website: https://spinternet.ohchr.org/ViewAllCountryManda tes.aspx?Type=TM&lang=en and https://spinternet.ohchr.org/ViewAllCountryManda tes.aspx?lang=en, accessed 12/1/2020.

68 OHCHR, "Special Procedures of the Human Rights Council," www.ohchr.org/EN/ HRBodies/SP/Pages/Welcomepage.aspx, accessed 12/1/2020.

69 Jo Becker, *Campaigning for Justice: Human Rights Advocacy in Practice* (Stanford University Press, 2013), pp. 78–79 citing Ted Piccone, *Catalysts for Rights: The Unique Contribution of the UN's Independent Experts on Human Rights* (The Brookings Institution, 2010), DOI: https://doi.org/10.1515/9780804784382

70 Becker, *Campaigning for Justice*, and Keck and Sikkink, *Activists Beyond Borders*, make a similar point.

71 There are two treaty bodies that monitor implementation of the Convention against Torture and Other Cruel, Inhuman or Degrading Treatment.

72 Only four treaty bodies accept individual communications or complaints. These are the Committee on the Elimination of Racial Discrimination, Human Rights Committee, Committee on the Elimination of Discrimination Against Women, and the Committee Against Torture.

73 United Nations, "Human Rights Treaty Bodies," www.ohchr.org/EN/HRBodies/Pa ges/TreatyBodies.aspx, accessed 11/30/2020.

7

AN INTRODUCTION TO THE HUMAN RIGHTS ADVOCACY TOOLKIT

One of the most important things I have learned about human rights is that anyone can help defend human rights and stand up to injustice. Getting started only requires belief in the inherent dignity and fundamental equality of all human beings and a commitment to justice. But understanding human rights and learning about the people, processes, and places where human rights change happens, helps make their enjoyment a reality. Hopefully, this book has captured your imagination and sparked new questions about human rights like: How does human rights advocacy work in practice? When can human rights be a tool for calling out injustice, promoting rights, and building inclusive communities? How do we translate what we've learned about human rights into our daily lives? How can we pursue rights-inspired activism? This human rights advocacy toolkit aims to help readers avoid becoming bystanders to injustice by offering tools and strategies for defending human rights in their communities, and organizing with others for collaborative, human rights-inspired change.

What is a Toolkit?

A toolkit is a collection of resources that help people achieve a particular purpose. Toolkits are designed to translate theory into practice by offering practical advice and guidance. An advocacy toolkit is designed as a resource on how to use advocacy and lobbying to advance the policy practices that are important to you.

The Human Rights Advocacy Toolkit offers practical ideas for building more inclusive communities, preventing bias, challenging hate, and increasing access to rights and justice. It was designed collaboratively by a team of citizen activists based on a combination of personal experience, empirical research, and the best practices of human rights practitioners. The toolkit includes factsheets and sample

DOI: 10.4324/9781003256939-8

activities to inspire your imagination and help you reach your goals. It is designed with multiple audiences and purposes in mind. You can read it cover-to-cover or you can use the table of contents to jump right to the information you need. There are ideas for things to do independently and strategies for working collectively with others and organizing group activities. There is something for all levels of comfort and experience. When you find something that works, we hope you will share these ideas and resources with others.

Why a Toolkit for Human Rights-Inspired Action?

We believe that human rights issues are all around us. If we look closely, we can find them in our neighborhoods, on our college campuses, and even in our closets. We can advance human rights by placing the well-being and dignity of others at the center of the decisions we make personally and as a community. Using a human rights framework helps us understand injustice in new ways. The language of human rights is powerful for claiming dignity, and existing human rights laws and norms are tools of political, social, economic, and legal change.

Organization of the Toolkit

The toolkit opens with a "Human Rights 101" factsheet that summarizes the basics of the human rights approach and a handout on the importance of protecting mental wellness while protecting rights. We believe that creating a culture of care is part of ethical human rights advocacy.

The rest of the toolkit is organized in two parts.

Part 1 focuses on the power of the individual to be an agent of human rights protection. Throughout communities in all regions around the world, individual defenders promote human rights education, publicize information on violations, support victims, work to secure accountability for abuse, and support more just governance and policy. Part 1 of the toolkit shows how individuals can chart their own path of activism for meaningful change.

Part 1 *Becoming a Human Rights Defender* includes:

- steps to becoming a human rights defender;
- things you can do…to promote human rights;
- tips for writing op-eds;
- communicating with elected officials and other decision-makers; and
- how to safely attend a protest.

Human rights defenders are intertwined in communities. They seek to grow and expand networks of support and they work collaboratively with others to protect human rights, including the very right to defend human rights. Some human rights defenders even critique the over-individualization of human rights work and instead stress the collective dimensions of effective human rights protection. **There is power in community and** part 2 **is all about collective approaches to making human rights change.** Part 2 invites readers to be a part of something bigger than themselves. It offers a map for applied action created by campus activists for activists-in-the-making who are grappling with how to effectively engage their communities and build their networks.

Part 2 *Organizing for Community and Campus-Based Action* includes:

- human rights advocacy 101;
- making a map for meaningful change;
- tips for organizing a protest; and
- beyond the standard protest: using creativity to promote your message on campus.

People whose rights are being violated may face threatening circumstances that prevent them from advocating for their rights or put them in extreme risk. The purpose of the human rights toolkit is to empower students and people of goodwill to harness their individual and collective power for human rights-inspired political and social change when they can safely do so. We give up some of our individual and collective power when we think that we don't have any. No one can do everything, but everyone can do something. It just might not look the same.

HUMAN RIGHTS ADVOCACY TOOLKIT
TABLE OF CONTENTS

★★★

Human rights are only respected, protected, and fulfilled to the extent that people, individually and collectively, demand that they are. We all have responsibilities for human rights and justice. The human rights advocacy toolkit that follows shows us how we can build a more equal, just, and rights-filled world by "living human rights" at home.

THE HUMAN RIGHTS ADVOCACY TOOLKIT

Carrie Booth Walling, Morgan Armstrong, Marco Antonio Colmenares Jr., and Caitlin Cummings

Advocating for human rights is a necessary, difficult, and rewarding challenge that every person can incorporate into everyday life. This toolkit introduces the basics of human rights advocacy in practical terms, using practical means. Whether you want to support an existing rights or justice campaign underway or create your own movement, this toolkit shows you how to get started.

Human Rights Basics Fact Sheet

Human rights are the rights every human is born with and are essential for a life of **dignity**.

Human Rights Are:

- **Equal & Universal**: Human rights must be guaranteed to all people without distinction of any kind. In practice, if human rights are not equally respected or realized this means that human rights are being violated, not that they don't exist.
- **Inalienable**: Human rights are not earned and cannot be taken away even if those in power don't recognize them. Individuals are entitled to human rights by birthright.
- **Interdependent**: Human rights are interdependent and indivisible. The violation of one right negatively impacts the fulfillment of other human rights.

DOI: 10.4324/9781003256939-9

How Do We Know What Our Human Rights Are?

The **Universal Declaration of Human Rights** is a historic document agreed to by the world's governments that defines the fundamental human rights to be universally guaranteed. It is a common standard for all peoples and nations. Its content has been legally codified into two international treaties: the **International Covenant on Civil and Political Rights** and the **International Covenant on Economic, Social, and Cultural Rights**. Combined, these three documents are known as the **International Bill of Human Rights**.

- **Political rights** include the freedom of peaceful assembly and the right to vote.
- **Civil rights** include due process rights and equality before the law.
- **Economic rights** include reasonable work conditions, fair pay, and right to form unions.
- **Social and cultural rights** include the right to education, the ability to participate in the cultural life of your community and to share in the benefits of science and medicine.

Who Must Protect Human Rights?

Individual human beings are rights holders. **Everyone** has a duty to not violate the rights of others, but governments are considered the principal duty bearers. **Governments have a three-fold responsibility** to respect, protect, and fulfill their human rights obligations.

- The **obligation to respect** means that governments must not violate, limit, or interfere with the exercise of human rights.
- The **obligation to protect** requires governments to protect individuals and groups from having their human rights violated by others.
- The **obligation to fulfill** means that governments must take positive steps to facilitate the enjoyment of human rights.

All human beings are born equal in dignity and rights. Human rights are only respected, protected, and fulfilled to the extent that people, individually and collectively, demand they are. All people, corporations, governmental and non-governmental organizations have responsibilities for human rights.

Human Rights and Mental Wellness

And we have brought healing to our movement, the ideas and practices that demonstrate that as we seek to care for communities, we must also care for ourselves.[1]

Patrisse Khan-Cullors, co-founder of Black Lives Matter (BLM)

The right to health is a fundamental part of human rights and is crucial to living a life of dignity. According to the World Health Organization, health includes "physical, mental and social well-being and not merely the absence of disease or infirmity." Protecting the health and wellness of all people, including the wellness of rights defenders, is an important part of any advocacy plan or social justice movement.

Human rights practitioners face risks to their mental health. Responding to injustice and human rights abuse is often accompanied by exposure to, or experience with, trauma. Trauma initiated by deeply distressing or disturbing events can overwhelm our ability to cope, cause us to feel severe distress and helplessness, diminish our sense of self, and wreak havoc on our emotions. Pre-existing mental illnesses can be worsened by exposure to trauma. And while protest is a powerful tool for educating and mobilizing people against injustice, participation in protest can also exacerbate symptoms for people with preexisting depression, anxiety, or other mental health issues.

Protecting the Mental Health of Human Rights Defenders and Justice Advocates

Rights protective organizations are increasingly attentive to the well-being of movement participants. Defenders cannot fight for the rights, safety, and well-being of others and not ensure that same level of dignity for themselves. The Black Lives Matter network includes restorative practices within its organization. This includes appointing health and wellness directors dedicated to ensuring a healthy organizational environment.[2] During the Ferguson protests held after Michael Brown's killing by a police officer in St. Louis, Missouri, BLM organizers set up a healing justice space in the basement of a local church. Protesters were invited to find healing with caregivers who provided massage, acupuncture, and talk therapy; experience comfort through prayer at the altar dedicated to people who passed; gain renewal by resting on the beds of pillows that had been pro-vided; and find release by painting or drawing what they could not name or speak through art.[3] Patrisse Khan-Cullors, one of the co-founders of BLM, explains, "We are envisioning and creating a new movement culture in which we care for the humanity of the people we're fighting for and *with*."[4]

Caring for our Humanity

You can live your values by prioritizing mental wellness in your organizing activities:

- Engage professionally trained counselors in your justice work. Offer work-shops on improving mental wellness and coping skills.
- Build networks of solidarity. Surrounding yourself with others who defend rights and share your values can be therapeutic. It creates a sense of

community, combats feelings of social isolation, and fosters the exchange of ideas and inspiration. Supportive relationships with others are beneficial to mental health.

- Know when to take a break from social media. While social media is a convenient tool for rights organizing, it also provides a platform for hate and can magnify discord. Heavy social media use can increase depression, anxiety, and loneliness.[5]
- Develop health coping mechanisms like meditation, exercise, or adopting new hobbies.
- Pay attention to physical health. Physical health and mental health are connected. Getting adequate sleep and eating regular, healthy meals generates the energy to defend human rights. Creating balance between justice work and self-care produces stronger results.
- Recognize progress and celebrate victories, even small ones.
- Set realistic personal or organizational goals, track and reward success, organize and balance the time you devote to work and self-care.

Cultivating Joy

People hunger for joy and connection. Human rights are about dignity and not just survival. Activism can include fun and joy – indeed, it's often necessary to counteract a hate-filled world.[6]

- Do what brings you joy, happiness, or solitude. Meditate, listen to music, create art, exercise, journal, dance, self-reflect.
- Creating art is therapy. It requires concentration. It focuses the mind and can quiet racing thoughts, allowing them to flow effectively. Art can express thoughts and emotions, contributing to a healthy mind.
- Dance. Dancing is a fun form of exercise. It promotes the release of endorphins or neurotransmitters that naturally alleviate stress. Dance is also an art form that expresses culture and tradition while also promoting good mental wellness.
- Walk through nature. New scenery can cultivate new ideas. Connecting with nature can inspire.
- Journaling can be powerful. It is an effective way to document experiences, process feelings, express emotion, and clarify thinking. It is a great problem-solving tool, a way to work through difficult issues, and can cultivate gratitude and joy.

Defenders of rights and justice should practice in their own lives the same values they seek for everyone in their communities – a life that is deserving of dignity, that strives for joy and well-being, not just survival.

PART 1: BECOMING A HUMAN RIGHTS DEFENDER

This section of the toolkit develops individual skills and competencies for becoming an agent of human rights protection. It's possible to promote human rights change in your own way, on your own schedule, and according to your terms. Throughout communities in all regions around the world, individual defenders promote human rights education, publicize information on violations, support victims, work to secure accountability for abuse, and support more just governance and policy. Use this part of the toolkit to develop your personal skills and chart your own path of activism for meaningful change.

What's included?

- *Steps to Becoming a Human Rights Defender*
- *Things You Can Do…to Promote Human Rights*
- *Tips for Writing Op-Eds*
- *Communicating with Elected Officials & Other Decision-Makers*
- *How to Safely Attend a Protest*

Steps to Becoming a Human Rights Defender

> Where, after all, do universal human rights begin? In small places, close to home-so close and so small that they cannot be seen on any maps of the world. Yet they are the world of the individual person…Without concerted citizen action to uphold them close to home, we shall look in vain for progress in the larger world.
>
> *Eleanor Roosevelt*

1. **Know that anyone can be an advocate for justice, equality, and human rights.**

   - Ordinary people in our community and abroad have used the human rights framework to expose injustice, confront perpetrators, demand political action, and generate just solutions to human rights problems.

2. **Believe that all people are equal in dignity and respect.**

   - It sounds obvious but human rights defenders cannot promote human rights change if we don't practice what we preach. We must defend the rights of ALL human beings – even those who deny dignity and respect to others.

3. **Hold ourselves – and our friends – accountable.**

   - Be mindful of our own stereotypes and biases. If our friends and family make insensitive comments, tell discriminatory jokes, or use labeling language, don't let it slide. Words have power. We use words to create the world we share. We must challenge ourselves and others to change our words and behaviors.

4.   **Develop empathy.**

- When we imagine ourselves in the place of others, our empathy increases. We can strengthen our empathy when we spend time listening to those whose ideas and experiences are different than our own. We can diversify our social groups, make new friends, and become an ally to others who are experiencing injustice. We must learn to see and understand injustice, and our role in it, if we want to stop it.

5.   **Model human rights: speak out and stand up.**

- Use inclusive language. Welcome others. Call out hate, bigotry, and discrimination when you witness it. Stand in solidarity with those who are targeted. Promote values of equality, dignity, justice, and rights and celebrate the diversity of identities in our community. Support those whose rights are violated.

- No one can do everything, but everyone can do something. Don't be a bystander. We have the power to interrupt cycles of violence, discrimination, and exclusion by speaking out against injustice, acting in solidarity with those who are targeted, documenting injustice, and intervening to prevent the abuse of others.

6.   **Build a network of like-minded people.**

- Invest in building community. Reach out to leaders, community organizations, campus groups, and other people who share your beliefs and values. Support each other, share ideas, pool resources, and learn.

7.   **Advocate for change.**

- Raise your voice against injustice and increase awareness of human suffering. Identify your sources of power (your talents, your networks, your resources, and your privileges) and use them to advocate for equality, dignity, freedom, and rights. Tell your personal story or share the stories of others to open hearts and change minds. Participate in the political process by voting, contacting elected officials, writing letters, and participating in advocacy events – virtually and in person.

8.   **Keep trying.**

- Activism is as much art as science. Human rights change takes practice, perseverance, and patience. When one strategy fails, try another. Understand that the conditions that foster human rights abuse did not emerge overnight, so implementing solutions may take time. Part of activism is being flexible, creative, and persevering against challenge.

9.   **You got this!**

Things You Can Do...to Promote Human Rights

> ...Indifference is always the friend of the enemy, for it benefits the aggressor – never his victim, whose pain is magnified when he or she feels forgotten.
>
> *Elie Wiesel, Holocaust Survivor*

Things You Can Do to Promote Human Rights in a Few Minutes...

Speak Up

- Don't be indifferent if you witness a bias incident or hear hate speech. Become an ally for the target whether that means safely intervening on their behalf, providing much needed comfort, or simply distracting them from the ugliness around them.
- If someone you know makes derogatory comments or engages in stereotyping, explain why and how those words and ideas contribute to a culture of harm and inequality.

Reconsider What You Buy

- Human rights issues shape our everyday lives as consumers. Learn if the products you buy and the companies you support with your purchases protect and promote human rights. For example, flower growers should protect workers from exposure to toxins. The people who sew your soccer ball should receive fair wages. Your chocolate should not be produced with child labor. Clothing should be produced in safe working conditions by workers who have the right to organize, and cell phones and electronics must not use conflict minerals that fuel war and violence.
- Download apps to your phone or electronic device that educate you on human rights, help you shop products and companies that have fair labor standards, and strengthen the human rights community.

Promoting Human Rights Online

- Post human rights stories and photos.
- Change your profile picture to support a rights-based cause.
- Retweet an empowering hashtag and make human rights trend.
- Sign an online petition and then spread the word.
- Visit the website of an international human rights organization like Amnesty International (www.amnesty.org), Human Rights Watch (www.hrw.org), or Physicians for Human Rights (www.phr.org) and join an online advocacy campaign.

- Contribute money to organizations in your community that promote and defend human rights, equality, and justice. Domestic violence shelters protect women's rights, food banks promote access to food, and a variety of local and national organizations promote civil rights.

Things You Can Do to Promote Human Rights in a Few Hours...

Register to Vote or Update Your Registration

- The right to vote in elections and participate in the political life of a community is a treasured human right and necessary for protecting a rights culture. Use it to protect and advance your rights and the rights of others.

Learn More

- Increase your human rights knowledge by researching a human rights issue you care about. Watch documentaries, read articles, and study human rights reports produced by independent experts and human rights organizations.
- Study how to resist human rights violations so that you are prepared when you see them occurring in your own community.
- Participate in free online training courses on human rights advocacy or safely documenting human rights violations. Free training resources are available through Witness.org, The Advocates for Human Rights, Human Rights Watch, and Amnesty International, among others.

Find Inspiration

- Read about human rights defenders. Learn how ordinary people have faced, resisted, and organized to overcome extraordinary injustice.

Practice Exercising Your Own Rights by Contacting Your Elected Officials

- In democracies, elected officials are accountable to the citizens. Calling, texting, emailing, and writing letters to elected officials at all levels of government (local, state, and national) incentivizes them to support rights-based policies.

Attend a Protest, Demonstration, Rally, or Meeting

- Voice your opinions and demonstrate your concern about human rights violations. Gathering with others who share your views generates solidarity, focuses attention, and also encourages brainstorming and creative problem-solving for how to solve human rights problems. Voices united become amplified and can lead to human rights change.

Write Letters

- Writing letters on behalf of people who need urgent help has become a hallmark of human rights activism. Each year Amnesty International hosts a "write for rights" campaign you can join.
- Write letters on your own or organize letter writing on your campus – write to campus decision-makers, elected officials, global leaders – and use the power of collective action to change minds and policies.

Things You Can Do to Promote Human Rights in a Few Days, Weeks, or Months...

Become a Volunteer, Ally, or Mentor

- Examine your own biases and challenge assumptions you may hold.[7]
- Participate in an anti-racism workshop or diversity, equity, and inclusion training.
- Approach organizations that share your values and people you want to support. Ask how you can be an effective ally to them. Listen to what they say. Amplify their voices and follow their lead. Respect the mantra, "Nothing about us, without us."

Investigate

- Are spaces on your campus and in your community equally accessible for all?
- Does your community have a plan to celebrate diversity, promote equity, and increase inclusion on campus?
- Are the cultural and religious traditions of all members respected?
- Does your community provide an inclusive and safe learning environment for people of all nationalities, races, religions, abilities, genders, sexualities, and gender identities?

Lobby for Legislation or Petition Campus Leaders for Rights-Centric Policies

- Understand your issue from multiple angles and develop a variety of frames for your argument (legal, moral, fiscal, political).
- Identify the appropriate targets for advocacy:

  a   know who you share common ground with and enlist them as allies;
  b   identify decision-makers who might be sympathetic to your cause;
  c   identify decision-makers whose support would be the most impactful.

- Write out a script for phone calls and in-person visits or a template for emails and letters.
- Make contact – and try to interact with your targets personally.

Create and Disseminate Educational Materials

- Once you've investigated human rights violations and gathered information about the possibilities for change, you can produce informational flyers, brochures, pamphlets, blogs, or a website to promote your findings, educate others, and organize action.
- Make your materials accessible to a wide audience. Use videos with captions or sign language, large fonts, and multiple languages that reach diverse communities.

Organize an Event to Promote Tolerance and Acceptance

- Raise awareness about violations, offer support to those affected, educate others, and teach others how they can help.
- Be proactive. Build community among diverse peoples by creating events that celebrate shared values, enhance cultural exchange, and promote friendship through food, music, and dance.

Join or Start an Organization to Carry on the Work Beyond Your Event

- Have a clear vision of the change you hope to make.
- Collaborate with like-minded people and organizations with goals similar to your own.
- Be inclusive and make your movement accessible to join.
- Raise awareness.

Tips for Writing Op-Eds

Writing an opinion-editorial (op-ed) and getting it published in a local, college, regional, or national news source is a great way to reach a new audience with your human rights or justice message. If you have a clear point to make, feel a sense of passion about your issue, and want to persuade others, writing your own op-ed can be an effective strategy for changing hearts, mobilizing support, and increasing pressure on decision-makers.

Before You Start Writing Your Op-Ed, You Should Do the Following:

- Summarize your argument in a 30-second thesis. This is the main point that you want your reader to understand.
- Identify your audience. Who do you want to write to and why? Are you writing to your college campus, small hometown, or big city? Conservative politicians or liberal policy experts? The answers to these questions will shape what you choose to say, how you say it, and where you will try to publish it.

- Have a specific media outlet in mind. Be sure to check their website for any submission instructions, such as word length (most are between 500–1,000 words), and to get a general sense for tone.

The best preparation for writing an op-ed is reading other op-eds found on the opinion pages of the news outlet you have selected.

Writing Your Op-ed

Most opinion pieces have three main parts: the opening, the body, and the conclusion.

The Opening

There are three main parts to your opening paragraph:

1. The first sentence is crucial. Your opening "hook" should grab the reader's attention with a strong claim, important fact, compelling story, interesting puzzle, or counterintuitive observation. The goal is to entice your reader to keep reading.
2. Establish relevance. Briefly explain how your hook relates to a contemporary news story, important date or anniversary, public debate, newly released report, or ongoing controversy.
3. Thesis statement. This is that 30-second summary from earlier. Remember to keep your audience and outlet in mind when crafting this statement. Write in accessible and casual language. This is not a college essay.

The Body

The body of an op-ed typically makes three to five main points (shorter is usually better). Each point that you make should have its own paragraph and has two main components:

1. Evidence. Reasons why readers should believe your claims. This includes in-text hyperlinks to accessible sources, facts and figures, quotes from validators, or your personal story.
2. Analysis. Your opinion as an extension of the evidence you have provided. An op-ed must have original analysis—without it, you are just writing a summary of someone else's argument.

With these components in mind, your body paragraphs should follow this format:

1. Preview the point in a topic sentence where you briefly highlight the main issue.

2. Back it up with your evidence.
3. Tell your reader what the evidence means (analysis) and how it proves your point (draw a conclusion from that evidence). Remember to tailor how you explain your evidence to your specific audience and outlet.

After you've made your key points, it can be effective to acknowledge counter-arguments. Briefly acknowledging the opposition can help bolster your credibility and strengthen your argument. A common way to do this is with a "to be sure" statement that addresses the strongest argument against your own.

The Conclusion

The final paragraph is your last chance to convince your reader. Be sure to end strong!

- Restate your thesis. Limit this to only two or three sentences.
- Connect back to your opening. The ending should make sense relative to your opening hook.
- Make your final words something your audience will remember.

Leave your reader with something to think about, provoke an emotional response, or mobilize action.

Getting Published

Email the editor of the news outlet you are targeting and take the following steps:

- Summarize your idea in a few lines.
- Explain why their readers will care about this issue.
- Explain the news hook and why it is timely to publish now.
- Explain who you are and why people should listen to you.
- Cut and paste your completed op-ed below your pitch. Don't send as an attachment.
- Include links to published news sources and facts that support your argument.
- Include your contact information.
- Only send to one news outlet. Most won't consider a piece submitted to more than one place.

If the editor says, yes, thank them for giving space to your issue. If the editor says no, thank them for their consideration. If it's still timely, send your op-ed somewhere else. If you don't hear anything after several days and are worried that your op-ed will be dated, send a follow-up email. Thank them for considering publication and tell them that if you don't hear back from them by a specific time, you will assume that they have declined to publish and will send the op-ed elsewhere.

Maximizing Impact

After your op-ed is published, promote it on your social media. Email links to friends and colleagues. Print or clip it and mail it to your elected officials and family members. If it doesn't get published this time, don't give up. You've gained valuable practice and you can turn it into a strong advocacy letter to your elected officials or self-publish it on social media.

Final Style Tips

Tone: What voice should I use when I write?

- Keep it simple: There's no room for subtlety or coyness in an op-ed piece.
- Clarity: Use a bold and active voice; avoid jargon, acronyms, and academic language.
- Be natural: Try to use a natural voice, as though you were talking to a good friend.
- Get to the point: Preferably in the first paragraph.
- When possible, engage or entertain: Remember that no one gets paid to read your piece.

Content: What should I include?

- Take a stand: Have a strong viewpoint. Don't feel the need to summarize other views.
- Make it logical: Include examples and facts to support your argument.
- Offer anecdotes: Make your piece visceral, human, and memorable. Personal stories can help make your point.
- Present solutions: Wrap up by recommending fixes for the problems you identify.
- Be accurate: Double check your facts and your writing. Mistakes harm your credibility.

Structure: How should I organize my op-ed?

- Start small and go big: Move from a specific problem, such as a personal story, to a broader public issue.
- Be brief: Short, declarative sentences work best. Paragraphs should usually contain a small number of sentences.

- Develop and integrate evidence: Don't repeat points. Present multiple pieces of evidence and connect them together.
- Don't use footnotes, formal citations, and bulleted or numbered lists. They disrupt the flow of your piece, and an editor will not likely accept them.
- End strong: Conclude with a new point that wraps your argument in a cohesive message.

Communicating with Elected Officials and Other Decision-Makers

Article 21 of the Universal Declaration of Human Rights gives everyone the right to participate in the government of their country either directly or through elected representatives. All people must have equal access to public services, and the will of the people should be respected, and expressed through free and periodic elections.

Decision-makers at all levels, whether elected or not, must protect the human rights and dignity of the people they serve. Contacting leaders charged with governance to share your views is a sacred right. Lobbying decision-makers in positions of authority to change laws, adopt new rules and develop inclusive policies is an important tool of social and political change.

1. Make contact.

- Directories with contact information for people in leadership at the local, national, regional, and international level can be found online. With access to internet technologies you can follow them and communicate with them through social media.

2. Do your research.

- Know the issue and gather the information and evidence you need to build your case. If you are responding to a specific piece of legislation, identify it by name and number. Know who supports it, who opposes it, and why.

3. Identify yourself.

- Say who you are and explain how their decisions impact you and the lives of those around you. If you are a constituent, identify yourself as one. Articulate the ways that you and the decision-maker are connected.

4. Be brief.

- Get directly to the point. Address a single issue at a time (and with no more than three reasons). Explain your position. Support it with evidence and a compelling story about how it affects you and those you care about. Keep written statements to one page.

5. Find your own voice.

- While it is perfectly acceptable to work from a common script, try to make your communication as personal as possible. It is your individualized effort that creates the greatest impact. Thoughtful, original ideas count for more than others' talking points.

6. Be respectful.

- Maintain composure and follow the appropriate conventions and formal protocol.

There are multiple ways to lobby leaders for change. The most effective are the most personal and demonstrate the most effort. In-person visits and phone calls have the most influence because letters, emails, online petitions, and social media posts are more easily ignored. Personal contact forces leaders to pay attention. Not ready for in-person? Leave a voicemail after hours. If you write a letter or email, being thoughtful and original has more impact than highly polished form letters. Don't discount the impact of online petitions and social media comments. Taking any action is a step forward.

How to Safely Attend a Protest

The right to peaceful assembly is protected by Article 20 of the Universal Declaration of Human Rights. This right protects your right to defend human rights.

Do Your Research

- Conduct background research on the people or organization(s) organizing the protest. Understand the purpose of the protest. Examine their goals and plans for the event.

Know Your Rights and Respect the Rights of Others

- Consult your student handbook and comply with campus policies on rallies and demonstrations or understand the costs of choosing not to comply.
- Know state and local laws. Public spaces don't typically require a permit if you don't block roads, sidewalks, or access to buildings and obey traffic signals.
- Private property owners set the rules for free speech on their property. You cannot lawfully protest in a private space without permission and could be subject to removal or arrest.
- Remember counter-protesters have the same rights as you. Do not engage in physical or verbal retaliation when others target you. Don't debate haters –

they thrive on attention and your focus gives them legitimacy. Ignore them and maintain your message.

- In most democracies, police are not permitted to end a gathering unless it threatens public safety. If a dispersal order is given, protesters should be given a reasonable opportunity to comply, including sufficient time and clear access to exit.

Safety First

- There is power in numbers. Never march or travel to or from a protest alone. Find a friend who is going or recruit someone to tag along with you.
- Wear comfortable clothing. Avoid clothes or shoes that might restrict your safety or limit your freedom of movement.
- Bring a small bag or backpack with water, ID, cellphone, emergency contact numbers labeled ICE (in case of emergency), essential medicine, money, and snacks. You may wish to carry a scarf to protect your eyes if aerosols are used to disperse a protest and other protective gear like an extra facemask or small bottle of sanitizer during a pandemic. Never carry anything that can be perceived as a weapon.
- Make sure your cellphone is fully charged and disable facial recognition and fingerprint unlock features on your smartphone. Turn off text preview to keep messages from showing on your screen. This prevents people other than you from accessing your phone without your expressed permission.
- Scout out the area. Identify a safe meeting place and multiple routes to reach it in case you are separated from your friends. Take the phone number of a person not attending the protest or an organization who you can call in case you need assistance.
- Do not run from or resist authorities and keep hands visible. Even if it seems unfair, be calm and polite. Memorize everything. Justice can come later. Do not lie but do not reveal unnecessary information like immigration status. State verbally that you wish to remain silent, that you want an attorney, and that you do not consent to a search.

There is joy in collective action! Enjoy the solidarity. Have fun and take time to build community with people who share your commitment to justice and human rights. Know you are an agent of change and your work may be felt for generations to come.

PART 2: ORGANIZING FOR COMMUNITY AND CAMPUS-BASED ACTION

There is power in community and Part 2 of the toolkit is all about collective approaches to making human rights change. This section invites you to become part of something bigger than yourself. Here you will learn the best practices of human rights advocacy and learn strategies for promoting your message and advancing human rights in institutions. It shows you how to create an advocacy plan – a road map for designing advocacy campaigns, building your network, and organizing with others. It is a toolkit of resources for activists-in-the-making who want to coordinate with others to promote change.

What's included?

- *Human Rights Advocacy 101*
- *Making a Map for Meaningful Change*
- *Tips for Organizing a Protest*
- *Beyond the Standard Protest: Using Creativity to Promote Your Message on Campus*

Human Rights Advocacy 101

Human rights advocacy refers to activity that aims to influence the creation or implementation of human rights norms, standards, law, and policy. Effectively deploying information and shifting power dynamics is at the heart of human rights change.

Credible research and documentation that spotlights patterns of abuse is the core of human rights advocacy. Careful and timely documentation enhances the credibility of advocates and makes it harder for policy makers to ignore violations.

Human rights advocacy relies on **skillful messaging**. The most effective messages are simple and clear. Some of the most powerful messengers include those most affected by abuses who can speak directly to their own experiences. Strong advocacy campaigns include multiple messengers representing a diversity of voices, all speaking to a unified, consistent message.

There is power in numbers. Successful advocacy often requires the creation of **diverse, broad-based alliances and coalitions**. Coalitions allow advocates to leverage and pool resources, generate momentum that can sustain the movement across time and place, and both generate and signal widespread support for the cause.

Human rights advocates are prepared. While it is difficult to predict when a window of opportunity will open, human rights advocates are prepared with their evidence and message to **take advantage of strategic opportunities as they present themselves**. Events, political developments, and a shifting social landscape can create unique opportunities to make progress on human rights. Effective advocates will find these opportunities and use them.

Human rights change often requires placing pressure on **multiple points of leverage**. This includes public campaigning and political lobbying for the adoption of, and compliance with, human rights standards. It may also include naming and shaming rights violators, mobilizing the media, and assisting victims and survivors.

Human rights advocacy must be **human-centered**. This means placing people at the center of concern, empowering victims, and uplifting their voices, and respecting human dignity.

Successful human rights change requires **persistent organizing, painstaking effort, and long-term commitment**. There is no quick and easy formula and no guarantee of success. Human rights practitioners creatively employ the tools and strategies available, adapting them to an ever-evolving political landscape. Human rights advocacy is likened to art more than science. Yet over the last seven decades, the world has experienced profound human rights change.

Making a Map for Meaningful Change

The purpose of a map is to guide us to a place we are unfamiliar with. Maps give us direction and can help us navigate our way around roadblocks and unforeseen obstacles. A map is an essential tool for the human rights activist trying to plot the route to human rights change.

A map is not the same as a model. A model is an example to follow or imitate. It offers step by step directions that must be adhered to in the designated order to achieve the desired outcome. In contrast, with a map you can identify multiple ways to get to the same destination. When a barrier blocks your path, you can try a different route. What follows is a map for organizing human rights-inspired political and social change. Identify your destination and use the map to guide your steps along your chosen path.

Identifying Injustice

Rights advocates must be attentive to the world around them and notice when injustice happens. The best organizers do their research. They make sure that they have a complete and accurate understanding of what has occurred. They check their facts, collect stories of injustice from those that experience it, investigate its underlying causes, identify those responsible, and initiate discussion with others on how to repair harm, restore dignity to victims, and chart a course of action toward meaningful change.

Don't overlook resources and services available to you that could help you spread your message or protect you through the advocacy process. Tap into the rich body of human rights research and the wide network of domestic and international human rights organizations. See what organizing looks like on other campuses. Don't recreate the wheel. You will save time and energy if you can access existing information and join forces with an established movement. And if your group decides to forge a new path, you still might gain inspiration from others who have done parallel work or have similar goals.

Building an Inclusive Movement

Build relationships on your own campus and by networking with activists and groups addressing similar causes in other places. Share ideas and best practices. This means including people with experience and ideas different than your own. By initiating a conversation about how people from different backgrounds understand the problem, you might identify amazing perspectives and new solutions.

Involve other campus leaders and student or community-based organizations that share your interests and values. There is power and legitimacy in numbers whether you come together to host a single event or coordinate a series of connected actions targeting different audiences. Ask each student and organization to mobilize their own network.

Gaining the support of elected student leaders can build solidarity and magnify your efforts in the eyes of administrators. It also helps you to leverage and pool resources and generate a broad support system.

It is difficult to sustain momentum when you are balancing activism with work, school, and a social life. Building a broad network removes the burden of organizing from a single individual. Delegating responsibilities can prevent burn out. Building a network of trustworthy leaders can sustain an organization or movement when energy ebbs and flows.

Your movement should reflect the values you profess to hold. If you are fighting for diversity, equity, inclusion, just treatment, and human rights, your organization or movement should demonstrate these same values in its membership and practices.

On a college campus, you might involve trusted faculty, advisors, or staff that can offer advice on how to raise awareness while staying within campus guidelines, provide feedback on your protest plans, or communicate your message to broader audiences. Allies who feel negatively impacted by communal harm and who want to speak out against injustice can serve as envoys to college administration and other decision-makers and help legitimate your message. Finally, allies can help you anticipate barriers and how to resolve them.

When appropriate, you might involve the cooperation of lawmakers, alumni, community members, or political representatives that are sympathetic to your cause. You can leverage their power and influence to address your issue.

Crafting the Message

In human rights advocacy, the message matters. Indeed, your argument and how you frame it is the central component of advocating for change. When crafting your message, link it to an accepted body of legal or social norms or directly to the human rights framework.[8] The most effective frames are those that tap into widely shared beliefs about equality, fairness, and protection of the innocent or vulnerable.[9]

Offer a compelling story about human rights abuse that identifies an intentional perpetrator whose actions can be directly linked to the harm suffered by the victim. Constructing problems in this way garners the most support for change because the injustice can be ended by either stopping the wrongdoer from committing the harm or eliminating an unjust policy.[10]

Storytelling and personal narratives that evoke an emotive response are the most effective at changing individual hearts and minds. Putting a face to a policy can foster empathy among the public and mobilize action by decision-makers, especially when personal experiences can point to a gap between an institution's mission or core values and its actual practices.[11]

The messenger who gives voice to the message also matters. Different types of messengers connect with different audiences. Credible and charismatic leaders are effective messengers for human rights. Witnesses and victims offering testimonials can humanize suffering and build empathy with the audience and can become "spokesperson" of the movement. Experts can win over a skeptical audience with independent research and compelling evidence. Community and national heroes inspire action and model behavior that an admiring audience will want to replicate.[12]

The right people to speak in defense of justice or to delegitimize hatred and violence depends on the audience you are seeking to reach. Sometimes "elite influencers" who come from within the community whose behavior you are trying to change have greater credibility than those who have been most effected by abuse.[13] Use both.

Movements can have many messengers. The most effective movements for change build cross-cutting coalitions based on common values.[14] When large numbers of diverse people assert values of justice and inclusiveness in public ways, political and social change within the community becomes possible.

Symbolism Matters: Performing the Message

Match your tactics to your targets. Identify the best way to capture their attention and focus it on your message.

Testimonials and storytelling are effective ways to "perform" human rights. There is power in hearing the lived experience of survivors and victims. Storytelling is also effective at garnering attention. Use your own story. Turn personal struggles into sources of inspiration for change. Share your passion, it will inspire others and rally them to your cause.

Make your message visual. By wearing the same t-shirts, carrying the same signs or flags, or coordinating use of a common symbol, you demonstrate unity while also controlling your image. This can also differentiate your movement from counter-demonstrators or potential spoilers who might seek to disrupt your message or subvert your cause.

Consider a range of possibilities and adopt the tactics that best represent your message (see handout on creative protests on pp. 163–167 of this toolkit). Is your goal to educate, raise awareness, protest or shame, generate pressure for specific demand? How can you best express the message to meet that goal? Is it protest? An art exhibit? A public dramatization? The use of satire or comedy? Be creative.

Using Media to Amplify the Message

Use social media to gain supporters, increase your membership, and amplify and control your message. Social media can circulate a large amount of information in a short period of time. You can use social media to promote rallies and demonstrations, advertise available campus resources, and to document or livestream events. Advertise your actions and invite others to join you – disseminate information widely using print and electronic means. Don't overlook the power of a personal invitation and the effectiveness of word of mouth endorsements.

Develop symbols or slogans that represent your purpose and your people. Include them in your communications. Visual images move people. Use photographs to strengthen credibility and change hearts and minds.

Create a press release and send it to the school paper, school administrators, and local or national media. Identify the people who will speak for your movement and make them available for comment. Be disciplined about your message. External media attention has the power to help or the power to harm your cause. Consider creating a list of "talking points" that members of your group can use to communicate a common message. Be sure to think carefully about how to shine a light on the injustice without inflicting unnecessary damage on the people and institutions you'll need to partner with to achieve your desired reform.

You can use your phone to document incidents of abuse but be thoughtful about how you circulate the evidence. Some footage could put individuals or communities at risk of harm. You should consider the safety, dignity, and privacy of the people captured in video before sharing it. You don't want to shame, revictimize, or endanger people you seek to help. Make sure you document what, who, how, and when the incident took place. Record the date, time, and location. Narrate, if possible, and be sure to capture landmarks that confirm the location. Only film if it is safe to do so and protect your evidence. Visit www. witness.org for best practices.

When taking collective action, document everything. Video record. Take pictures. Live stream. Collect written accounts of participants and journal your own experiences. This will help you maintain control over and amplify your message and it will help you generate ideas later when you evaluate what worked well and what you might change in the future. Just be sure to protect people at risk.

The Ask: Empowering Action

Document your demands for easy dissemination and be sure to have a clear ask. Be clear and vocal about your goals. Explain what supporters can do to help advance those goals. Once you have an engaged audience, you want to empower them to do something. Make sure you are clear about how your audience can help make meaningful change.

You also want to be clear about what specifically you want the target of your action (the violator, perpetrator, or decision-maker with power) to do to restore the rights and dignity of those who are being harmed. Clearly articulate those demands and be prepared to meet with those who have the power to meet them – even your advocacy targets.

What Happens Next?

Injustice doesn't typically end after a single event. Stay passionate yet patient. Meaningful change takes time. Activism can and should continue. Effective advocacy uses multiple points of leverage. This means organizing multiple actions often focused on different targets.

Check in with the people you are fighting with and for. Debrief the participants in your activities. Plan for the future by sequencing a series of actions that help you achieve your goals: restoring rights and dignity to victims; achieving justice for the community; and securing accountability.

Follow up with the people whose behavior you are seeking to change. Deliver evidence of support for your cause. Return focus to new expectations or continuing demands. Decide whether it is more effective to partner with them or to take an adversarial approach. Be deliberate and thoughtful about your choices but don't confuse means with ends.

Tips for Organizing a Protest

It is better to protest than accept injustice.

Rosa Parks

There may be times when we are powerless to prevent injustice, but there must never be a time when we fail to protest.

Elie Wiesel

1. Clarify the purpose for your protest.

- Know your issue and its underlying causes.
- Create clear and measurable goals – are you seeking to spread awareness and garner attention or are you trying to change a specific policy or demand accountability?
- Clearly articulate your demands.
- Identify the target for your protest action – whose actions are you trying to change?
- Clarify the purpose at the event and ask participants to honor them.

2. Plan.

- Match your strategy to your cause (Will you have a march or rally? Will you have a silent protest, peaceful demonstration, occupation of space, walk out, or boycott?)
- Anticipate potential challenges and how you will solve them.
- Disseminate your plan among supporters.
- Have action items prepared for protesters to do in the days and weeks beyond the protest.

3. Generate solidarity.

- Encourage diversity and unity. A protest is not a movement, but it can help build one if you leverage it to develop relationships.
- Join forces with like-minded organizations and identify potential allies. Involve individuals who can use their platforms to generate support.
- Songs and chants create unity among demonstrators and force the audience to see them as a group. Songs can communicate the political message of the protest and help establish legitimacy of the cause. Make sure you identify chant leaders in advance and equip them with what they need to be heard.

4. Craft a unified and inclusive message.

- The message matters – what message will persuade your audience and third parties?
- Align your message with your college mission statement or with widely accepted social norms. Decide whether human rights language connects with your audience. Use frames that resonate. Tactically you may need to abandon language that doesn't. Achieving justice is what matters.
- Find the right messengers for your message. These should be individuals with compelling stories or experiences and individuals whose influence can sway audiences. Provide them with a platform and direct media inquiries to them.

- Make sure that participants understand and communicate the same message through social media, on their signs and banners, in their chants, and in statements to media.

5. Protect privacy.

- Consult victims – nothing about us without us!
- Do not reveal identities or disclose personal information about victims without permission. Be sure to minimize risk to vulnerable participants.

6. Location, location, location.

- Identify a location that is safe, accessible, and consistent with the protest message.
- Pick a convenient time and location relative to goals. It should be convenient for participants, accessible to media, and visible to your target audience. Know whether you need a permit and apply for one in advance if needed.
- Know state and local laws and follow them. Public spaces don't typically require permits if you don't block roads, sidewalks, or access to buildings, and obey traffic signals.
- Private property owners set the rules for free speech on their property. You cannot protest in a private space without permission and could be subject to removal or arrest if you choose to do so.

7. Know your rights and respect the rights of others.

- The right to peaceful assembly is protected by Article 20 of the Universal Declaration of Human Rights. This right protects your right to defend human rights.
- Consult you student handbook and comply with campus policies on rallies and demonstrations or understand the costs of choosing not to do so. Have an attorney in your network? Run your plans by them and seek their advice. See if they'll be on call in case an emergency arises related to the event.
- Remember counter-protesters have the same rights as you. Do not engage in physical or verbal retaliation when others target you. Don't debate haters – they thrive on attention and your focus gives them legitimacy. Ignore them and maintain your message.
- In most democracies, police are not permitted to end a gathering unless it threatens public safely. If a dispersal order is given, protesters must be given a reasonable opportunity to comply, including sufficient time and unimpeded access to exit.

8. Safety first.

- Embrace nonviolence and get some training on civil disobedience. A safe and peaceful protest will attract wide participation. Multi-generational and intersectional participation increases legitimacy and strengthens the message. When possible, gain support from authorities.

- There is power in numbers. Encourage participants to travel to or from the protest location in groups. Better yet, coordinate walking groups or ride-sharing. Don't let a single individual be the focus of harm or negative consequences.
- Encourage participants to bring a small bag or backpack with water, ID, cellphone, emergency contact numbers labeled ICE (in case of emergency), essential medicine, money, and snacks. As the organizer you should plan to have emergency supplies and water available on-site. If possible, invite medical and legal professionals to participate. If you anticipate arrests are possible, organize legal aid or coordinate a community bail fund in advance. Have a list of emergency contacts available in case anything goes wrong.
- Enable communication channels between organizers. Make sure the contact information for all organizers is clearly labeled in your phone. Know who is in charge of what. Consider duplicative systems like walkie-talkies to enable communication.
- You may wish to carry a scarf to protect eyes if aerosols are used to disperse a protest and other protective gear like an extra facemask or small bottle of sanitizer during a pandemic. If possible, make these available to others. Never carry anything that can be perceived as a weapon.
- Make sure your cellphone is fully charged and disable facial recognition and fingerprint unlock features on your smartphone. Turn off text preview to keep messages from showing on your screen. This prevents people other than you from accessing your phone without your expressed permission. Encourage organizers and participants to do the same.
- Do not run from or resist authorities and keep hands visible. Even if it seems unfair, be calm and polite. Memorize everything. Justice can come later. Do not lie but do not reveal unnecessary information like immigration status. State verbally that you wish to remain silent, that you want an attorney, and that you do not consent to a search. Share this information with your participants. You might even go over safety information at the start of the event.
- If you believe that rights are being violated, cooperate with authorities in the moment but pay attention and record details. Document, film, or write down everything you can. Memorize names, and badge and patrol car numbers. Write down contact information of witnesses. Make prior arrangement with lawyers, legal aid societies, and civil society or rights organizations who you can contact in case external assistance is needed. Better yet, invite those people to join you at the protest.

9. Adopt a Code of Conduct.

- Human rights-based activism must have principles of conduct. Participants should commit to nonviolence, respect rights, share values, and communicate the message.
- Set the tone. At the start of the event, remind participants of the purpose and ask them to respect the values and the ground rules of the event.
- Ask participants to adopt a human rights-based attitude. You are advocating for something.
- Everyone should understand the risks and rewards of their participation.

10. Attend to needs.

- Be prepared to provide accommodations for participants of all abilities and ages.
- Ensure access to water, food, and restrooms. Have a first aid kit or multiple depending on expected crowd size.
- When possible, involve counselors, healthcare, and legal professionals on-site.
- Protest can be hard. Provide an outlet for self and communal care or a healing place where you can care for the humanity of the people you are fighting for and with during or after the event, or both.

Don't forget to have fun while you build community with people who share your commitment to justice and human rights. Find the joy that comes through solidarity. Know that your organizing work is part of a broader movement for change – it builds on the work of those that have come before you and paves the way for those that will follow.

Beyond the Standard Protest: Using Creativity to Promote Your Message on Campus

Injustice ends when silence ends. Rights advocates and justice warriors promote justice, equity, and inclusion in a variety of ways. Advocacy can be more than protest and can inspire hope as well as give voice to pain. Effective movements engage in creative acts of disruption that draw attention to their cause and push others to think in new ways. Art, music, poetry, and performance give meaning to ideas that are otherwise impossible to articulate. These approaches to activism have the power to touch souls, change hearts, inspire hope, and mobilize change. Sometimes, the creative arts can speak when words fail.

Use Your Talents and Training to Promote Human Rights

Poetry can promote rights as much as a policy paper. Artists can design posters, create paintings, design a photography or art exhibition, or use spoken word to promote human rights or protest a rights violation. Podcasts, food as activism, and even silence are tactics by which to promote your platform and push for change. Think beyond the scope of traditional methods to engage diverse people.

- Damaris Akhigbe is a Nigerian poet, podcaster, voice actor, and youth advocate. She uses art and spoken word to promote gender equality and the rule of law. In 2019, her recitation of her spoken word, "I am Change" decrying corruption and promoting youth leadership won a prestigious United Nations competition. You can listen to Damaris Akhigbe's submission on YouTube.
- Shirien Damra, a young Palestinian American, sees art as an advocacy tool. Damra uses digital illustrations to raise awareness of injustice and to inspire others to imagine what the world could be. In the aftermath of the 2020 racially motivated murders of Ahmaud Arbery, Breonna Taylor, and George Floyd in the United States, Damra used her art to draw attention to the beauty of their lives and the injustice of their deaths. Describing this work as a gesture of solidarity with the Black community, Damra hopes to combat racist stereotypes and dehumanization tactics prevalent in American culture.[15] You can follow Shirien Damra's viral art on Instagram.

On your campus…

- Create participatory public art. Design a wall of positivity in a high traffic area on campus where students can contribute art and display words of encouragement to support peers affected by injustice.
- Bring artists together to create a series of original posters to raise awareness about an important human rights cause affecting members of the campus community. Individual submissions maintain the creativity and individuality of each artist while collectively promoting a unified message. Hang the posters in high traffic areas around campus. Host an exhibit opening where artists contextualize their creations and answer questions about their cause.
- Many college campuses have a campus landmark, often a campus rock which students paint with messages to serve as a billboard of student communication. At Albion College, "the rock" promotes community by advertising campus events and generating school spirit. It also communicates culture. Decorating the rock with positive messages of inclusion and change can promote rights and send a powerful message of belonging to campus peers.

Performances are a Powerful Way to Communicate a Message

Use music, dance, drama, or comedy to highlight injustices and advance equality.

- Plan a party instead of a protest. After the election of openly anti-LGBTQ American Vice President Mike Pence, groups started spontaneous queer dance parties outside his home. People danced and played music for hours as a form of protest against a discriminatory policy agenda. They used joy and pleasure as a tool of advocacy.

- In 1993, the UN World Conference on Human Rights was being held in Vienna, Austria. Women and the gender-specific aspects of human rights were not on the agenda. On 15 June, women human rights activists opened the "Global Tribunal on Violations of Women's Rights" in Vienna to draw attention to the persistent pattern of human rights abuses against women. Thirty-three women survivors of human rights abuse and their advocates presented public testimony on gender-specific human rights violations and demanded accountability. Their public testimonies described human rights abuse in the family, war crimes against women, violation of women's bodily integrity, socio-economic violations of women's human rights, and gender-based political persecution and discrimination.[16] The Vienna Declaration and Programme for Action adopted by the delegates at the end of the Conference reaffirmed that the human rights of women and girls were an integral part of universal human rights and fundamentally changed the UN's human rights work.

On your campus...

- Invite a justice advocate to be a campus speaker. Professional speakers often use audience participation, music, and comedy to help engage the audience in their message. Check to see if your campus has a speaker policy and honor the terms to avoid your event from being cancelled or postponed.
- Stage a teach-in on your campus quad to generate awareness about injustice. Intermix teaching with music, food, and fun activities. Including music and food from different cultures promotes inclusion and promotes resilience.
- Perform Eve Ensler's award-winning play, "The Vagina Monologues" to raise awareness of violence against women and girls, and to raise money for your local domestic violence shelter or other local organizations working to protect women's rights. Address the problem of sexual abuse by organizing a campus book reading of *The Apology*, [17] an imagined apology from the perpetrator of sexual, physical, and emotional abuse to his victim.

Be inspired by these other examples of creative activism...

Make the Unseen Visible and the Silenced Heard

Invite others to see human rights around them.

- Students at the University of Dayton identify and celebrate upstanders who take risks in support of human rights through The Moral Courage Project.[18]

Students take testimony and engage in human rights storytelling to disrupt existing narratives on race and immigration. They elevate and bring the stories of upstanders to life through audio-recordings, photography, and music.

- In 2017, Day Without Immigrants (USA) and Day Without a Woman (International) boycott actions were organized to highlight the contributions that both groups make to daily life and the economy. Immigrants and women, respectively, were encouraged not to work and not to spend money (except at women and minority owned businesses) to protest anti-immigrant and anti-women government policies. Removing them from life for a day shows how integrated these groups are within their societies and how much they are relied upon without recognition of their contributions.

Symbolism Matters

Connecting your protest to an important date, event, milestone, or common practice can increase the power of your message.

- On one college campus, students delivered a "report card" to their administrators identifying specific ways the institution was not living up to its stated mission.
- On another campus, students scrubbed down the school mascot statue with mops and buckets of soapy water to symbolize the need to clean up a racist campus culture. Similarly, Peruvian women gathered in the main plaza in Lima in 2000 to publicly launder Peruvian flags to protest government corruption.
- In 2014, Emma Sukowicz used performance art to protest campus sexual assault at Columbia University and the mishandling of her own rape complaint by university officials. Titled, "Carry That Weight," Emma's performance art included carrying a 50- pound mattress wherever she went on campus to draw attention and protest policies related to campus sexual assault.
- In 2019, students at Albion College organized a silent march to draw attention to the fact that underrepresented students felt they were not heard by the administration when it came to racial bias incidents on campus. The silent march tapped into civil rights history by borrowing the idea from the 1917 Silent Protest Parade. By linking the two events, the organizers highlighted the justness of their cause.

Organize Remote or Virtual Protests

Sometimes organizing physically is not possible; creative forms of protest can be impactful even when conditions make it difficult to organize *en masse*.

- In Paris in 2015, climate activists were barred from protesting during climate negotiations due to heightened security restrictions following a terrorist attack. Instead, they gathered and displayed thousands of pairs of shoes representing their supporters from around the world and displayed them outside the building where negotiations were being held, ensuring that delegates would see them as they walked by.
- During the coronavirus pandemic when social distancing policies prevented large protests, hundreds of thousands of runners around the globe participated in a 2.23 mile run in their own communities to honor the life of Ahmaud Arbery by posting photos with the hashtag #RunWithMaud. Arbery was a 25-year-old Black man who was chased and shot by armed white men while out for a jog in the United States.

Harness the Power of Social Media and Online Organizing

- In 2018, March for Our Lives, a student-led movement, organized the largest single day of protest against gun violence in US history. What started as a march became a movement that protests gun violence, promotes gun control, and registers and mobilizes voters to support their anti-gun violence policy agenda. Their "Our Power" campaign has harnessed the power of digital technology and the creative arts to tell stories rooted in the trauma of gun violence and to advocate for change.
- Attaching a hashtag for a cause organizes the information effectively and gives the campaign a recognizable slogan. This also is a convenient way for people to get involved, because hashtags can be quickly and easily reposted. #BlackLivesMatter and #MeToo have effectively mastered the organizing power of social media. Over the period of one month in the summer of 2020, more than 4,700 demonstrations (an average of 140 a day) were held in about 2,500 communities across the United States, making Black Lives Matter possibly the largest movement in US history.

We hope that this toolkit has shown you that anyone can defend rights and justice and that it has inspired you to action. We have learned that despite the injustices we face, these practices can build solidarity, cultivate hope, and strengthen community. Sometimes, they even lead to more rights and greater justice. This toolkit is only the beginning; we invite readers to adapt, innovate, and add their own tools to the kit and share them with us and others.

Carrie Booth Walling (cwalling@albion.edu) is a Professor of Political Science and Faculty Director of the Gerald R. Ford Institute for Leadership in Public Policy and Service at Albion College.

Morgan Armstrong (armstrongmorgan74@gmail.com) is a passionate mental health advocate and devoted human rights defender who earned her BA in

Psychology from Albion College in 2021. Her commitment to serving the underrepresented in her community through civic engagement has enriched her experience as a student, teacher, and friend. Morgan is continuing her education in psychology and social work at the University of Michigan to promote social justice in her field.

Marco Antonio Colmenares Jr. (marcocolmenares98@gmail.com) is from San Francisco, California. Marco received a BA in Political Science from Albion College in 2020 and is a full-time law student at Indiana University McKinney School of Law with a personal interest in civil rights law.

Caitlin Cummings (cfc11@albion.edu) is from Gurnee, Illinois and a student at Albion College studying political science with aspirations to go to law school. Her passion is in human rights and advocacy work. She enjoys music, sports, and reading.

BOX 1 HUMAN RIGHTS BASICS FACT SHEET

Human rights are the rights every human is born with and are essential for a life of **dignity**.

Human rights are:

- **Equal & Universal**
- **Inalienable**
- **Interdependent**

How Do We Know what Our Human Rights Are?

The **Universal Declaration of Human Rights** is a historic document agreed to by the world's governments that defines the fundamental human rights to be universally guaranteed. It is a common standard for all peoples and nations.

- **Political rights** include the freedom of peaceful assembly and the right to vote.
- **Civil rights** include due process rights and equality before the law.
- **Economic rights** include reasonable work conditions, fair pay, and right to form unions.
- **Social and cultural rights** include the right to education, the ability to participate in the cultural life of your community, and to share in the benefits of science and medicine.

Who Must Protect Human Rights?

Everyone has a duty to not violate the rights of others, but governments have a special responsibility to respect, protect, and fulfill their human rights obligations.

- The **obligation to respect** means that governments must not violate, limit, or interfere with the exercise of human rights.
- The **obligation to protect** requires governments to protect individuals and groups from having their human rights violated by others.
- The **obligation to fulfill** means that governments must take positive steps to facilitate the enjoyment of human rights.

All human beings are born equal in dignity and rights. Human rights are only respected, protected, and fulfilled to the extent that people, individually and collectively, demand they are. Everyone is responsible for human rights.

BOX 2 STEPS TO BECOMING A HUMAN RIGHTS DEFENDER

1. Know that anyone can be an advocate for justice, equality, and human rights.
2. Believe that all people are equal in dignity and respect.
3. Hold ourselves – and our friends – accountable.
4. Develop empathy for others.
5. Model human rights: speak out and stand up.
6. Build a network of like-minded people.
7. Advocate for change.
8. Keep trying.
9. You got this!

BOX 3 COMMUNICATING WITH ELECTED OFFICIALS AND OTHER DECISION-MAKERS

1. Make contact.
2. Do your research. Use evidence to build your case.
3. Identify yourself and explain how their decisions impact you.
4. Be brief. Get directly to the point.
5. Find your own voice and use your own words.
6. Be respectful.

BOX 4 TIPS FOR ORGANIZING A PROTEST

It is better to protest than accept injustice.

Rosa Parks

There may be times when we are powerless to prevent injustice, but there must never be a time when we fail to protest.

Elie Wiesel

1. Clarify the purpose for your protest and ask participants to honor them.
2. Create a plan that matches your strategy to your cause.
3. Generate solidarity by joining forces with like-minded people and organizations.
4. Craft a unified and inclusive message.
5. Protect the privacy of victims.
6. Identify a location that is safe, accessible, and consistent with your message.
7. Know your rights and respect the rights of others. Do your research on what is permitted, when, and where.
8. Put safety first.
9. Adopt a code of conduct for participants.
10. Attend to the needs of participants of all abilities and ages.

BOX 5 BEYOND THE STANDARD PROTEST: USING CREATIVITY TO PROMOTE YOUR MESSAGE ON CAMPUS

1. Use your talents and training to promote human rights in a way that is true to you.
2. Performances are a powerful way to communicate a message.
3. Make the unseen visible and the silenced heard. Be creative in inviting others to see human rights around them.
4. Symbolism matters. Connect your action to an important date, event, milestone, or common practice to increase the power of your message.
5. Organize remote or virtual protests for when gathering physically is not possible.
6. Harness the power of social media and online organizing to support your action (before, during, and after the event).

Notes

1 Patrisse Khan-Cullors and Asha Bandele, *When They Call You a Terrorist: A Black Lives Matters Memoir* (St. Martins, 2017), p. 250.
2 Khan-Cullors and Bandele, *When They Call You a Terrorist*, p. 251.
3 Khan-Cullors and Bandele, *When They Call You a Terrorist*, p. 222.
4 Khan-Cullors and Bandele, *When They Call You a Terrorist*, p. 251
5 Zachary Laub, "Hate Speech on Social Media: Global Comparisons," *Council on Foreign Relations*, April 11, 2019, www.cfr.org/backgrounder/hate-speech-social-media-global-comparisons, accessed 3/11/2021.
6 Khan-Cullors and Bandele, *When They Call You a Terrorist*, p. 252. See also Aja Monet and phillip agnew, "A Love Story About the Power of Art as Organizing," November 2018, TEDWomen2018, www.ted.com/talks/aja_monet_and_phillip_agnew_a_love_story_about_the_power_of_art_as_organizing?language=en, accessed 3/11/2021; William Paul Simmons, *Joyful Human Rights* (University of Pennsylvania Press, 2019).
7 Project Implicit Bias, https://implicit.harvard.edu/implicity/takeatest.html, accessed 3/1//2021.
8 Alison Brysk, *Speaking Rights to Power: Constructing Political Will* (Oxford University Press, 2013).
9 Margaret E. Keck and Kathryn Sikkink, *Activists Beyond Borders: Advocacy Networks in International Politics* (Cornell University Press, 1998).
10 Carrie Booth Walling, *All Necessary Measures: The United Nations and Humanitarian Intervention* (University of Pennsylvania Press, 2013), p. 23; Deborah Stone, "Causal Stories and the Formation of Policy Agendas," *Political Science Quarterly*, 104:2 (Summer 1989), 281–300.
11 Jerusha O. Conner, *The New Student Activists: The Rise of Neoactivism on College Campuses* (Johns Hopkins University Press, 2020), p. 167.
12 Brysk, *Speaking Rights to Power*.
13 Elizabeth Levy Paluck and Michael Suk-Young Chwe, "Confronting Hate Collectively," *PS Political Science and Politics*, October 2017, pp. 990–992.

14 Alison Brysk, "Speaking Rights to Power," *PS Political Science and Politics*, October 2017, p. 1008.

15 Madison Feller, "The Social Justice Artist Behind the Powerful Portraits You Keep Sharing on Instagram," *Elle*, May 28, 2020, www.elle.com/culture/career-politics/a 32688070/shirien-damra-instagram-tributes/, accessed 3/11/2020.

16 Charlotte Bunch and Niamh Reilly, *The Global Campaign and Vienna Tribunal for Women's Human Rights* (Center for Women's Global Leadership and the United Nations Development Fund, 1994).

17 Eve Ensler, *The Apology,* (Bloomsbury Press, 2019).

18 University of Dayton, Human Rights Center, "Moral Courage Project," https://uda yton.edu/artssciences/ctr/hrc/moral-courage/index.php, accessed 3/11/2020.

INDEX

Taylor & Francis Group
an **informa** business

Taylor & Francis eBooks

www.taylorfrancis.com

A single destination for eBooks from Taylor & Francis
with increased functionality and an improved user
experience to meet the needs of our customers.

90,000+ eBooks of award-winning academic content in
Humanities, Social Science, Science, Technology, Engineering,
and Medical written by a global network of editors and authors.

TAYLOR & FRANCIS EBOOKS OFFERS:

A streamlined
experience for
our library
customers

A single point
of discovery
for all of our
eBook content

Improved
search and
discovery of
content at both
book and
chapter level

REQUEST A FREE TRIAL
support@taylorfrancis.com

 Routledge
Taylor & Francis Group

 CRC Press
Taylor & Francis Group